DEATH IN A G

ONE WEEK LOAN

Also by Ruth McManus

Exploring Society (with G. McLennan and P. Spoonley)

Death in a
Global Age

Ruth McManus

palgrave
macmillan

First published 2013 by
PALGRAVE MACMILLAN

Palgrave Macmillan in the UK is an imprint of Macmillan Publishers Limited, registered in England, company number 785998, of Houndmills, Basingstoke, Hampshire RG21 6XS.

Palgrave Macmillan in the US is a division of St Martin's Press LLC, 175 Fifth Avenue, New York, NY 10010.

Palgrave Macmillan is the global academic imprint of the above companies and has companies and representatives throughout the world.

Palgrave® and Macmillan® are registered trademarks in the United States, the United Kingdom, Europe and other countries

ISBN 978-0-230-22451-3 hardback
ISBN 978-0-230-22452-0 paperback

This book is printed on paper suitable for recycling and made from fully managed and sustained forest sources. Logging, pulping and manufacturing processes are expected to conform to the environmental regulations of the country of origin.

A catalogue record for this book is available from the British Library.

A catalog record for this book is available from the Library of Congress.

10 9 8 7 6 5 4 3 2 1
22 21 20 19 18 17 16 15 14 13

Printed in China

To my mum, Ruth Gray McManus, and grandparents, Isabella and James McManus, and Elizabeth and Raymond Forsyth

Contents

List of Tables and Figures

Tables

Figures

Acknowledgements

Thanks to Jim, Ishbel and Fionn for always being interested and encouraging. Also to the anonymous reviewers, students from 'On Death and Dying' classes at the University of Canterbury, New Zealand, friends, colleagues and family, especially Alison Archer, Chris Brickell, Gregor McLennan, Kaylene Sampson and Andrew Sepie, who have all read various versions of the manuscript. And to the various 'death and dying' scholars who have listened to seminar presentations that became the building blocks of this book, including my colleagues at the University of Canterbury Sociology Department, NZ, the York Cemetery Colloquium and colleagues at Bath, Nijmegen and Durham conferences on death and dying. Also to Maggie Rowe and others who offered support in many ways, including Professor David Thorns for suggesting the idea in the first place; the University of Canterbury College of Arts for internal funding for conference presentations in 2009 and 2010; Glasgow Caledonian University and the Glasgow School for Business and Society and Professor Elaine McFarland for organizing my stay as a visiting scholar in 2008; and Dunoon Grammar School, Argyll, Scotland, for hosting a couple of Kiwi teenagers on sabbatical. A special word of appreciation to Esther Croom for her perseverance and patience during the production of this book, especially as it became derailed temporarily by the Christchurch earthquakes of 2010 and 2011.

RUTH MCMANUS

Acknowledgements

The author and publishers wish to thank the following for permission to reproduce copyright material:

Table 2.1 Transplant tourism web sites available 21 March 2007 from Y. Shimazono (2007 'The state of the international organ trade: a provisional picture based on integration of available information', *Bulletin of the World Health Organization,* vol. 85, no. 12. By kind permission of the World Health Organization.

Figure 3.2 Russian male mortality rates, 1950–2008. By kind permission of Lokiit from Wikipedia. http://en.wikipedia.org/wiki/File:Russian_Male_Death_Rate_since_1950.PNG.

Figure 5.1 Tartan coffin. By kind permission of j.funerals: www.jfunerals.com/coffins.htm. 2012.

Figure 5.2 Resomator with bag of ashes. By kind permission of Finn O'Hara / Gallery Stock / Snapper Media.

Figure 9.1 Worker prepares a carnival float. By kind permission of Tranz International (representing Reuters Image in New Zealand). Photographer Sergio Moraes, Brazil, 2008.

Extracts from *Endings: A Sociology of Death and Dying* by M.C. Kearl (1989) p. 310. By kind permission of Oxford University Press.

Extracts from *Cicely Saunders Founder of the Hospice Movement: Selected Letters 1959–1999* by David Clarke (2005) words from p.7. By permission of Oxford University Press.

Extracts from *The American Way of Death Revisited* by J. Mitford (2000) words from p.22. Vintage Press. By permission of the Heirs of the Jessica Mitford Estate.

Every effort has been made to contact all the copyright-holders, but if any have been inadvertently omitted the publishers will be pleased to make the necessary arrangement at the earliest opportunity.

Introduction: Death Is Integral to Life

We are born, we live and we die, and we do so together, but in the normal scheme of things, we tend to think about death only when confronted with it directly. Customarily, we tend to understand that death is something that happens to us, and that we as individuals and groups react against, either by trying to prevent it, or by grieving when it comes close to us. Death, from this everyday point of view, lies outside a sense of ourselves as individuals and as members of a given society. In this view, death is separate from the social world. Yet we must stop and consider that an individual's interest in death and dying may stem from a perplexing personal experience of death. Someone's death may have propelled them through a set of social conventions that they usually would neither comply with, nor believe in. They may relish the rigours of profound ethical debate that issues such as euthanasia and organ transplants raise. Alternatively, they may wish to understand international responses (or the lack of them) to mass deaths from natural disasters such as earthquakes, tsunamis and floods. Perhaps they are people who deal with death in a professional capacity, be that as a chaplain, a hospice nurse, an embalmer or a grief counsellor. Or they may be intrigued by the explosion of death imagery in contemporary entertainment and the news media. In this diversity of interests there is a common thread, and it is that death and life are inseparable.

As social relations are the foundation of society, we can say that death can shape our social world in positive and constructive ways. Let us just think about how much is 'death-in-life'. Regardless of how we feel at the time, when confronted with death we invariably draw upon systematic yet complex social practices that involve social relations and meanings, as well as a degree of social construction. From making funeral arrangements for relatives, to watching Hollywood blockbusters, we are engaged in death practices that shape, and are shaped by, our social worlds. Death practices shape our social worlds because they give structure, meaning and resonance to what we do. At the same time, each time we organize a funeral, contemplate a disquieting set of medical test results or go online to chat about the most recent pop idol who has overdosed, we also engage our creative talents to help complete and make sense of these experiences and events through our worldviews. The mid-twentieth-century hospice movement is an example.

1

Death is socially mediated – an example

In 1948, Cicely Saunders, a nurse turned social worker, encountered David Tasma, a Polish Jew dying of rectal cancer in a busy London teaching hospital. Inspired by her conversations with him, and her subsequent work as a volunteer at St. Luke's Home for the Dying Poor, Cicely Saunders studied medicine at St Thomas' Medical School in London, England. In 1967, after becoming a physician, she opened St Christopher's Hospice in south London as the first academic hospice. It was a place where patients could go for 'total pain relief', with its physical, psychological, social and spiritual dimensions all being considered.

Cicely Saunders is credited with founding the modern hospice movement. Her ideas took hold at a time when attitudes to death were changing. It was no longer acceptable to die a painful death at a time of great advances in the pharmacology of pain relief. Moreover, Saunders' work gained momentum because of the great advances in medicine made since the discovery of antibiotics. As more people were surviving infectious and preventable illnesses, in later years they became susceptible to degenerative diseases and cancers. More people than ever before were living long enough to die of cancers. People were more receptive to Saunders because of the context of the times in which she lived. The modern hospice movement emerged from a new and unique set of social circumstances. Attitudes to, and causes of, death were changing, and this created the space for a new social movement, with Cicely Saunders at the helm. Moreover, with the emergence of the British hospice movement and the growing acceptance of palliative care worldwide, expectations about and experiences of dying have changed profoundly for those able to receive palliative care. Public debate has also flared over those who cannot reap such benefits when they are dying.

Nowadays, in countries that have stable health care and public policy systems, such as the UK, Australia and New Zealand, individuals may feel well within their rights to expect some kind of palliative care in the public health system when they are diagnosed with a terminal illness. In response to this growing expectation, government advisory groups have written reports and drafted national strategies for the provision and monitoring of palliative care services, and there is now some degree of state-supported palliative care in these countries.

The impact of the hospice movement demonstrates the ways in which social institutions and personal experiences of death are intertwined. The kinds of life we live influence the way we organize our social institutions, and, in turn, institutional forms and transformations influence the kinds of lives we can live. By being entwined, they influence or *mediate* each other. The notion that death is *socially mediated* underpins the ethos of this book, as it lays out the enduring concerns of the sociology of death and dying, and explains the ways in which death is integral to life in our contemporary, globally-orientated age.

Why study death?

Why study death? Death, of all the social subjects, is fascinating yet difficult. A single death can have world-shaking consequences – Archduke Franz Ferdinand's assassination in 1914 triggered the First World War, for example, while the killing of Osama bin Laden by US Special Forces in 2011 is regarded by many as a mission accomplished for America's presence in Afghanistan. How can a single death set in train such extraordinary events and so come to influence relations between millions of people? Alternatively, a person's sorrow can shape the mourning rituals of a generation of British people, as did Queen Victoria's inconsolable grief over the loss of her husband, Prince Albert. Or it can become a global tourist draw. The Taj Mahal, a mausoleum built by the Moghul emperor Shah Jahan in memory of his third wife, Mumtaz Mahal, attracts two to three million visitors a year. How is it possible for death, grief and mourning to have such presence in what people do, feel and think? What is it about the one thing that all humanity shares? Why does death run so deep and spread so wide for the living? Questions about death's depth and span of impact help to explain the fascination it holds for many scholars. Its forms and significance for everyday life are important to know and understand, because that knowledge can lead to many insights about the world we are living in, and allow us to evaluate that world, for good or bad.

Death around the globe

At the most general level, this book introduces what the sociology of death and dying is all about. It focuses on thinking and rethinking death and society using real-world events. It also provides a critical discussion of the ways that death has been thought of, analysed and explained, and encourages a deeper understanding of the ways that the conceptualization of death has changed over time and space. It also aims to draw out the ways that sociologists focus on the ongoing relationship between the empirical/real world and conceptual/symbolic realms. The motivation that underpins this book is to inform readers of the main aspects of the sociology of death and dying, including its core topics, approaches and debates. It addresses that core aim by approaching it from a global perspective. It highlights how contemporary changes in the social world (such as increased mobility, interconnectivity and global communication networks) are present in death as they are in life.

As in every age, people are quite precise about what makes our time on earth distinctive from all that has gone before. One of the unavoidable themes of contemporary life is that we are living in an age defined through global social relations. At the same time, the nature of death, dying and loss seems to be changing. If we look around us, we can see at times startling and as yet difficult to understand changes in the ways that people are dealing with death and dying. There are, for example, the global social movements associated with both palliative care and euthanasia; the burgeoning of interest in personally tailored funerals; the growing practice of online grieving; the dissolving apprehension over showing dead bodies in global media reports; and the recurring scandals over the illegal and para-legal trade in body parts, including vital organs. In addition, the deceased social member has increasing influence over the living – not only in the form of posthumous performances by musicians and actors, but also in the proliferation of halls of fame, incentive trusts controlling the actions of heirs, lengthening copyrights and so on. What does the *Zeitgeist* mean? And what is to be made of the increasing politicization of the euthanasia debates and the irony of its symbols, Karen Anne Quinlan, Nancy Cruzan and Terry Schiavo, being young females? As the USA witnesses rates of inequality unseen since the Great Depression of the 1930s, there has been a building boom in mausoleums. There are other ways that death is integral to life in a globally informed age. These include, for example, the Bhopal disaster in 1984 in India that raised global awareness of how the developed world is exploiting factory workers producing toxic products to the developing world. It is also present in questions about growing fundamentalisms, with their multiple and at times contradictory views on death – how the American abortion debate leaked into other societies, while bombing abortion clinics and killing abortion doctors in the homeland. And the global coverage of radical Islam, with 72 virgins promised to suicide bombers, and the honour killing of daughters and wives. It is important to reflect on their interconnections, which we shall do in more theoretical detail in Chapter 1.

Aims and limitations of this book

The book uses sociological discussions about death to present the sociology of death and dying as a series of ongoing critical questions about social practices, conventions, dominant ideas and sets of social relationships. It aims to increase readers' confidence and capacity to apply sociological insights to death in the twenty-first century.

As with any scholarship, the biggest limitations of this book fall from the head into the lap of the author and I take full responsibility for the failings, illogical connections and misplaced presumptions about death in a global age. Although the book draws on literature on death practices from around the world, including Australia, New Zealand, Japan, the USA, South America, the UK, continental Europe and China, and the resources used span disciplines and areas of study beyond sociology, including anthropology, social policy, geography, demography, philosophy, and ethics, it is beyond the capacity of the book to fully engage with all the available fields of research and analysis that feed into death studies.

Sources are restricted to those published in English, and this is in part because of the linguistic limitations of the author. But some of the limitations come from the social environment that is explored in the book. The book draws on wide-ranging materials, but it has to be acknowledged this will not generate an even-handed account of events that are unfolding across the globe. There will, inevitably, be an over-reliance on nations that continue to dominate the world scene as sources of accounts of, and innovations in, death and dying. This is because the systemic asymmetries that shape global social relations also shape the global world of death practices more generally. Sociologically oriented death studies are concentrated in Western nations. British, Australian, US and European societies are sites of cultural innovation and do dominate many death issues and drive debates. This is a consequence of existing path dependencies and enduring power differentials that tend to prevail in global social relations. Among this global patterning is the cultural phenomenon of layering, where long-standing traditional practices co-exist with mainstream modern and cutting edge innovations in death practices.

It is also beyond my abilities to generate a fully representative account of the panoply of death issues, debates and dilemmas that individuals, communities and societies face round the world today. In its place, this book draws on a small selection of sociological theories chosen for their attempts to comprehend, engage with and critique the global dimension of contemporary trends in death and dying. The number and choice of vignettes and examples is also limited. Focused on illustrating a key aspect or concern under discussion, they are not intended to present the breadth of contemporary death practice around the world. Notwithstanding these limitations, it is hoped that the reader will engage with the arguments, examples and issues in terms of their own understanding, circumstances and experiences of death and dying. Also, as death studies advance, scholars from more diverse locations will add to the critical edge of scholarly thinking about death and dying globally.

The content of the book

The book follows a series of core ideas in the sociology of death and dying, including death paradigms, demography, grief and mourning, caring for the dying, body disposal, mass death, death and religion, and death in the media, to connect advances in sociology with the aims of contemporary death studies.

Chapter 1 discusses key concepts and dominant intellectual perspectives in the sociology of death and dying as a way to introduce the core issues and debates for contemporary scholars in the field, and sets the conceptual scene for the other chapters. These take a substantive approach to examine ways that specific death practices and global relations come together, and the book progresses from the most to the least tangible aspects of death and dying; from the dead body to the virtual representation of death.

The decision of which social aspect of death and global feature to include was guided by circumstances. During early research for the book, certain social dimensions of death emerged consistently when dealing with specific kinds of global relations, and vice versa. This early and insistent co-presence was taken as a justification for a more thorough examination. Each chapter discusses a core aspect of the sociology of death and dying, then assesses this main aspect from a global perspective so that the book generates not only a sense of what is novel and beneficent but also what is *not* in contemporary death and dying. For example, Chapter 2 focuses on what is called the *death paradigm*. This is the term for general attitudes toward and beliefs about death that inform a range of social practices. From a global perspective, it is clear that there are significant changes taking place in the dominant death paradigm of Western societies, to the extent that there may be a new death paradigm in the making. These are linked to globally scaled networks.

Chapter 3 is all about how patterns of life and death are linked directly to social formations (how societies are organized). As societies change to become more global through the increased mobility of money, people and commodities, new and distinctive patterns of life and death emerge, accompanied by new responses and solutions.

In Chapter 4, an examination of the changing roles of doctors and funeral directors addresses sociology's abiding concern with the institutional organization of dying and the disposal of bodies. These professions have undergone a transformation as a direct consequence of global trends towards what is called prosumerism, where customers do some of the work; for example, when customers collect their own food in a restaurant and clear their own table (such as happens in McDonald's). This is having a significant impact on people's attitudes to and experiences of end-of-life care and funeral organization. Sociology is also concerned with the connections between people's interpersonal relations and the subjective understanding of their world.

Chapter 5 is concerned with funeral rites, mourning and memorialization, and how these play an integral part in fostering a sense of belonging and identity. The chapter then examines how communicative technologies that allow people to stay connected to others without being physically present all the time, significantly alter these rituals of remembrance and memorialization and so, perhaps, reconfigure how people can foster a sense of belonging and identity from a global perspective.

The sociological concern with belonging introduced in Chapter 5 is taken up in a different way in Chapter 6. It focuses on a long-established sociological understanding that, when a death occurs, it rips apart the social fabric, which then has to be re-made. The chapter explores this social breaking and re-making through the topic of grief and grieving, and how online technologies allow many grieving people to do this effectively through virtual social relationships.

Chapter 7 moves the discussion on to the territory of mass death. Different kinds of mass death (from massacres to mass starvation) are associated directly with forms of large-scale institutional organization, and resistance towards them. Again, the idea that social formations shape mortality patterns resurfaces, but in this chapter, the focus is on global aspects of mass death (its management, prevention and remembrance) which are increasingly pragmatic and task-focused.

The moral dimensions that can precipitate mass death come to the fore Chapter 8 with religion and death. Religious beliefs and death are very closely tied together. In fact, it is suggested that death is a fundamental wellspring for religion. The spiritual dimensions of many religions inform both how people treat their dead and what people believe happens at death. These in turn shape mourning practices and afterlife beliefs as well as more general moral and ethical codes. Chapter 8 explores these more general ideas and debates about death and religion and connects them with a discussion of the claims for a de-secularisation of society that is linked to the fall of the communist bloc and the resurgence of religious fundamentalisms around the world.

Chapter 9 focuses on representations of death. Much of life is understood through images and texts. These are representations; they do not reflect the original source directly. Rather, they construct a particular way to understand and make sense of the original source. Death has been represented for millennia in texts, images, literature and artwork, and the way that death is represented highlights much about the beliefs, expectations and taboos that give shape to the core values of a given society. Much of contemporary life is lived through global communication media such as the internet and mobile phones. Chapter 9 discusses the representation of death and theories about how such representations are to be understood, before assessing death representations from a global perspective and exploring how the representation of death has shifted as a result of what is called global convergence.

The conclusion, Chapter 10, sets out to evaluate the claims made about death in a global age in the previous chapters, and speculates on the future under this scenario. For example, how will we die (and *will* we die?) a hundred years from now? How are we to think about this? How can some of the cases and forms discussed in the book help in forming such questions? What is going on in global society which might suggest that, in spite of death being always with us, its social forms and significance might change.

Having noted the influence of images and texts on how death and dying is understood, it is appropriate to point out that there are some images and discussions in this book that readers may find challenging.

This is not a deliberate strategy to sensationalize the text. Each image and example has been carefully chosen as a means to illustrate a significant dimension of a complex death and dying issue that people may currently face.

Chapter 1

Perspectives and Theories on Death and Dying: New Horizons

Introduction

The subject of this book is the sociology of death and dying, so understandably, its focus is on the social aspects of death studies. Nevertheless, it is important to gain a sense of the contribution that other disciplines interested in social relations make to death studies, as their insights simultaneously inform and contextualize the key debates and concerns of the sociology of death and dying. Anthropology, history and psychology each offer distinctive and very useful contributions to death studies, and some important contributions are discussed here.

Anthropology has always taken a keen interest in the death-ways of non-modern societies. At the outset of the discipline, anthropology's interest in death was to study the death practices of what was referred to as simpler societies, as a means to highlight the distinctive (and as was thought evolutionarily more advanced) characteristics of modern death-ways. While professional attitudes to studying other cultures have shifted dramatically since then, the dimensions identified in early anthropology have withstood the test of time and continue to underpin useful discussions on the social aspects of death. These include the recognition of the importance of the symbolic realm to death; that a significant component of death rituals is to repair social relations damaged by the loss incurred, and to enact the core values of a society. Anthropology's study of death has also highlighted the strong bond between the cultural and moral dimensions of social relations. As anthropology has contributed core concepts to the lexicon of death studies, they are paid some attention here.

A general aspect of the anthropological contribution to death studies is the way in which anthropology brings the connections between material and symbolic dimensions of human activity together – there is never one without the other. All the physical things that people do in relation to the dead, from enacting rituals to speaking with the dead, to fabricating life gems out of the carbon extracted from human remains, are always imbued with meaning and symbol. The mutual inclusiveness of the symbolic and the material realm must always play a part in any examination of death. Moreover, it is *also* the key to society in general. Death as a human experience, even as it is

9

inevitable for every last one of us, is regarded as the great crucible of human activity: culture and society are ultimately systems of symbolic representation constructed in response to death. As Peter Berger puts it, 'every human society is, in the last resort, men banded together in the face of death' (1967, p. 52).

Led by the French sociologist, Émile Durkheim (who was the first-ever Professor of Sociology), a group of scholars straddled sociology and anthropology in their quest to understand and explain social solidarity – how people band together in the face of death, and why that makes society. They developed a cluster of connected concepts that included religion, the sacred and profane, respect, taboo and pollution to help them. Powerfully articulated by Durkheim in *The Elementary Forms of Religious Life* (Durkheim, [1912]1995), religion is the key to society. From this perspective, all religions are made up of both beliefs and rituals that share a common feature: they classify 'The division of the world into two domains, one containing all that is sacred and the other all that is profane – such is the distinctive trait that is religious thought' (ibid., p. 34).While anything can be categorized as sacred or profane, the two states are mutually exclusive: 'sacred things are things protected and isolated by prohibitions; profane things are those things to which the prohibitions are applied and that must be kept at a distance from what is sacred' (ibid., p. 38). What this means is that, once something is imbued with a sacred status it is very important *never* to treat it as if it is profane because the profane defiles the sacred. Once it is defiled, it has become polluted. The division between what is sacred and what is profane is regulated by taboos. Taboos[1] highlight the strong connections between the cultural and moral aspects of social life. As Mary Douglas ([1960]2004) puts it in *Purity and Danger*, taboo is about the ordering of the sacred and the profane, and 'is a spontaneous coding practice which sets up a vocabulary of spatial limits and physical and verbal signs to hedge around vulnerable relations ... taboo confronts the ambiguous and shunts it into the category of the sacred' (ibid., pp. viii–xi). The purpose of taboos is to maintain the boundary between the sacred and the profane, and taboos manage this because we use them continually to adjudicate (that is, assess and judge) whether our own and others' actions are good and therefore right, or bad and therefore wrong. The American flag is a useful example here. The star-spangled banner is a sacred emblem – it represents the American identity and a distinctive way of life. When American flags are treated as everyday objects – for example, as face cloths – they are being treated with disrespect. The values and beliefs enshrined in that sacred object are seen to be under attack and there is a strong sense that it is wrong to defile the flag. From a Durkheimian perspective, morality, a person's sense of what is right or wrong, good or bad comes from what taboos tell us are sacred or profane.

This cluster of connected concepts helped to initiate a deeper sociological understanding of death and dying. The ritual practices that act out symbolic dimensions of death also give shape to the specific worldviews of particular societies. The role of death in the constitution of society was first publicly discussed in two studies that focussed on, respectively, death as a rite of passage and death as a source of collective representations (or shared worldviews). Arnold Van Gennep ([1960]2004) illustrates the idea that death, among other events including birth and marriage, is a key *rite of passage*. Central to this explanation is that a death is very disruptive to the status quo of social relations (as are both birth and marriage). They rip apart the configuration of relations through death, birth or the creation of another family. To manage that disruption, symbolically-driven rituals reconfigure the status of those involved. The status of an individual undergoes a significant and ritualized transformation. The individual begins the ritual with a particular social identity and goes through a liminal phase that ends with the designation of a new social identity. Thus a funeral is a ritual that transforms the deceased from being a living member of a community into an ancestor. This social restitching and repair is a core symbolic function of death rites.

Not only do death rites repair damage to specific social relations affected by death, they also play a part in continually re-establishing the shared worldview of broader society. This was eloquently posited by Robert Hertz ([1960] 2004). The Indonesian communities he studied did something with their dead that was, to him, very unusual: they were buried twice. At the first, provisional, burial, the deceased is placed in a coffin with leak holes to allow suppurating fluids to drain and objects associated with the dead person are destroyed. The corpse can be left for anything between eight months and six years to allow the body to decompose and the bones to dry out. Only when it was fully disintegrated could the corpse be buried again. This final ceremony achieves multiple ends – transferring the remains to their final resting place is considered to free the soul of the deceased because 'it liberates him from the isolation in which he was plunged since his death, and reunites his body with those of his ancestors' (Hertz, [1960]2004, p. 55). At the same time, it brings mourners together into a large collective celebration that involves not only the mourners, but the entire social group. The long intermediary period allows the family to accumulate the large store of foodstuffs necessary to accommodate the many guests attending the great feast. Often, a number of families will pool their resources in this collective observance. The final ceremony completes the separation of the dead from the living, and ensures the soul's entry into the community of sacred ancestors. The 'living are freed from their mourning obligations. They return to normal activities and resume their interrupted social relations. The celebration marks the end of a perilous time ... the dark period dominated by death is over, "a new era begun"' (ibid., p. 56). Hertz suggested that these mortuary rituals embodied significant collective life transitions that were a central means through which Indonesian society, in fact *any* society, was lived.

People modulate their beliefs and behaviour when they engage with complex socialized engagements such as death rituals because of the capacity of death rituals to join what people do to what they believe. This means that death practices are a significant avenue for social control. This aspect will be explored in Chapter 9, which focuses on death and the media. Anthropology's interest in the symbolic realm and its focus on culture has furnished death studies with significant insights into the role and place of death in society. The role of history in delivering accounts of previous death-ways is likewise integral to understanding death as socially mediated.

Historians of death and dying have furnished death studies with detailed accounts that show how people change their death-ways as the broader fabric of a society transforms. The historians Rosemary Horrox and Colin Platt (Horrox, 1994; Platt, 1996), in their different ways, use catastrophe to reveal the impact of death on society. Using first-hand accounts and the visible scars that still remain on the physical landscapes of Europe, they tell of the social transformation set in motion by the widespread terror and hardship brought about by the Black Death that haunted the European populations of the Middle Ages. Phillipe Ariès (1974) and Norbert Elias (1985) each weave evolutionary tales about the transformations in European attitudes towards death and dying from their historical studies of cultural writings, art and popular books on manners. They highlight the importance of approaching the past as another country, and caution against using current sentiments to make sense of life and death in bygone ages.

Yet other historians have generated detailed analyses of more minor passages of history that have, even so, offered incredible insight into present times. For example, *The Puritan Way of Death* by David E. Stannard (1977) explains how various social forces, including migration to a physically hostile environment and religious politics, help to make sense of how a minor, though ideologically significant group, the New England Puritans, viewed death and set about their death-ways. The core beliefs they lived by helped to set the tone for how subsequent generations of Americans could resolve the thorny tensions that death perennially throws into the paths of the living. History helps us to ask *How has death changed over time, and what are the major influences that have brought about change?* It also helps to identify the path dependencies that inform death in the present.

Psychology offers perception of the internal workings of the mind in relation to death, dying and loss. There are various connected aspects to psychology's contribution to understanding death and dying. One is that it has offered significant analyses of the Western psyche, so much so, in fact, that one of the most influential and widespread explanations for Western death-ways is psychologically based. This is the theory that modern Western societies are characterized by their denial of death. This theory will be discussed in more detail in the pages to come. As a way of approaching human relations, psychology has had a profound effect on the understanding of particular aspects of death – especially grief and loss. These have become psychologized in modern Western societies, which is testament to the institutionalization of a particular approach to understanding death.

Because sociology aims to understand how all the facets of a society are pieced together at a given time and place, its tendency is to develop accounts that synthesize the material and symbolic with the past and the psychological, in its overarching quest to make sense of the multi-dimensional, constantly transforming whole that is human society. The first aim of this book is to focus on the central aspects of the sociology of death and dying, with a secondary aim of assessing these main aspects from a global perspective. Anthropology's concern with culture and the symbolic, history's insights about the transforming nature of society, and psychology's concern with inner machinations, will reappear in the service of these sociological aims.

Enduring issues in the sociology of death and dying

Death is a manifestly deeply important, deeply sensitive and deeply social area. How, as a sociologist, is it best to approach this subject? It requires respect for the attitudes, feelings and hopes that underwrite people's experiences of death. It also requires a critical, explanatory attitude, so that sociological sense can be made from everyday experiences of death and dying. Social practices need scrutiny because they have consequences for people's living and dying. These consequences can be more-or-less positive, and more-or-less intended, and they are not always apparent. Indeed, when new social practices begin to emerge and coalesce, the question of whether they are in fact new, and if they are here to stay or merely a passing fad, needs to be established before their true effects can be fully revealed, evaluated and acted upon for the greater human good. This raises the issue of how best, as a sociologist, to scrutinize emerging death practices.

The next section introduces the enduring issues concerning the sociology of death and dying. When it comes to death, a good way to understand what sociologists are interested in, and how they go about developing that interest, is to reflect on the emergence of sociology as an academic discipline. It emerged as a discipline of study in the mid-nineteenth century and enthusiastically sought to comprehend, engage with and critique social practices. The point of sociology was to apply scientific methods to society for the common good. Sociology raises awareness of the consequences of human activities and actions on individuals, groups and communities, and is used ideally to identify and evaluate trends in human activity so as to develop ideas that might change our societies and institutions for the better.

Key sociological concerns are to describe, interpret, explain, critique and evaluate the social. As will be discussed below, there are different ways to achieve these aspects, but broadly speaking, sociologists develop these key concerns by paying attention to the ongoing interplay between societal formations (systems of social organization), social change (history), social institutions (infrastructure) and social identities (selfhood) to make sense of human activity. Because its interest is in helping the world to become a better place, it has a particular emphasis on power and inequality in those examinations.

When death and dying are brought into the mix, sociologists tend to study the ways in which these different facets of society link to people's deaths. A useful way to think of how social formations and death are linked is to examine patterns in life and death – the difference in life-chances between, for example, babies born in Singapore and Somalia in late 2011 is profound. Singapore has the lowest infant mortality rate in the world, at 2.6 per 1,000 live births, whereas Somalia is ranked at 190 with an infant mortality rate of 113 per 1,000 (United Nations, 2011a). These two rates speak of widely divergent societies organized in ways that are more, and less, able to supply the basic necessities of life to its resident population. The difference between the two nations' standards of living speak of the vast yet connected inequalities in life-chances round the world today.

Sociologists also have an abiding interest in how social change affects people's lives. Shifting mortality rates are again a very strong indicator that something significant is changing in the social make-up of that society. A drop in mortality rates suggests that social institutions are working effectively to keep people alive. Conversely, when there is a leap in mortality rates, it clearly indicates a drastic change in the capacity to organize society to meet basic human needs. Famines are just one example, when the capacity to procure and distribute basic necessities such as food and clean water fails – again, Somalia is a case in point, as it suffered two failed harvests and millions of infants died of malnutrition in mid-2011. Understanding mortality rates within and between societies shows how death connects to the central sociological interest in social difference and social change.

Another common concern of the sociology of death and dying is what can be called social institutions. These are 'activities which are repeated or continuous within a regularised pattern that is normatively sanctioned and reproduce itself' (Bullock *et al.*, 1988, p. 426). Sociologists usually speak of four major complexes of institutions:

- *political institutions* regulate the competition for power;
- *economic institutions* are concerned with the production and distribtion of goods and services;
- *cultural institutions* deal with religious, artistic, and expressive activities and traditions in society; and
- *kinship institutions* focus on the question of the reproduction of individuals.

Death is present in all of these institutions, but its presence varies in form and purpose. For instance, the place of death in cultural institutions such as religion is visible when, for example ceremonies associated with the rite of passage of death are conducted through the auspices of the church. Less directly visible, but nevertheless present, death is embedded in political institutions and can be observed in, for example, coroners' investigations into unexpected deaths, such as workplace accidents and suspected murder. Death's presence in economic institutions can be seen in the production and distribution of the accoutrements for the rites of passage of internment; for example, caskets or coffins, hearses, burial plots and cremation facilities. And in terms of institutions of kinship, death triggers many inheritance and status changes within kinship networks. Under a monarchical political system, the death of a monarch shows ways in which all of these institutions can come together – when a king dies, not only is there a change in who heads the political institution when an heir-in-waiting becomes monarch, but also, culturally, religious orders will organize the ceremonies and rites of passage, while kinship positions also alter as the individuals who are designated to fulfil certain roles are reshuffled – for example, a princess becomes a queen. Speaking very broadly, it is useful to think about how society organizes for death using this idea of social institutions. It also helps when considering dramatic changes in a society. Accounts of social change can be discussed in terms of how these four social institutions are changing, and how those changes may affect death practices.

The place of death in identity, including its formation and transformation, is another enduring theme in the sociology of death and dying. Deaths transform people's individual status. For example, a dead husband makes a widow, and dead parents make an orphan, and these changed identities can have significant consequences for the people involved, not least emotionally and financially. The place of the dead in the broader identities of the living is also of sociological concern. Holocaust victims have a significant presence in the lives of the survivors *and* the broader international coalition of countries that fought in the Second World War. The dead are used to help define the guiding principles of societies that follow in their wake. At the same time, as is the case with the victims of 9/11, the dead can also be used as a reason to wage war on others. As a theme, death and identity go a long way towards explaining an individual and societal sense of self.

Using these kinds of aspects, it becomes possible to understand the myriad and complex ways that death is socially mediated. However, to understand that death is socially mediated is one thing, but there is much debate over how best to explain the patterns that are observable in those mediations.

Sociological perspectives and approaches

Auguste Compte (1798–1857) is said to have invented the term sociology to describe his intellectual endeavours to unify history, psychology and economics through the scientific understanding of the social realm. His focus was to try to understand the social world, in particular the malaise linked historically to the brutal fall-out from the French revolution. Alexis de Toqueville (1805–59) paralleled Compte's quest in *Democracy in America* (Toqueville, [1835]1998) with his exploration of the effects of the rising equality of social conditions built into the individual and political infrastructure of the newly forged United States of America. These early sociologists put their faith in the application of the scientific method of methodical observation and its analysis to discover the workings of the laws of society, with the aim of making societies better. They considered that the best way to understand how society works is to use the scientific method, because it will focus on the true nature of what is under investigation and not be marred by political interests, religious fervour or philosophical speculation. So the history of sociology is a history of the scientization of the study of society; the systematic investigation of social practices as a means of furthering the knowledge, understanding and evaluation of the social world. Like other disciplines, sociology takes a distinctive subject-matter for analysis, one that represents an independent and complex reality, and it generates systematic knowledge about that reality rather than merely producing a personal or political opinion. Herein lies the rub, however, because, as sociology began to cohere into a discipline, founding thinkers struggled with what they saw as their task – to outline what a science of society should and could look like, and therefore *how* to conduct social enquiry.

The underlying question of how best to achieve this systematic investigation has been an enduring source of productive debate in sociology. And the contention rests on the realization that there are different ways to acquire knowledge. While avoiding a digression into the philosophy of knowledge in the social sciences, it is relevant to discuss the basis of these different ways of thinking about knowledge and society, because it helps to make sense of why there are numerous and at times rigorously competing theories that seek to explain social behaviour, including death practices.

One way through this morass is to consider three dimensions to this knowledge: ontological, epistemological and axiological. These are how we understand the way that the world works, how we enquire by way of that understanding, and the morals and values that underpin and inform the ontology and epistemology. As Durkheim was such an influential sociologist in the discipline as a whole and in the sociology of death and dying, it is worth giving a bit of space to his sociology as a way to show how these three dimensions come together. One of Durkheim's greatest intellectual achievements was to develop a coherent empirical approach to the study of the social. Others had preceded him, such as Compte and de Toqueville, but they lacked precision. In terms of *ontology*, Durkheim believed in objective reality that can be observed and measured (what he called 'social facts as things') independent of the way that we personally experience it.

Epistemologically, he regarded himself as a positivist, believing that knowledge can only come from what is observed, and a methodological naturalist.[2] Durkheim's aim was to identify and elaborate on the laws of society through the rational application of an empirical examination of the world. *Axiomatically*, he believed in what is called 'the fact–value distinction'. This involves two interconnected sets of assumptions about the influence that beliefs and values have on knowledge: whether new knowledge could appear without the influence of people's wishes, and whether science should use this new knowledge for the good of society. Durkheim assumed that value-free sociological knowledge was both feasible and desirable. But he rejected the fact–value distinction of science not being required to contribute to the betterment of society. Precisely because they are scientists, morally sociologists can and should develop and offer solutions that will help society. This issue underpins recurring debates about the moral responsibility of scientists who develop technologies that are then used to make weapons with the potential to kill millions of people, such as nuclear weapons, germ warfare and chemical warfare.

In contrast to Durkheim's ideas, Max Weber (see Weber and Turner, 1991) proposed an equally influential version of sociology. Weber was not convinced that natural science has what it takes to make the best sense of the social, for he understood that human behaviour is spontaneous and creative. He strongly believed that it is not possible to exclude how people think and feel about their lives if you want an accurate as possible account of the social. In contrast to Durkheim, Weber considered that the best way to have a science of society was to incorporate rather than exclude how the world is personally experienced. This is called *subjectivism*. Ontologically, Weber believed that the world was more than just our personal human perceptions; however, the way to get to these more objective truths about the world was to find out if and how an individual's understanding and motivations about the world were shared by others. This common sense of purpose and activity would be what shapes a society, and would be the source of the patterns and trends that made up society, including death. Understanding the beliefs and motivations of people who go to war is as vital as understanding the bigger political context that prompts the wholesale uptake of arms. One of Weber's abiding contributions to sociology is the concept of *Verstehen*, which is a method adopted in an attempt to appreciate the motivations, values and beliefs of people that inform what they do – their meaningful action. For Weber, sociology is a science that employs interpretative understanding of social action to explain the workings of society.

The two perspectives of Durkheim and Weber are pegs in the sand that mark contrasting ways to understand the social. One the one hand, we have Durkheim's positivism that only takes observable phenomena into account, and on the other there is Weber's interpretivism, that personal motivations and beliefs are at the centre of any real, accurate account of the social. This debate has never been fully resolved, and one of sociology's distinctive features is the diversity of theories and research methods that are drawn upon to make sense of the social world. Lest the character of sociology comes across like a long washing-line with various positions neatly filling the continuum between positivism and interpretivism, the next section focuses on four main approaches to sociology that have come out of this long-standing tension, and help to organize the sociology of death and dying.

Sociologists focus on explaining the social world. As already noted, debates about the best way to do that are influenced by the tensions between positivism and interpretivism. Four approaches relevant to the sociology of death and dying have arisen from the productive space between these two poles: *structural functionalism*, *critical realism*, *discourse analysis* and *symbolic interaction*. Macionis (2008) emphasizes that each approach puts forward a basic image of society that guides thinking and research. The structural-functionalist approach is 'a framework for building theory that sees society as a complex system whose parts work together to promote solidarity and stability' (Macionis, 2008, p. 15). It emphasizes a macro or big picture approach that sees societies as systems of interrelated parts that are relatively stable, with each part working to keep society operating in an orderly way. Durkheim was a structural-functionalist. A later discussion will explain his theory of society and how it approached the place of death in modern society. A structural-functionalist approach most commonly underpins studies that emphasize objective, empirical accounts of the world. Statistical studies of the social world would fit that bill. This approach has been particularly influential in American sociology from the 1950s, and in post-Second World War European sociology. Talcott Parsons, no less, discussed the role of death in facilitating cultural change – older generations take their 'out-dated attitudes' with them to the grave, and so open opportunities for cultural growth and flexibility (Parsons *et al.*, 1973).

Critical realism is neither positivist nor interpretivist. It holds that there is a reality independent of our thinking about it that can be studied, but we cannot assume that what is observed is an accurate depiction of that reality – the social world is not just out there to be studied. A critical realist approach works with a layered ontological model that includes the empirical domain consisting of experiences, the actual domain consisting of events, and the real domain consisting of causal mechanisms. Critical-realist sociology is the study of society that takes seriously the fact that the call to study society is also the call to change it for the better. It is linked most closely to theories that understand the social world as being driven by conflict and tension, which are ultimately generated by real, underlying, difficult-to-observe causal mechanisms at work. This approach emphasizes how social patterns benefit some people while hurting others, and is often associated with research that focuses on revealing underlying inequalities.

A symbolic interaction approach is interpretivist. It views society as an ongoing process which arises from meaningful interactions between people. It is very much drawn from Weber in that it is a study of society which focuses on discovering the meanings that people attach to their social world. This social world is always variable and changing rather than driven by objective laws or underlying causal mechanisms.

A discourse analysis approach takes a different perspective again. Its orientation seeks to step aside from the debate about which view of the social world is true. Instead, it emphasizes how truths are produced and sustained through the different ways that texts, language, policies and practices tussle with each other. Even the concept of society is subject to discursive analysis as this is seen as a way of understanding the world that has come to be taken as true by those cultures in which the discourse of science as *the* method for establishing truth has been in the ascendant. Discursive approaches tend to underpin studies that focus on the ways in which discursive meanings and practices change over time. For example, suicide has undergone discursive shifts in the way it is considered, from being caused by the devil to being a mental illness and then to being a category of risk (McManus, 2005).

This brief overview of sociological perspectives has highlighted four main points of view with regard to tackling the study of society, and each has influenced sociological theories about death and dying. It is to these that we now turn.

Sociological theories on death and dying

Sociological theories are about explaining the social world. The first classical sociological theories sought to describe and explain the patterns of modern society, and theories of death and dying made an early appearance. Sociologists tend to focus on modern societies. Modernity is both a historical (temporal) and a substantive or normative category. From the temporal perspective, it is the period of time that begins with the discovery of the Americas and the Copernican revolution in astronomy during the late Renaissance. From the substantive perspective, it is the emergence of new attitudes and ideas such as progress, secularization of the worldview, emancipation from natural and political restraints, and breaks with tradition (Kumar, 1996). The transition to modernity is when a society is organized along secular rather than religious lines, so that life and the world are understood in terms of reason, science and progress, rather than as through the will of God or fate. Another feature is that these societies tend to be bureaucratized, industrialized, capitalistic and urban (Hall and Jarvie, 1992). This modern way of living brings with it particular constitutive cultural sentiments – core beliefs about what it means to be a person in the world. These sentiments shape powerfully the ways that people live and die in the world. These societies are often labelled Western because many of these profound and specific social changes first gained momentum in Western European countries: Germany, Scotland, the Netherlands, France and England, and later extended to their colonial settlements – America, Australia, New Zealand and South Africa.

Long-accepted trends in modern society include: the transformation of the economic sphere away from local artisans and markets and towards large-scale industrialization (Fordism); the shift away from religion as central official pillar of society; and a growing acceptance of the secularization of society. A parallel shift is the social weight accorded to science and the incorporation of scientific thinking into many aspects of society, including medicine. Also, the emergence of the nation-state as the central governing institution of modern societies was closely linked to democratic governments of these nation-states. The personal, human consequences of all these widespread and deep changes to the organization of these societies are distinctive in the accord given to individuality – the individual becomes the paramount concern in terms of their autonomy, productivity and spiritual relationships.

Early classical social theorizing set out to both chart and evaluate the modern world and its consequences for people, and the study of death and dying has played a central role. Émile Durkheim, who held the chair of sociology at the Sorbonne in France, staked his claim to the discipline through a study of suicide, one of the most deeply unsettling types of death.

Durkheim was concerned to make sense of the consequences of what he regarded as a radical transformation of the organization of societies when they shifted from traditional to modern systems. He took serious note of the widespread social concern about the numbers of suicides in many European societies. Applying his distinctive method of comparative analysis (in this case of suicide rates), he developed the theory that people kill themselves when they are unable to resolve a deep internal conflict, and that this internal conflict arises from the psychological effect of specific social forces. These forces, in stable times, generated particular types of what we would now call 'suicide ideation' (anomie, egoism, altruism, fatalism). But when societies were themselves undergoing rapid and widespread change, these forces shifted out of equilibrium and this caused an observable escalation in suicides. The type of suicide (egoistic, altruistic and so on) depended on the kind of change a society was undergoing, but at its root, the crisis point was reached when the gulf between people's beliefs and values (their ethics) and the new material conditions of their lives became too great to bear psychologically.

When Durkheim focused his attention on modern societies, he was deeply concerned because, using this approach, he understood that the rapid industrialization, secularization and individualization he observed in modern Europe was having dire effects on newly-modernized people. There were increasing suicide rates in societies when people's beliefs and understanding of the world fell out of step with these kinds of rapid material change. For example, a personal worldview that considers religion to be central is deeply challenged when an alternative approach – say, in the power of science – is used by the world around them to explain and resolve human concerns. Or when community-oriented beliefs and practices, which in times past would have supported small networks of market production, are confronted by mass urbanization, industrialization and mass markets. Durkheim saw that social equilibrium was being disrupted by radical social change. As a sociologist, he was deeply worried about the long-term consequences for modern people if they did not recognize and attend to the inherent social dangers of modernization. While fretful for modern people, he also recognized that modernization also held the secret to a beneficent future, which was rooted in a new form of ethically oriented professional practice that he believed would help to recalibrate and rebalance the material and conceptual worlds of modern people.

As a social theorist, Durkheim was trying simultaneously to document, explain and evaluate the social trends he was witness to in the rapidly modernizing societies of Europe as the twentieth century approached. There are many criticisms and limitations to Durkheim's social theories of the modern world, and there are convincing alternatives to his explanation for death by one's own hand. What is significant for this discussion, however, is that he developed his theory of death in society to make sense of and to help alter what he could see going on around him. His intention to describe, explain, evaluate and change the social world remains central to social theorizing in general, *and* the social study of death and dying.

Since Durkheim, many social theorists have grappled with the conundrum that is death in modern society and they have done so with a keen awareness of the debates over how best to study the social aspects of death in modern societies. There is an important stream of social theorizing about suicide and society. While it will not be addressed in this discussion, key theorists representing different sociological perspectives and who draw on studies from America and Europe include Émile Durkheim (1897), Peter Sainsbury (1955), Lois Dublin (1963), Jack Douglas (1967), Harold Garfinkel (1967), R. W. Maris (1969), Anthony Giddens (1971) and J. M. Atkinson (1975).

Though only able to hint at the depth and breadth of sociological scholarship in suicide studies, as this book is an introduction to the sociology of death and dying, it is vital to gain a sense of the broad theoretical terrain that underpins it if we are to draw out the broad concerns of the sociology of death and dying, and approach these aspects from a global perspective. The next section brings together the main debates and concerns, with the caution that they illustrate rather than review all the available accounts.

Sociology tends to be concerned with modern, industrial societies rather than traditional, agrarian ones. Industrialized, mechanized, mass modern societies have equivalent death practices. In the numerous accounts of the trends and characteristics of death in modern societies, certain things are commonly accepted as happening, even if explanations and evaluations of them differ. Broadly, these include:

- the medicalization of death;
- the institutionalization of dying;
- the professionalization of undertakers;
- the commodification of funerals;
- the secularization of ceremonies;
- the industrialization of disposal (for example, the rise in the number of cremations); and
- the psychologization of death, grief and mourning.

All these changes in death practices are associated with the individualization of society, which is taken as the hallmark of modernity.

Some sociologists have taken upon themselves the task of explaining these profound and widely adopted changes in death practices in ways that link to the overarching characteristics of modern society. The next section introduces four contrasting sociological explanations for both the ways that modern society organizes its death practices and why they have changed in the ways they have.

Modern death as death-denying

The fear of death is a deeply established account of death in modern (Western) society, and whether its elaboration by scholars is a self-fulfilling prophecy or not, it is present and is real in its consequences for people living in Western nations, in their lives, beliefs and attitudes to death and dying. As a theory with much influence, it has to be considered in any talk of changing death practices, therefore the *denial of death* thesis will be outlined here, with the emphasis on how the trappings and characteristics of modern death practices have been interpreted in terms of the overriding characteristics of modern society.

The death denial thesis claims that modern society's death practices are marked by a discomfiting contradiction – on the one hand, the personal experience of death is of loneliness and isolation in hospital wards surrounded by professionals, whilst at the same time modern funeral rites are marked, especially in America, by their lavishness and ostentation. The tension lying at the heart of this contradiction, according to many scholars of modern death, is that because modern society is marked by growing secularization, one of the consequences of this lack of faith is that it becomes impossible for modern individuals to hide the existential contradiction that defines humanity. This contradiction is that humans are both bodily and conceptually aware entities, meaning that, at one and the same time, humans can see beyond themselves while recognizing that they will die and be no more. This capacity to think symbolically in a finite body is experienced as a fear, or terror, of death. Rooted in the evolutionary urge for self-preservation, death is seen as the ultimate threat to our symbolic and biological existence. This capacity to appreciate death as an ending raises a deep tension in every person, which acts as the ultimate propellant; the fear of death is 'the mainstream of human activity' in that it fuels the pursuit of heroism, which is at the core of all social activity (Becker, 1973, p. xi).

Alongside Becker's unrelenting psychoanalytic lens, mid-twentieth-century social theorists such as the German, Norbert Elias; the American, David Stannard; and the Frenchman, Philippe Ariès, focused their not inconsiderable talents on elaborating the modern death contradiction. Stannard, for example, dug deep into the internal, contradictory world of early-settler Puritan communities as a means of showing how modern societies, in their own times and contexts, falteringly engage with the great human dilemma that death brings. Stannard interprets the death contradiction not so much as the struggle for life in the face of death, but as knowing death is inevitable but never being able to truly experience it. In *The Puritan Way of Death* (Stannard, 1977) he argues that the Puritan settlers, while being in isolated communities, were one of the wellsprings of the distinctively modern, American way of death. Their now curious, but sense-making culture, was permeated by fear and confusion in the face of death, and this fear came from the combined effects of political, social and theological movements. Escapees from political turmoil and social upheaval in Britain and Europe in the seventeenth century, the Puritans sought out the brave new world of New England to renew and reform their Christian doctrines. Isolated from the need to compromise with other churches and communities, the Puritans entrenched their religious beliefs into tight doctrines that were rigorously upheld in their small and vulnerable new communities. Theologically, New England Puritans held the death dilemma close to their faith. Strong beliefs in predestination and saving grace were infused with a deep dread rooted in 'the acute awareness that man was both powerless to affect the matter of his salvation and morally crippled by his natural depravity' (Stannard, 1977, p. 88). A Puritan's fear of death was a consequence of three very strongly held beliefs: of their own depravity linked to the first fall from grace in the Garden of Eden; of the omnipotence of God; and of the terrors of Hell. This tension became untenable in the new world, as Puritan communities were becoming swamped by the rising tide of urbanization and commerce going on around them. The contradiction burst out, according to Stannard, because key Puritan patriarchs died during this time of retrenchment and isolation, and much work had to be done to re-establish social bonds. This work was done at death, in what has become the striking New England Puritan practice of embellishing graves, embalming and offering fulsome funerary accoutrements to their dear departed. Stannard's account of the Puritan way of death deftly recounts the origin story of the distinctive American resolution of the death dilemma – of the existential and physical isolation of the dying alongside the ornate funeral embellishments for the dead.

The tensions generated by the inherent contradiction that death presents in modern society has been, to all intents and purposes, resolved in modern societies, it has been argued, through *denying* and *fearing* death. When death practices are understood using this rubric they seem to make sense. They help to explain why people would flock to funeral directors when perfectly adequate domestic and informal customs were already in place (for example, local women would come and sit with the dying, then prepare them for their funeral rites). It helps to explain the dramatic shift in the places where people died. In a matter of a generation, the majority of people died in hospitals rather than their own homes. Similarly, it seems to explain the sudden shift from Victorian to Edwardian sensibilities. During Victoria's era, the dead were acknowledged and commemorated in post-mortem photographs and jewellery made from parts of the lost loved one, such as locks of hair. Over a brief decade or two, such artefacts were deemed to be distasteful and in some way morally ambiguous. The theory of death denial makes useful sense of these rapid and quite drastic departures from the status quo at the end of the nineteenth century and into the twentieth. The theory of death denial assembles these components of modern society to say that the overall effect of these modern ways of organizing for death, from the medicalization of dying in hospital to the individualization of death, is to reduce the material presence of death in modern people's everyday lives. People usually will not see a dead person until relatively late in their lives, and even then, the dying or dead person will have been sequestered into an organization such as a hospital or funeral director, and away from the intimate exchanges of everyday life, and that personal experience of dying will be deeply internalized.

Rooted in the denial of death thesis is a deep concern that modern societies are profoundly damaged because, through urbanization and individualization, people are no longer able to re-knit their communities in the face of loss in the time-honoured way, where death rituals bound relations across families and neighbourhoods. This pejorative approach echoes the worries of earlier classical social theorists, and, as Norbert Elias did in *The Loneliness of the Dying* (1985), lambasts the isolation of dying as the ultimate alienation, and finds the fine funerary accoutrements as the galling frippery of the mass commercialism of modern capitalist economies, so deftly decried in Jessica Mitford's *The American Way of Death* (1963). The self-deprecation of twentieth-century scholars of twentieth-century death practices is perhaps another example of the dilemma that is death in the modern age.

The influence of the theory of death denial is felt across different sociological approaches to this day. Recall that structural-functionalist, interactionist, critical-realist and discursive approaches to the social world each emphasize different aspects of the social, and so tend to produce different *kinds* of explanation. In Becker's case we can see the influence of symbolic interactionism – where Becker emphasizes that the ongoing personal experiences of death being more socially invisible means that the symbolic meanings associated with death are oriented towards fear of the unknown. The macro-oriented tendency to explain death denial as the driving force of modern society can also be found in the more structural-functionalist explanations offered by, for example, the European sociologists Mellor and Shilling (1993) and the American scholar, Robert Jay Lifton (1983).

Mellor and Shilling (and Lifton in parallel) argue that the professionalization and individuation of death is the characteristic way of organizing death practices and meanings in modern societies. For Mellor, death is hidden rather than forbidden in modern society, being treated as a private and personal concern, and placed in secluded environments such as hospital wards. For Mellor, death is sequestered, and he has set himself the task of explaining why. Mellor draws on Giddens' (1991) theory of how modern society as a whole works, to explain the sequestration of death. For Giddens, modern society is individually oriented. Giddens sees that, for every society, our ontological security, our sense of ourselves as human beings who have a place and meaning in the world, is driven by the meaningfulness of our day-to-day actions. But our sense of meaning is contingent, always shadowed by the chaos that lurks behind our need to make our own meanings. When events shake our everyday reality and sense of meaning, we become terribly insecure, so we seek to avoid these dangers as best we can. Modern society is chronically insecure because we know that our meaningful lives can easily be thrown into doubt and we do it to ourselves quite frequently, because as a society that lives through reason and science we are *always* questioning what we know. This ontological insecurity creates a sense of dread about the world and, as we cannot live our day-to-day lives in a state of constant dread, as a society we organize things in such a way as to bracket out those questions that might be raised about the social frameworks through which we conduct our lives and elaborate the meaningfulness of our daily existence.

For Mellor, death is always a potential challenge to our everyday meaningfulness, and consequently a challenge to our elaborate social frameworks, so in modern society we have bracketed off death by hiding it away in lonely hospital beds. Why does death rock the modern world so much? It does so,

> because death signals the end of reflexive planning, the point at which reflexively constituted knowledge can no longer be applied, thereby opening up individuals to the 'onslaught of nightmare' where an understanding of what is meaningful and what is real disappears. Death has been sequestrated because it is a challenge to modernity itself. (Mellor, 1993, p. 25)

So, according to Giddens' theory of ontological security being the cornerstone of modern society, societies must deny death to a certain extent to allow people to go on in their everyday life with some sense of commitment. We are always on the brink of existential angst and one way we cope is to bracket death off. Hence modern society does this bracketing by making death a personal/subjective/individual/private experience that happens in secluded places.

So, for Mellor, death plays a central (though negative) role in the constitution of modern society. He stretches this explanation of current death practices to the contours of mainstream sociology, arguing that sociology does not look death directly in the eye. Instead, it hides it away in secluded sub-disciplinary culs-de-sac where a few sociologists work out applied problems; for example, how to make hospice care more acceptable and accessible.

Alternative theoretical accounts have emerged. Walter (1994) develops a different reading of modern death practices. First pointing out, in agreement with Mellor, that death is individualized in modern Western society, but then disagreeing with Mellor's contention that death is hidden behind the professionalization of medicine, Walter says it is inaccurate to say that death is secreted within the medical establishment. For Walter, death is everywhere, and particularly in the mass media. As far as Walter is concerned, the move towards individualizing death in fact signals a revival of death rather than an attempt by Western society to hide it. This reading of individualization allows Walter to develop a different explanation for the role that death plays in the organization of society. For him, modern society is still defined by its individualization. But whereas this was a reason to deny death for Mellor, for Walter this places death in a more positive role in that he sees there has been a revival of death over the course of the twentieth century, seen in the rise of the hospice movement and the growing practice of arranging one's own funeral.

Yet the revival of death, or the cult of dying my way is not as individually determined as it seems at first sight. For Walter, these private feelings are in fact a manifestation of more public interactions that emphasize 'the authority of the individual – only individuals can and should determine how they want to die or grieve' (Walter, 1994, p. 185). According to Walter, modern people are shown, through public dialogue, how to 'do' death individualistically: 'Within hospices, and other institutional settings committed to patients dying their own way, role models are presented by both staff and by other dying patients; dying is learned and mutually constructed. Even when people die their own way, the death has been constructed together with others' (Walter, 1994, p. 189). For Walter, the interactions between individuals and institutions, including the mass media, that at first glance may seem incredibly atomistic are in fact an ongoing process of meaning-making, and as such they constitute society. Evolving traditions based on negotiations of meanings and practices is at the root of Walter's theory of death practices, and his theory of society. Walter gives us a social interactionist theory of modern death practices.

We now turn to the fourth, discursive perspective, laid out in Armstrong's article 'Silence and Truth in Death and Dying' (Armstrong, 1987). Armstrong develops his theory of death in modern society by taking a discursive approach to understanding the social world. This perspective approaches current death practices as elaborations of particular regimes of truth with associated institutions, infrastructure, symbolic referents and habituated responses to particular events that have come to be known as dying. One trick with this perspective is that all reality (all the things we know to be true, and that we take for granted as happening beyond our control) is really shaped by what we think of and regard as being true, and shaped by ways of knowing death. Under this perspective, death is what we say and think death is. Armstrong deals directly with the issue of sequestration. He explains that the conventional debate over whether death is hidden in contemporary society misses the mark. Mellor, Lifton, Becker and Walter are trying to explain changes in people's activities and how they talk about death, and each explains the changes from traditional to modern in terms of death shifting from the home to the hospital, from everyday community talk to medical talk, and a further shift from medical to cathartic talk with and by the dying in hospices and public forums. Armstrong does not dispute these events, but he argues that these transforming death practices have arisen because there has been a succession of different ways of knowing, a succession of different regimes of truth rather than a profound transformation in the constitution of society. The fate of death as not sequestered then sequestered, and now coming out of seclusion, is really three distinct ways of knowing the truth of death, three distinct ways of speaking about death, and three distinct ways of organizing and co-ordinating social procedures surrounding death: three distinct *death discourses*.

According to Armstrong, in the traditional phase of death,

> in the old regime, the patterns of ceremony, speech and silence had existed in a context demarcated by the domestic, the family and neighbour. In the new (modern) phase, it was the administrative authorities, particularly in the form of medicine, which demanded the ritual of death certification and registration. The death of a body was thereby removed from its private domestic setting and exposed to a truly public visibility. (Armstrong, 1987, p. 652)

Attention to the process of dying gave way to a preoccupation with the dead. And this has given way to a new diagram of power. The human body was no longer the dominant space of truth – the cause of death was fragmented, each sign became ambiguous – death stretched into life, and dying became a process. 'This new discourse of death took over the medical analysis of death and required the confession of the clinician while the new discourse of dying encouraged the dying as subject to speak' (Armstrong, 1987, p. 685).

The different kinds of theories that the four perspectives (critical realism, interactionism, structural functionalism and discursive) generate are all in response to, though not always in agreement with, the theory that modern society is death-denying. They scope out the range of sociological world views available to explain death, dying and bereavement practices.

The discussion so far highlights how scholars of the sociology of death and dying have been concerned to explain the trends and practices associated with modern industrial death-ways. The thesis that death is denied in modern society still has much cachet, and it remains a powerful account in and for modern societies. Even so, there are numerous useful critiques of the various sociological theories about death in modern society. Howarth (2007) succinctly surmises that mid-twentieth-century accounts of modern death were children of their times – overly-psychologized and focused, it seems with hindsight, on the behaviours and beliefs of those who corroborated their theory. And given the self-justifying form that the denial of death thesis takes (if you deny that you are repressing your fear of death, you are repressing that which you deny) it was, for some time, difficult for questions and challenges to be taken seriously. Other key criticisms are that the thesis that modern society is death denying is limited because it tends to over-generalize and neglect marginal experiences and practices surrounding death and dying. These criticisms point to the growing realization that the contemporary world of the twenty-first century is vastly different from the modern world of the twentieth century. Modern societies are moving away from the mass organization closely associated with the twentieth century. As new trends in economic and political life have taken hold where we live in a world of global markets and radical-fundamentalist politics, new trends in death practices are also becoming visible and in need of documentation and evaluation.

Death and globalization

The general idea of globalization; of growing interconnectedness associated with technological advancement, improved communications and capitalist economies, has been around for a long time and can be traced to eighteenth- and nineteenth-century intellectuals such as the Comte de Saint-Simon, Karl Marx and Émile Durkheim. However, the term globalization was first used in the 1960s and 1970s, when people seeking to comprehend a rapidly expanding political and economic interdependence were dissatisfied with available thinking that kept a strict separation between internal and external affairs. The talk of globalization accelerated when the Berlin Wall came down and the East opened up to the West in the late 1980s and early 1990s (O'Byrne, 2003).

Globalization is used to chart a profound shift in social life around the world. These changes include the increasing and deepening interconnectedness of societies in different parts of the world, the almost unimpeded flows of financial capital, news and cultural images across the world, the rising activity and power of multinational companies (MNCs), and rising economic growth accompanied by increasing inequalities in many countries. It also incorporates a global consumer culture in the making, more travel and migration by more people from more countries to greater numbers of countries, faster methods of transport, and electronic communication. There is also a greater awareness by the public of what is happening in the world, and of the possible implications for their own country. Also, 'it seeks to include the rapid growth of governmental and non-governmental supranational organisations that supplement, supplant and support the activities of the nation-state' (George and Wilding 2002, p.2).

This chapter has already outlined some theories about the place of death in modernity – thus, according to Durkheim, suicide deaths are a means of identifying whether a society is functioning in equilibrium or pathologically. Mellor, Lifton and Becker propose that, if we understand that death is denied in modern society, many of the death practices *specific* to these kinds of society make sense. Also, many of the (often viewed as negative) consequences can be understood by reference to society being 'death denying' *and* that improving the situation can be achieved by working to shift social perceptions of death – much in the manner of Cicely Saunders' achievement with palliative care for the dying. What needs to be developed is how contemporary global social organization has an impact on contemporary death, in a similar manner to the way that modern life has shaped modern death. And sociology, with its concern to identify, explain and evaluate new trends in social practice is an appropriate vehicle with which to do so. How is sociology interpreting these widespread societal transformations?

Advanced modernity

Social theorists such as Anthony Giddens (1991; 1999; 2004; 2007) and Urlich Beck (1992; 2006a; 2006b) understand these recent social transformations as a shift to *advanced modernity*, which is marked by a series of complex shifts in the material, scale and cognitive dimensions. In the material dimension, for example, it involves a shift to global flows of trade, capital and people. In terms of scale it is a shift from international to global proportions. The cognitive shift is seen in the growing public recognition of links between distant events and local fortunes that denotes an 'awareness of and an ability to relate directly to the globe' (O'Byrne, 2003, p. 90).

Advanced modernity is marked by advances in technology that allow us to communicate around the globe in real time. These changes have had a profound effect. Everyday life breaks out from the hold of tradition as people share and trade ideas and goods. Many countries, Western and non-Western alike, are actively re-negotiating the role of tradition. We are all finding out about other ways of living and, it is argued, becoming more cosmopolitan in outlook. Our understanding of who we are, at a personal level, is now much more informed by anxiety and contestation between traditional and cosmopolitan ways. This stands in contrast to former times, when self-understanding was informed more by stability and continuity within different traditions. New anxieties are fuelled by the heightening awareness of new vulnerabilities that are a direct consequence of newly manufactured risks such as mad cow disease (bovine spongiform encephalopathy – BSE). This disease appeared as a consequence of feeding meat by-products to cattle that were intended for human consumption. This feeding practice emerged as a money-saving response to rising costs associated with fluctuations in the global commodity market (Giddens, 1999, part 2, 'Risk'). This pervasive sense of vulnerability is also a result of the resurrection of old natural risks, such as floods, that are devastating because they threaten (and take) life because of the ways in which we live today. Loss of life in the Pakistan, East Australian and Brazilian floods of late 2010 and early 2011 are a case in point.

Advanced modernity is gaining credence in sociological accounts of the contemporary world. It argues that many aspects of social life, including politics and economics, identity, representation, technology and religion, are experienced in terms of new global flows of social practice that shift and dissolve pre-existing boundaries. A useful way to approach the study of advanced modernity is to adopt the stance of methodological cosmopolitanism. This means shifting sociology's *unit of analysis* away from the nation-state and towards complex and interconnected global relations (Beck and Sznaider, 2006). It means examining empirically everyday situations and events that emerge from a coming together of global forces, such as global communication technologies and worldwide financial network, all the while recognizing the continued presence of long-standing social practices. The point of looking for the new in social relations *and* the new things people are doing as a result of these new relations, is that it is important to be able to identify what is new, whether it is just a fad or whether it will have an enduring presence, and the likely consequences for people's lives and deaths of these new ways of doing things.

All these effects have implications for the ways in which the living deal with the dead. With advanced modernity, there are new meanings to be read into poet John Donne's *no man is an island*. We have a growing sense of complicity in each other's deaths. Consider the global responses to the photograph that epitomized famine in Sudan. Kevin Carter won the Pulitzer Prize for his striking image of a starving Sudanese child being stalked by a vulture where she had slumped, collapsed on her way to a feeding centre. Haunted by what he had seen in Sudan and other war-torn nations, Carter committed suicide in 1994. The new vulnerabilities wrought by globalization are well illustrated by mass extinctions, global warming and associated extreme geological and meteorological events such as the devastating 2011 earthquakes and tsunamis in New Zealand and Japan.

What do these accounts of connection add to our understanding of death in a global age? Do they signal particular kinds of connection between people in the world today? Put together, do they point to an unavoidable sense of awareness of oneself in global connection with others? This heightened level of conscious-connection could be one key to understanding death in a global age. Perhaps it is the *Zeitgeist* of death in a global age? Living in a global age means to live in a consciously-connected world, one in which we engage socially with death, emphasizing deliberate choices, negotiations and engagements. These social changes have prompted a significant rethink of how sociology can best approach the study of death in advanced modernity.

One theory developed by Walter (1994) adopts an interactionist approach, to suggest that recent changes in the way that people engage with dying and with funerals is marked by multiple practices and personal agency. Tempering this optimistic view, in *Guns, Germs and Steel,* Jared Diamond (1998) draws on a structural-functionalist analysis of environmental factors. For Diamond, this socio-environmental approach is used to explain the particular constellation of inequalities that exist in the advanced modern world. He explains why modern society is closely associated with Western nations. It is not because of genetic superiority, but through the specific material conditions that fostered particular social formations – the four dimensions of material capability, according to Diamond, of the variations on wild flora and fauna that could be domesticated. The second was diffusion within the large continental land masses – because when there were relatively few mountains and seas across particular latitudes, the domestication of plants and animals could spread. Added to this, diffusion between land masses had a direct effect on the circulation of innovation and material goods. It is not difficult to understand why the greatest traffic has been between Eurasia and Sub-Saharan Africa over recent centuries.

The usefulness of these very broad historical takes on death and dying is that they offer ways to come to grips with the place of contemporary societies in the broader span of human existence. Not only do these broader accounts put modern societies in a social context, they also make clear the influence of the specific constellations of material conditions that lie at the root of their high profile and relative power over societies that are not as explicitly modern. They also allude to the enduring complex interplay between different societies. For example, the long-term histories of people from different continents highlights that recently the north has come to dominate southern continents, the West has come to dominate the East, and modern societies have come to dominate traditional ones. Sometimes this is a history of conquest and massacre, such as with the Spanish and Portuguese conquistadores against the people of the Americas; also the colonial slave trade that used brute force to subjugate and transport millions of people from Africa to the Americas. Or the twentieth-century preference for mechanized mass death in the upheaval of the two World Wars that brought many millions of European people from the rural to the urban world. The concern with the interplay of different societies today, and how death shapes and is shaped by those interchanges, is a central feature of the discussions on changing death practices. Does the turn to global networks spell an end to the relative inequities between peoples and nations? And what effect do these new networks have on death – is poverty increased, thereby escalating death by that means? Or is it decreased? Or do these new networks simply redistribute death in unexpected ways?

In similar fashion, Kellehear (2007) links the relationship between death and society in terms of the material environment to explain the particular death co-ordinates of advanced modernity. He explains how physical environments across the millennia have shaped how, where and who have died at a given time and place – which in turn makes for specific kinds of death experience. Kellehear suggests that contemporary dying (what he calls cosmopolitan death) is still overwhelmingly in denial about death.

Walter, Kellehear and Diamond represent different positions in relation to optimistic and pessimistic takes on the multiple and fluid nature of contemporary life and death. Contemporary evidence neither confirms nor denies either interpretation. Both are possible, but neither is likely to tell the full story of death in advanced modern society. A more robust account has to come in a way that can combine the insights from both – that contemporary death is distinctive as a source of creative personal freedoms, while at the same time recognizing that contemporary societies are just as likely to embed injustice, inequality and inhumanity. This book introduces the enduring concerns of the sociology of death and dying, and it does so by assessing their main aspects and existing explanations from a global perspective.

Conclusion

Why the need for this analysis of advanced modern death practices? There has been a shift in people's death practices and they do not sit comfortably within the generally accepted account that modern society is death denying as a result of the massification of its various death practices, so there is a pressing need to incorporate more peripheral practices into the account rather than seeing them as anachronistic.

This author harbours no illusions that the ensuing chapters fully describe and explain the new turn in death practices. At best, they identify several constellations of factors and offer a critical engagement with social theories that are working to explain them. And the conclusion reaches ahead and imagines some of the potential benefits and more daunting consequences of death and dying in a global age. Overall, the hope is that this book is convincing enough in its accounts and arguments to sensitize the reader's watchful eye and keen ear to the harbingers of future death ways.

The first step on that journey comes next, in Chapter 2. The dominant model for understanding death in modern times has been to regard it as a bio-mechanical process. Death occurs when there is a systemic shut-down of the whole (human) entity. This way of comprehending death is linked very closely to the historical scientization of medicine in the eighteenth and nineteenth centuries, and the medicalization of death in the twentieth century, complete with centralization and massification of health care provision in medical hospitals. Within this modernist paradigm, life and death are mutually exclusive states: a person is either biologically alive or dead. Life and death exist at the level of the organic entity – our bodies. Another way to say this is that life and death are *embodied*.

It is striking to note that, over recent years, medical science seems to have taken a quantum leap forward in its bio-technical capabilities. Successful multiple vital organ transplants are becoming commonplace; and body parts that are core to individuals' identities, such as faces and hands, are readily swapped between the dead and the living. Those who are irreversibly brain dead can be kept as beating-heart cadavers almost indefinitely; the bio-switches that control life and death within cells can now be turned off and on in Petri dishes, and in experimental treatments for cancers and paralysis. The list extends by the day. Medicine can, it seems, breach the divide between life and death in multiple, reversible and technically controllable ways. Chapter 2 will show how these kinds of advances rely on interdependencies between technical breakthroughs that reduce body matter into its smallest component parts, and the global rescaling of production, distribution and consumption networks. It then explores some of the new risks that come with these capabilities to discuss what this all may mean for people's actual life and death, and how we may usefully theorize the paradigm of death that operates in advanced modernity.

Questions

This chapter presented an overview of how sociologists have approached the study of death and society, and introduced current issues associated with the transition from modern to advanced modern society.

1. Explain the phrase 'death is socially mediated'.
2. Drawing on theoretical approaches outlined in the chapter, describe two ways that death plays a central role in the constitution of modern society.
3. Explain what is meant by the individualization of death. Give two examples to illustrate your explanation.
4. How might contemporary global relations challenge the theory of 'death-denial'?

Chapter 2

The Social Organization of Death and Dying: A New Paradigm Emerges

Introduction

On 23 December 2005, it was reported in the UK's Guardian newspaper that

> the bones of the late broadcaster Alistair Cooke, whose legendary *Letter from America* became one of the BBC's most treasured dispatches, were stolen shortly before his cremation. As his life's work drew tributes from both sides of the Atlantic, a criminal gang allegedly surgically removed his bones and sold them for more than $7,000 (£4,000) to a company supplying parts for use in dental implants and other orthopaedic procedures. (Younge and Jones, 2005)

The body-snatching scandal involving Alistair Cooke unravelled accidentally when two separate strands of the operation fell apart. In New York, the police had been called by a new funeral home owner to complain that the previous owner had stolen down-payments for funerals. When a detective went to the premises to check out the complaint, she was surprised to find its embalming facilities set up as an elaborate operating room. At the same time, while going through the company records to check for the alleged fraud, she noticed that the funeral home had engaged in many transactions with tissue processing companies. Sensing something more suspicious than funeral down-payment fraud, the investigation team widened its investigation to interview relatives of the deceased – out of 1,077, only one family had given permission for the cadaver to be harvested. At the other end of the country, in Colorado, a doctor had been employed by a group of tissue bank companies to review patients' medical charts. His job was to trawl through patients' death certificates to see whether any cadavers that might have the potential to contaminate tissue banks could have slipped through their safety checking procedures. He found a case he thought should be followed up: a patient's record stated chronic bronchitis. Realizing that this could have been caused by an acute infection (and so possibly contaminate harvested tissue) he telephoned the patient's doctor to verify the type of bronchitis. The telephone number given drew a blank. Trying subsequent records and numbers, many doctors named on the forms were not contactable. This suggested the falsification of medical records. Both the issues of lack of consent and falsified records were traced back to a New York-based tissue-banking company owned by a struck-off dentist Michael Mastromarino. One of his patients was Alistair Cooke, who had been suffering from lung cancer that had metastasized to his bones (*Horizon*, 2008).

When investigated further, an elaborate operation was uncovered where bodies procured by a ring of funeral homes were stripped of profitable body parts. The missing tissue and bones were concealed with PVC piping and other objects before the bodies were returned to relatives to be buried. The body parts were then sold on to various tissue-processing companies with falsified records assuring consent and safety.

Though sensational, the story of Alistair Cooke's bones chimes with the three central points of this chapter. First, this chapter is about the social organization of death and dying. The social organization of death means the ways in which death is managed collectively. It is about how webs of infrastructures and organizations deal with dying and death on a daily basis. A focus on the social organization of death involves two interlocking concerns: the practical configuration of these social structures; and how the meaning of life and death embedded in them shape people's experiences of dying and death.

The fate of Alistair Cooke's bones draws attention to the illegal trade in cadaver body parts and tissues. If we look more closely at what needed to be present for such a thing to happen, we can begin to see powerful social institutions at work. For Alistair Cooke's bones to be usable – and therefore sellable – the four main social institutions that inform death practices (economic, political, cultural and kinship – see the Introduction) were aligned with each other in specific ways. America's liberal economic infrastructure made it possible for a funeral director to simultaneously and legally become a tissue broker, despite the inherent conflict of interests. While the state regulation of the dead (in the form of death certificates that must be completed by a medical professional and legally required permission slips from the next of kin) gives the legal imprimatur to harvest organic material from the dead, culturally, the belief that it is perfectly feasible and acceptable to procure, trade in and use dead human tissue in the pursuit of improving human health and life, has to prevail in general American social beliefs about death and dying. This kind of cultural outlook sees the human body as an organic system that can be compartmentalized and commodified. In terms of kinship, the ways in which family members deal with their dying and dead in contemporary American society, through hospitals and funeral homes, meant that they were relatively easy to deceive. A bag of ashes was enough to suggest that their requests had been fulfilled.

It is not possible to talk of the social organization of dying and death in generic terms, because the ways in which it is carried out are always historically and culturally specific. As Locke and Nguyen (2010, p. 1) put it: [it is because] 'the ways which culture, history, politics, and biology (environmental and individual), are inextricably entangled and subject to never ending transformations'. Even so, there is a shorthand way of talking about the overall effect of all these interconnected factors, and that is to couch the organization of death and dying in terms of a *paradigm*. A paradigm is a whole way of understanding and working within that understanding. It is a way of thinking about the world that influences all the actions that take place within it. For example, people who adhere to a particular set of religious beliefs that guide their decisions and day-to-day practices are working from within that religious paradigm. When we consider how societies organize dying and death, we can see the distinctive ways that death is organized in a given society, and that there is a distinct paradigm in operation.

A few words of clarification are needed before going any further. The social organization of dying and death is a particularly demanding aspect of death studies, and with good reason. Understanding how societies organize death and dying is core business for sociology. Also, since getting-to-death more often than not is through an ailing body that falters and fails within medical settings, other branches of sociology, such as the sociology of health and illness, and the sociology of the body, share the same concerns: issues connected to dying and death are at the same time issues about health and illness, and issues about the body in society.

One example is a shared concern within sociology to discern and explain social systems of inequity and disadvantage in the world, be that through exploitative practices connected to organ harvesting or social disempowerment embedded in the sick role, or the unfair social consequences of sex/gender differentiation. Inequities in death and dying are also likely to appear as as inequities in relation to health and illness and the body. These shared concerns highlight that some of the core debates in the sociology of death and dying have been developed and discharged in other areas. For example, the medicalization debate has taken place both in the sociology of heath and illness and in the sociology of deviance and crime. This overlap explains why significant contributions to that debate are not always drawn from the field of death and dying. To prevent the discussion from becoming unwieldy, only issues *as they are relevant to death and dying* are dealt with in this chapter, on the understanding that readers should be able to follow up particular discussions armed with the most relevant concerns for the sociology of death and dying.

A central concern of this chapter is therefore to outline the death paradigm in modern Western societies in the twentieth and twenty-first centuries. The second point of the chapter is to discuss how various sociologists of death and dying have explained and criticized the prevailing death paradigm of the twentieth century; and third, how it may be changing in the twenty-first century as a consequence of global relations. It begins with a brief consideration of ways of thinking about the meaning of death, then goes on to outline the modern death paradigm and how it came to be. This is followed by a discussion of how the sociology of death and dying has sought to explain and critique this social formation, in particular in light of recent global trends.

Conceptualizing the boundary between life and death

There are numerous archaeological, historical, anthropological and religious academic tracts which seek to recount the many ways that human societies have perceived the boundary between life and death, and how people negotiate its crossing. While hearing Kellehear's (2007) caution that it is not wise to second-guess the symbolic and spiritual motivations for the burial practices of ancient cultures, it is still evident that the dead were recognized as being different from the living and given special treatment, which hints at a belief in death as separation of some essence of the person from the flesh. For example, in the ancient Neolithic and Cro-Magnon burials of 35,000 years ago, peoples' remains were painted with red ochre, consistently placed in a north–south orientation, and provided with items in the grave that would be useful on a journey. This suggests that 'Stone Age people believed that death was another type of life' of a different order to the embodied one of flexing flesh and pumping blood (Kellehear, 2007, p. 24). How the boundary between life and death is understood, and how people cross between the two varies by history and culture.

The following passage from a popular book about spiritual traditions also illustrates in a more vernacular way different ways of understanding the transition from life to death: 'I'm a Buddhist. When I drop the body, I will become pure consciousness. I'm Hindu. I am pure consciousness already. Who are you kidding? When you're gone, you're gone. Period. That last voice is the voice of materialism, which regards death as final because it sees life only in the physical body' (Chopra, 2006, p. 30). Chopra reminds his readers that a working definition of death is directly linked to how one understands the universe, and that the world is a mix of diverse and distinct cosmologies that alter over time.

There is a close link between how death is conceptualized and how it is socially organized. For example, when death is understood as a passage from a material to a metaphysical state – which is the case in Christian religions, for example – the social organization of dying and death is most likely to be organized in a way that reflects and embodies these views. Historically, in Europe and America, when death came knocking, it would be the priest rather than a doctor who would be called, because the vital social role would be to help the dying person's soul depart his or her body absolved from sin. In modern societies, death and dying are organized primarily through medical institutions and infrastructures (hospitals and health care systems). It is helpful to explain medicine's dominance over dying and death by how it came about. Historically, it has been a two-pronged process; one is the *scientization of medicine*; and the other is the *institutionalization of medicine* as the profession to provide health care and death care for the populations of many modern countries.

The scientization of medicine

The story of modern medicine and how it has defined the modern death paradigm begins in the ancient world. Before the scientific revolution of the seventeenth century, learned medicine practised in Europe and the colonized Americas drew on the ancient Galenic tradition, itself a product of Greco-Roman medicine that had been filtered through Arabic traditions as it travelled up through the European continent. As with any medical tradition, the Galenic approach was based on particular ideas about how the body worked, what had gone wrong when it did not work, and ways to try to right it. As doctors learned their profession through the close study of ancient books handed down through the generations, it was a medicine based on the interpretation of historical texts handed down from the ancient Greeks and Romans. The Galenic understanding of the body was, to put it simply, based on three organs – the heart, the liver and the brain, each of which governed a specific bodily system; the heart, for example, formed the principal member of the organs of the chest. These three organs were associated with three virtues (the spiritual, the animal and the natural). Of the three, 'the brain was the principle member of a collection of organs that included the spinal cord and nerves. This system controlled thought, motion, and sensation: the animal virtues' (Lindemann, 2010, p. 89). The main point of the Galenic system was that food, after being ingested, was transformed by natural warmth in the stomach into different substances. Parts of these were useful to the body and were transported by the blood to the different organs, while the waste was excreted. The main products of this process were the four humours: blood, mucus, yellow bile and black bile. These humours were combined with the four primary qualities: coldness, warmth, dampness and dryness. If the four humours and the four primary qualities were in a state of mutual equilibrium, the person was healthy.

Galenic technologies for understanding the body and diagnosing death involved looking at and touching the outside of the body, feeling and looking for signs that would denote an excess or shortage of heat, cold, wetness or dryness (Foucault, [1963]1994).Treatment was based on attempts to rectify imbalances: 'Standard therapies and preventives depended on re-adjusting perceived imbalances by siphoning off a humour that had either grown too strong or become corrupt. The practical means of doing so were bleeding, purging, vomiting, or opening lesions in the skin to allow proper draining' (Lindemann, 2010, p. 14). The Galenic tradition was naturalistic and holistic. As a doctrine it was concerned with the whole person in two ways: 'Illness normally arose from inner, constitutional developments, not pathogenic attacks from the outside. And the body and mind interacted so that emotions might produce illness' (Lewis, 2007, p. 43). Galenic medicine, as it affected the vast majority of the population, remained relatively stable over the centuries, where 'most doctors were content to enquire about previous illnesses and present appetite, to feel the pulse, and to observe the appearance of the eyes, tongue, urine and faeces, in that order of interest' (Conrad *et al.*, 1995, p. 19). Doctors attended to those who could afford to pay, and those who could not turned to self-treatment or traditional healers.

Since it was believed that disease resulted from the imbalance (*dyskrasia*) of the humours or the predominance of one or another quality (hot, cold, wet and dry) death was the result of intolerable imbalance or leakage of these vital fluids (Nutton, 2005). Galenic physicians depended on a few basic observations to determine death. Life had passed into death if the heart did not beat and air did not flow into and out of the lungs. Simple tests could be added, if necessary – for example, finding no response when the skin was pinched or pricked, or no involuntary reactions when the body was moved to a different position. Apnoea (no breath) became the cardinal sign of death, and mirrors and feathers were used for centuries to confirm the absence of breathing (Park, 2004, p. 625). Doctors were seldom present at the deathbed, because the church was the official organization that managed a person's dying and death – priests were the sanctioned professionals who oversaw the care of a person as their spirit passed from this mortal life into eternity. If doctors were present, it was only to estimate the probable time of death so that the priest could be called in time to officiate and give the last rites.

Many social histories of modern medicine debate the various trends and challenges that ultimately overthrew the Galenic order of medicine. Despite a lack of consensus on the specific set of incidents that mark the end, there is much agreement that the practice of anatomy played a significant part in its overthrow, as did the popularity of Paracelsus (1493–1541). Anatomy is about examining (that is, cutting open) bodies to understand physiological structure and processes. Evidence of early civilizations possessing a knowledge of human structure has been found among remains from various cultures. Some noted exceptions, however, are those of the Babylonians, Syrians, Egyptians, Chinese and Hindus, whose religious or philosophical beliefs conflicted with such desecration of the human body.

Anatomy encouraged change because it became a practical focus for the radical transformation in thinking about the body that Paracelsus epitomized. He denied the effect of the humours and thought that diseases were caused not by humoural imbalance but were entities in their own right, in the way that these days diseases are understood as being caused by pathogens (for example, bacteria and viruses). Within living memory of Paracelsus, Flemish physician Andreas Vesalius (1514–64) and Englishman William Harvey (1578–1657) had each trained at the Padua medical school and independently developed significant advances in understanding the human body by way of anatomical dissection. Vesalius's and Harvey's approach was to use methods of close observation and experimentation to (respectively) correct some errors in Galen's descriptions of the major organs (for example, that the liver was not five-lobed); and to demonstrate the circulation of the blood through the body. While neither spearheaded a revolution against Galen, their work paved the way for a tipping point, when 'A medicine based on experiential knowledge, observation, and experimentation thus came to replace a medicine of texts' (Lindemann, 2010, p. 66). The impact of anatomy on medicine, and the scientific method of experimentation and observation on knowledge acquisition was profound because, through close observation and dissection (of human as well as animal bodies) not only did a new, more mechanical understanding of the human body emerge, but also a new way of understanding both illness and death.

In terms of disease, thinking moved from a humoural to a pathological understanding. In this view, disease came to be understood as being caused by localized pathologies of the body. Diagnosis of disease was oriented towards close observation and note-taking of physical symptoms that were linked to anatomical abnormalities (called the anatomo-clinical approach). These explanations approached ill-health as the physical consequence of the mechanical breakdown of organs and tissues caused either by damage or disease. Of interest in terms of the relationship between patient and physician, the anatomo-clinical method of diagnosis does not rely on a patient's verbal reports but on observable physiological abnormalities. This new way for physicians to understand and interact with the human body came to be known as the bio-medical approach to health and illness. The bio-medical approach is mechanistic (it views the body as a machine with interlocking working parts) and materialistic (the human body is *only* made up of the material – there is no space for the concept of a soul or spirit, or a holistic approach to understanding illness and treatment).

When the body is viewed only as a biological system, the meaning of death changes. It shifts from one based on the extreme imbalance of the humours that has resulted in the separation of the soul from the human form, to a materialist one where death itself is no more than an extreme example of disease. From this perspective, death occurs when the complex organic system of the human body irreversibly shuts down and begins to decompose – this is known as systemic death (as opposed to cell death).[1]

As the term suggests, *systemic death* is when the whole system goes into irreversible shut-down. Systemic death has profound observable effects on the body: loss of consciousness after cardiac arrest occurs in seconds, while other functions of the brain may take minutes to stop. Some organs may take hours to stop functioning, while connective tissue may take days to die. To reflect the process of systemic shut down, systemic death is divided into somatic, clinical, higher brain and brain stem death. Somatic death is when the heart and breathing stops and anoxia (the pathological state when tissues do not get enough oxygen) sets in. Without a supply of oxygen, cells begin to die very quickly. Clinical death is when the heart and lungs have stopped but before the vital organs have become damaged through lack of oxygen. This lasts for about six minutes. Starved of oxygen, brain cells die rapidly. Serious brain damage and brain death occur within two to three minutes of somatic cessation. Higher brain function stops first (such as, vision, abstract thought, personality) followed by the death of parts of the brain-stem, also known as the vital centres involved in the maintenance of the respiratory and circulatory systems. Once death has occurred, other physical changes also begin that signal systemic shut-down. These include algor mortis, livor mortis and rigor mortis (Mims, 1998).

While the transformation of medicine from Galen to science marked significant leaps forward in the mechanical understanding of the human body and its treatment, it occurred on the back of significant criminal activity and general social injustice. These injustices are important to appreciate, not only for their dramatization of the past, but also as a reminder that influential social changes are never solely beneficent.

One irony of medicine's advance is that it came to rely very heavily on dead bodies to advance the science that aimed at the preservation of life. The new scientific medicine relied on dead bodies both to train future doctors and to expand the understanding and knowledge of pathology. But, bodies were difficult to obtain as dissection had been restricted, on cultural and legal grounds, to the bodies of murderers who had been hanged on the gallows. Medical schools were legally restricted to only one body per year to dissect. However, a confluence of social factors were building momentum alongside the anatomists who were questioning the long-held beliefs of Galenic medicine: there was much social change and great economic pressures in the social milieu of continental Europe, Britain, America and the colonies of the time. Religiously grounded prohibitions on dissection and vivisection were loosening as a new spirit of humanism took hold. There were large numbers of powerless and sick people in the early-nineteenth-century cities of Europe, America and the colonies. As a profession, medicine was growing in social status, and medical practitioners were accorded social worth and considerable freedom to pursue their scientific research unhindered. The demand for cadavers for dissection far outweighed the legal supply, and given the laws of supply and demand, less legal avenues of supply flourished.

One summer's day in 1818, villagers of Ipswich, Massachusetts, buried eight empty caskets. Their hollow ceremony was a virtuous attempt to rectify their shock and shame because, during the previous winter, eight of their graves had been plundered 'for anatomical purposes'. The culprit was local physician, Dr Thomas Sewall (Sappol, 2002, p. 13).

Within a decade of Ipswich's sorry ritual, the sensational trial of resurrectionists[2] Burke and Hare stunned the British population. William Burke and William Hare had only been caught because they had been greedy. For some time before they were apprehended they had been supplying relatively fresh cadavers to the Edinburgh medical school for dissection. Their scheme was to steal bodies as soon as they had been buried – digging them up on the night they were interred. The fresher the better, as dirty and foetid corpses had a lower premium. The lure of extra income overpowered them, however, and they began to procure extremely fresh corpses that had never been in the ground. Given the welter of isolated and itinerant people fresh in from the highlands and islands of the west of Scotland, and the droves of Irish people escaping the starvation of the potato famine, it was relatively easy to befriend then pressgang a new client for the dissection table of Dr Robert Knox, the sophisticated and well-heeled anatomy specialist at Edinburgh's medical school. It was only because of the gregarious nature of a recent Irish immigrant, Mrs Docherty, that they were caught. Having befriended other tenants in her lodgings, her absence was noticed and the police were called in to investigate. Finding her fresh body on the table of the local medical school, with the marks of foul play clearly evident, the noose began to tighten on Burke and Hare's scheme. They were brought to trial throughout that Christmas and New Year season of 1828, and though they were suspected of murdering between 13 to 30 people, there was never enough evidence to get a conviction on more than one body – that of the unfortunate Mrs Docherty. When the case finally came to trial, Hare turned evidence against Burke, and Burke was found guilty of murder. He was executed on 29 January 1829 and his body donated to the Medical School for what they called useful dissection. Nearly 200 years after his death, Burke's skeleton remains on display at Edinburgh University's Medical School. Though Dr Knox was named as the recipient of the bodies, he was never charged with any crime, nor was he brought to trial (Fido, 1988).

The exploits of Sewall, Burke and Hare reveal who the main targets were – groups who could offer little resistance and who would not be missed by the rest of the community: paupers were the main targets on both sides of the Atlantic (Humphrey, 1973). Within a few brief years of Burke and Hare's own demise, a new British law came into force: the 1832 Anatomy Act. This act addressed the shortfall in legitimate corpses for the dissecting table in a way that laid bare the class lines of Victorian society and fuelled the explosion of burial societies in poorer communities. The 1832 Anatomy Act allowed the state to seize unclaimed corpses from workhouses and sell them to surgical schools (Richardson, 2001).

The institutionalization of medicine

The rise in the institutional authority of medicine was less dramatic but equally significant. The high social status of medicine meant that physicians who could gain the patronage of rich and powerful people were assured significant personal wealth and status. However, because medicine was not organized collectively it could not develop a significant power-base as a profession in its own right. This situation began to change in the nineteenth century, when many European, American and colonial state authorities set up boards of health as bureaucracies (such as the London College of Physicians and the American Medical Association) to oversee the new medical corporations. The health boards and licensing corporations had two functions. They were gatekeepers to the profession, as their members decided who should be admitted to the profession and be allowed to practice legally. At the same time, once a physician had been granted a licence to practise, he or she automatically became members of that corporation. Medical corporations were then simultaneously policing and recruiting physicians, and thus fostered their monopoly on the right to practice medicine (Lindemann, 2010, p. 177). This had the dual effect of excluding non-bio-medical forms of medical practice (for example, homoeopathy) while raising the social stature and authority of bio-medically based medicine in late-nineteenth and early-twentieth-century modern Western societies. The institutionalization of bio-medicine as the *sine qua non* of treating illness gained significant ground in the early decades of the twentieth century. In Europe, Britain and the Antipodes the bio-medical profession was in the best position to sign up to oversee and provide health services to budding welfare states which sought population-wide health-care. American bio-medicine gained a central foothold in private and public health insurance schemes. While not sharing the same route of government-sanctioned health providers, American and European bio-medical institutions came to dominate both the thinking and the practice of health care in Western nations in the twentieth century. Medical practice was provided through extensive infrastructures of general practitioners, referral clinics and teaching hospitals that, in combination, came to dominate the provision of health care in twentieth-century modern societies (Lewis, 2007).

The growing influence of bio-medicine in the twentieth century organization of death is evident in different ways. One is its authority to verify death – the first, necessary step in the legal process of certifying a death. Up to the 1960s, common law in use around the world presumed that all vital signs had to cease before death could be declared or certified, and verification of systemic death was carried out by medical professionals using long-standing practical methods already referred to in this chapter (Youngner *et al.*, 1999, p. 122). Once verified, a death can then be legally certified. Deaths need to be certified to allow burial to take place and for criminal law purposes (where death is the criterion for the commission of a crime).

The certification process is also the trigger that sets in train a series of other official responses which may include, for example, succession and the distribution of property, as well as the inclusion of the death in statistical and epidemiological records.

Another form of influence is in the causes of death. The impact of bio-medical treatments, especially those able to treat infections, combined with the state's public health mentality translated into two effects on the health of the population. Not so many women would die in childbirth, fewer children would die in infancy of contagious diseases, and, in general, fewer people would die of infections. This meant that the age at which the majority of people died shifted from infancy to late adulthood, and the nature of fatality also shifted, from infections to age-related chronic degenerative diseases. This double shift in what people die of, and when they die, is called *the epidemiological transition*. The management of dying also shifted, from being in the care of religious orders to being in the hands of the burgeoning medical professionals: 'If in the mid-seventeenth century a good death required courage and faith as the final test of the Christian, 150 years later the good death was being medically managed, as an extension of the doctor's therapeutic role, to be as smooth as the transition to sleep' (Lewis, 2007, p. 66). Also, before the twentieth century, the vast majority of deaths occurred in people's own homes, but with the growing influence of medicine in the capacity to relieve if not to fully treat conditions, many more people entered hospital for chronic illnesses that would result in their deaths. There was a rapid move towards what is called the *hospitalization of death* in the early to mid- decades of the twentieth century. In Canada, for example, the rates escalated from the 1930s to 1966, reaching a peak in 1994, with 80.5 per cent of all deaths taking place in a full medical environment (Wilson *et al.*, 2001). By the late 1980s, in England over 60 per cent of people died in hospital settings (Mulkay, 1993, p. 36).

The death paradigm at the centre of bio-medicine has come to inform how dying and death have been understood and managed in modern societies of the twentieth century. When death is merely a cessation of the biological system that is the body, it is caused by the mechanical breakdown of the internal parts through injury, disease or dysfunction. Death tends to happen in hospitals as people are treated towards a cure up to the point that it is certain that life will not continue, and it is often too late or too complicated at that point for patients to return home to die.

The bio-medically shaped way of organizing death is referred to as the *modern death paradigm*. In this paradigm, death is biologically defined (to the exclusion of any other dimensions such as spiritual, religious, holistic and so on). It is also embodied. This means that, when death occurs, it has happened in a discrete body made up of the system of organs and tissues that has ceased to function. Another way to say this is that death is understood as a bounded entity – it is linked to the beginning and end of a human life that is lived out within the confines of one particular body. These distinctions, of being biologically defined, of being embodied and bound by the singular human form, are significant because, as it turns out, though they form the basis of a strongly held and deeply embedded definition of death, they have been subject to change over recent decades.

The social control of death by medicine

Sociologists have sought to explain and critique the growing presence of medicine in twentieth-century death. Powerful intellectual critiques of biomedicine and its relation to health were made 'by Ivan Illich about physician-induced illness and the medicalization of what were problems of living; by Vicente Navarro about capitalism's unending search for profit and thus the promotion of health-care markets in the growth of technological medicine; and by Thomas McKeown's minimization of the role of curative medicine in the great mortality decline' (Lewis, 2007, p. 53). Illich, Navarro and McKeown, like many others, focused on the negative, if unintended, consequences of the medical organization of medicine, the manner in which it was practised, and the overinflated belief in its capacity to improve the quality of life. Called the *medicalization thesis,* the basic point was that medicine had totally overreached itself and was shaping up as a social institution intrinsically involved in social control.

Illich's approach argued that medicine, by labelling aspects of life as illness, could exert significant control over certain behaviours and activities. From this approach, medicine is a moral enterprise that defines and manages individuals deemed undesirable by the broader culture. For example, since early in the twentieth century, deviance has increasingly been medicalized, as is evident in public discourse: one is no longer a drunkard, but rather suffers from alcoholism, and the slow learner in school is no longer stupid but rather has a learning disorder. Intervention is in terms of medical treatment and ongoing medical surveillance, as those who deviate from the norm of healthy behaviour are now stuck with the label of lifelong patients. Illich's attack on medicine sought to reveal the limits and negative consequences of medicine in terms of people's autonomous action. One way that he sought to reveal the structural exploitation at the heart of modern professional medicine was to suggest that medicine was not as good at healing as it claimed, but that many of its practices actually made people ill (this is known as iatrogenic disease: iatrogenic meaning the adverse effects, complications or death caused by or resulting from medical treatment or advice), thus they needed more medical treatment, so furthering the profitable possibilities of medicine. He showed the connections between the way that medicine was organized and its cultural context in American society, where economic relations are capitalistic and based on the commodification of goods and services for profit.

While Illich was not concerned specifically with death and dying, the general questions he raised echoed studies taking place at that time. The *medicalization of death* seeks to make sense of how and why the medical establishment has made significant inroads into death practices. The first step in the critique is to elaborate ways in which medicine has involved itself in problems of living. One way is the aforementioned hospitalization of dying. When death takes place in hospital, it is medical professionals who are in control of where and how it occurs – of the drug-induced, pain-free coma. Medicine's control over death is also seen in the increasing dominance of bio-medical thinking in the treatment of the dying, where the focus is on intervention for a cure, or the control of physical symptoms. More ammunition against the medicalization of death is used in the iatrogenic diseases argument. Iatrogenic deaths are statistically significant: in 2004, a HealthGrades study of 37 million patient records concluded that during the years 2000–2 an average of 195,000 Americans annually died because of in-hospital medical errors. According to the report, 'the United States loses more American lives to patient safety incidents every six months than it did during the entire Vietnam War. This also equates to three fully loaded jumbo jets crashing every other day for five years' (HealthGrades, 2005).

One other critique of medicine's capacity to control death concerns the unequal distribution of health care. Despite themselves being a source of economic revenue, those who are the most economically prosperous gain the best access to medical health care and suffer the least. In estimates of the total burden of suffering and life-shortening conditions, interesting comparisons can be made. According to the World Bank Group (2008), 'Developing countries account for 84 percent of global population, 90 percent of the global burden of disease, and 20 percent of global GDP, but only 12 percent of global health spending'. Seen in reverse, developed countries make up 16 per cent of the global population; suffer only 10 per cent of the global burden of disease but account for 80 per cent of the total spending on health care. Premature death frequently occurs in those unable to afford medical treatment or who for some reason are defined as undeserving of drastic measures. According to Kearl (1989), this explains the 59 per cent longer wait by African-Americans for kidney transplants, and the 89 per cent higher rates of bypasses for whites than blacks.

At a more personal level, a ground-breaking study of dying in hospital conducted by the interactionist sociologists Glaser and Strauss (1968) found that patients were subjected to what they called *social death* by the ways in which the hospital professionals engaged, or more to the point, did not engage with them when they were dying. They were able to examine social interactions to explain how the medicalization of death de-humanized the dying. Dying patients were treated 'as if they were already dead'. They found that hospital staff interacted with patients in a very particular way – if a patient was near death they were often moved into a secluded side-ward, staff would not talk directly to them and would have conversations about them while in their presence. Glaser and Strauss coined the phrase social death to capture what they saw as the disempowering, dehumanizing consequences of dying in modern medical hospitals (Glaser and Strauss, 1968).[3] Social death is about changes in social relations. It is about attitudes that can be held toward others that we recognize and treat in particular ways. If we treat others as being socially dead and deny them the benefits of living in society, this is a form of inequality. In this way, Glaser and Strauss's work proved to be a useful way to unravel the power relations embedded in medicine's approach to dying and death.

Feminist and critical realist perspectives have also been used to further the cause of the medicalization of death. Feminist analyses explored the gendered nature of the definition of illness and the treatment of patients, and their main concern has been to reveal the ways in which medical treatment involves male control over women's bodies and identities. During the heyday of the medicalization thesis, feminist critiques tended to argue for the recognition and reclamation of womanly skills in care for the dying, against the male-oriented, technologically focused and ultimately inhumane practices of 'male-stream' medicine. Classics include Ehrenreich and English's (1973) *Witches, Midwives, and Nurses*, which recounted how 'regular' physicians took over healing practice from women and 'irrevocably split' curing from caring (Lind, 1989). Other studies sought to reveal the hidden histories of how women from working-class backgrounds managed dying and death without the privilege of medical care (Adams, 1993).

In critical realist approaches, the main focus is on how the definition and treatment of health and illness are influenced by the nature of economic activity in a capitalist society. These approaches retain a focus on the power of the professions and mediating organizations such as pharmaceutical companies, and government regulation and less emphasis on the individual. Navarro (1976) developed the most notable account, which set out some features that define medicine as capitalist: medicine had changed from being an individual craft or skill to become 'corporate medicine', and had become increasingly specialized and hierarchical (Bilton *et al.*, 2002, p. 362). In terms of the medicalization of death, analyses drew attention to the effects of the capitalist imperative at the heart of medical attitudes to the dead and dying, especially in America. When Sudnow (1967) studied the social organization of dying in a US West Coast charity institution and a Midwestern private general hospital, he sought to discover how the handling of the dying and the dead was governed by the practical organizational concerns of the hospitals. He found that, for the charity hospital, the dying and dead were organized on a 'mass' basis, and he linked it to a particular attitude of the medical profession towards non-paying patients and the 'peculiarly impersonal environment of the charity institution' (Sudnow, 1967, p. 170). Canada, like the USA, has a dual system of health care that spans charity and private organizations. Many of the other modern Western nations have taken the path of state health care where treatment is provided free of charge through a nationwide system of general practitioners and general public hospitals. The cost of health care is covered from taxes and distributed through central government bureaucracies such as the National Health Service (UK), Department of Health (NZ), and Medicare (Australia).

Despite the different welfare systems used to organize death in these capitalistic societies, the massification and de-humanization of dying and death remain a central refrain in what has culminated in claims that modern societies are denying death and are all the worse for it.

A new social organization of dying and death: 9/11, hybrid humans and intercontinental organ farms

Within hours of the terrorist attacks on the World Trade Center in New York on 11 September 2001, the United States Department of Health and Human Services, the American Association of Blood Banks and the American Red Cross issued calls for people to donate blood. The call went out because supplies were dangerously low, as people had pretty much stopped donating blood in any great quantity. Even though people had got out of the habit of giving blood, immediately after that call went out, people flocked in their thousands to donate. They waited in line for hours. The NY Blood Centre (which supplies most of the New York City hospitals) collected more than 5,000 units of blood and fielded 12,000 calls in the first 12 hours – a mind-boggling response. When the collection centres closed for the day, many people queued through the night and at 6:30 the next morning there were huge lines outside blood-banks not only in the USA but also in the UK and at other centres around the world. In the weeks following the terrorist attacks 11,475,000 units of whole blood were collected – but only 258 units were used, and the vast majority of the blood donated had to be discarded (Glynn, 2003). What was going on here? Why did the citizens of the USA rush to give blood, after years of decline? To ask a wider question, what does this confounding scenario offer for an understanding of the social organization of death and dying through global relations?

In the latter decades of the twentieth century, global networks began to play a significant role in the practice of bio-medicine. The means through which bio-medical products and services were sourced and routed to their final destinations began to be reformed. Distribution networks, previously corralled by national boundaries, spread new nodes and supply chains, legal and otherwise, across the globe between wealthy urban and poor rural communities regardless of their geographical distances and political borders. The products and services proffered by medicine were similarly transformed. They were broken down into their primary component parts, later to be reconstituted as novel products with newly created service industries in attendance. Medicine's monopoly over the practice of managing death has waned and the influence of its conceptualization of death has wavered: the social organization of death has been re-constituted.

The interconnected histories of blood banking and organ transplantation can usefully illustrate the key alterations to the organization of death. Blood storage and transfusion (that is, blood banking) has its origins in the Spanish Civil War (1936–9). Blood banking methods came about because, when Barcelona and Madrid were being bombed, resistance doctors developed new technologies. Frederico Durán Jordá developed an ampoule that could draw blood without air. This minimized haemolysis (fizzy blood caused by the rupturing of red blood cells) which resulted from shaking during transit. At the same time, the anti-fascist resistance networks were good at organizing donors and distribution to the field hospitals that needed the blood. As soon as blood could be drawn, stored and transported, it could be used to save lives. A total of 9,000 litres was collected during the course of the war, and the donors received certificates entitling them to extra food. The capacity and knowledge to run blood banks was further advanced during the Second World War. Small blood bank networks were set up in London and other British cities early in the war. The USA collected civilian blood to send to the UK, and the Free French created a facility in Algeria to assist their fighting forces in France and Corsica. In each place, citizens came forward in large numbers to give blood for their troops as a fundamental contribution to the war effort.

After the Second World War, the organization of blood banking was based on different belief systems regarding civic participation. The easiest way to think about them is in how the blood was collected. The first draws directly from the principles that underpinned the Spanish Civil War and is the *voluntary* donation of blood – where blood is defined as a gift. The other is to sell blood – where blood is defined as a *commodity* (Titmuss, 1970). The two systems emerged around the same time. Europe, Australasia and the UK, in line with their welfare state systems, supported a donation procedure for blood banks. In this model, the donation of blood is voluntary, without financial compensation and distribution of medical need rather than ability to pay. This model fitted very well into the universalistic post-war model of the welfare state, whereby access to such things as health care and blood transfusion was on the basis of need rather than an ability to pay, or who had the right to access it. Makers of health policy in New Zealand, Australia and the UK have also favoured the gift model for managing human tissues for transplantation.

Rather than opting for a national welfare state, America chose to develop an intricate web of private insurance systems to organize and provide care for the needy: a mix of the market and charity. In terms of blood donation, America has a unique situation, with three systems of blood banking: voluntary, credit or commercial. The voluntary system (developed by the Red Cross) was built on donation, like the welfare models seen in New Zealand, Australia and the UK. There was free voluntary donation and transfusion. Community blood banks tended to use a credit system, where recipients (those who received the blood) were required to give the blood bank a donation, either from themselves or from a friend or relative. Both systems occasionally used paid donors to supplement voluntary donations when the need arose from the third, commercial, system of blood collection. For-profit blood banks grew, especially during the 1950s, by exploiting the various gaps in supply and demand left by the voluntary and credit systems. In the absence of a federal licensing system, non-medical entrepreneurs could, and did, set up blood banks with minimal medical supervision, buy blood (often from poor and indigent people) and sell it to needy hospitals. This commodity-based system of blood banking stands in sharp contrast to the gift system, but it is important to note that the US complex system of blood banking in fact reflects the dominant post-war American social values of entrepreneurship and the rejection of nationalistic welfare states (Starr, 1998).

These systems of blood collection as a gift, credit or commodity represent the pre-global conceptualization of the world as being made up of a range of different and independent nations that basically were able to set up their own internal systems in ways that reflected their specific social values –state-run redistribution versus market distribution of well-being. Like the medical organization of dying and death, the spatial limits of the whole blood economy were also the limits of the nation, and blood banks were primarily points for the exchange of whole blood units between one person and another.

The first major shift leading to the globalization of blood banking occurred when biochemists broke down blood into its component parts. In 1944, Edwin Cohn, an American biochemist, developed *fractionation*, the process of separating blood plasma into its different components. The fractionation of blood meant that it could be used in more flexible, strategic and clinically targeted ways than could whole blood. Greater clinical and financial profit could also be made, because it was possible to treat many more patients than by the one-to-one transfusion of whole blood:

> Normally, if you collect 4 units of blood you can treat 4 individuals. But, if you first separate the liquid into red cells and plasma, you can then treat 6 people – 4 with red cells and 2 with plasma – you can increase the blood's usefulness again if you fractionate the plasma into albumen, gamma globulin and other products ... you can treat a total of 23 people, all with the original 4 units. (Waldby and Mitchell, 2006)

The second dramatic shift involved the *internationalization* of blood bioproducts, and this story can be told through the discovery of Factor VIII. In 1965, Dr Judith Pool discovered that the precipitate left from thawing plasma was rich in Factor VIII. She called this *cryoprecipitate*. Pool found that it could be infused to control serious bleeding. However, as a highly concentrated substance, a great deal of blood product is needed to make small amounts of Factor VIII. The pharmaceutical companies producing Factor VIII in the USA made it by pooling plasma from thousands of paid donors into huge vats. Even though these companies had long-standing collection programmes in poor communities in the USA, the demand was so great that companies turned to offshore and less legal means to access blood. Even though nation-states could supply the very small quantities of whole blood needed, they could not meet the need for the complex blood products, and so plasma became a global commodity sold by the poor of the developing world and the USA to the citizens of Western Europe and Australasia.

As blood became an increasingly mobile, flexible and specialized substance needed for more kinds of treatment, such as cancer therapy, it also became a global commodity brokered by international pharmaceutical companies (Starr, 1998; Waldby and Mitchell, 2006). By the late 1970s, the blood services complex had become an interlocking network that mingled the blood and plasma of millions of people living in regions thousands of miles apart.

Generally, the intermingling of bio-fluids has proved to be beneficial. The fractionation and internationalization of blood services revolutionized the treatment of haemophilia and organ transplants, and more people were able to receive life-saving blood products than ever before. However, the new distribution networks also brought peril. Integrating the world's blood products network did more than increase the efficiency of supply – it also established optimum conditions for the spread of emerging viruses. A consequence of the new, relatively cheap, life-giving properties of fraction-ated blood is the new history of many people in locations around the world contracting relentless and potentially fatal conditions. The likelihood of contamination increases dramatically when blood products are pooled from many donors. The results are well documented. In 1982, at a time when some gay men were exhibiting symptoms of a mysterious new illness, later labelled as the Human Immunodeficiency Virus (HIV), US Centres for Disease Control identified a handful of haemophiliacs with a similar symptom profile. This was eventually termed the Acquired Immune Deficiency Syndrome (AIDS).[4]

From blood products to transplantation

In J. Whale's Hollywood film *Frankenstein: The Man Who Made A Monster,* Doctor Frankenstein exclaimed at the birth of his creation, 'It's alive. It's alive. In the name of God! Now I know what it feels like to *be* God!' (Whale, 1931).Technological and organizational advances have has made the unthinkable and the undoable not only possible, but commonplace and rela-tively cheap. It is now possible to keep human bodies functioning indefi-nitely, even though there is no life remaining. Similarly, it is perfectly feasible to live for many years minus diseased or damaged vital organs. Under these conditions, what it means to die and what it means to live take on a particular character unique to the contemporary age.

Frankenstein's monster was put together from body parts of the dead and infused with life by electricity from the sky. Though *Frankenstein* is a fantastic story by Mary Wollstonecraft Shelley, the use of the body parts of others has become possible in the contemporary age. The idea of transplanting animal or human parts dates back many centuries, though the first successful transplant of human-to-human *tissue* (a cornea) was achieved on 7 December 1905. The first successful *organ* transplant (a kidney) took place in Chicago, USA, in 1950, and by the early 1960s doctors had discovered how to match donor and recipient tissue more closely. They also began to use a combination of radiation (to destroy certain cells) and drugs to suppress the immune system (immuno-suppressants). In effect, this shut down recipients' immune systems to prevent the rejection of alien objects and tissues inserted into the body. The first successful *vital organ* transplant, a pancreas, took place in 1966. Soon after this, in 1967, Christiaan Barnard, a South African surgeon, became a worldwide celebrity for achieving the first successful heart transplant. Barnard took the heart of a young black woman and implanted it in Louis Washkansky, a 55-year-old white grocer. Though Washkansky survived for only 18 days, Barnard's second patient, dentist Philip Blaiberg, lived for 17 months. With improved surgical techniques and powerful medicines (such as cyclosporine) to prevent rejection, life expectancy after transplantation increased dramatically during the 1980s. By the 1990s, more than 70 per cent of transplant recipients were surviving for more than three years.

Spurr (1993) outlines a number of factors that have contributed to this growth in demand for organ transplants. Most potential transplant recipients are older people, who are more susceptible than others to organ failure. The share of this segment of the total population in advanced modern nations has grown because of increases in life expectancy and other demographic changes. Moreover, the real income of the elderly population has also increased, along with the number of people covered by government programmes that subsidize transplants. At the same time there has been relatively slow progress in the development of the most important substitute – artificial organs. While research is being done on xenografts (the use of animal organs), most transplant specialists consider this possibility to be at best a long-run alternative (Spurr, 1993, p. 189). At the same time, many countries rigorously restrict the supply of human organs. People waiting for transplants far outnumber those who voluntarily donate a non-vital organ, or donors who are accidentally killed. Ironically, as public health strategies lower death rates (for example, speed limits and seatbelts lower the numbers of car crash fatalities), so allowing more people to live to an age when organs degenerate, the availability of vital organ transplants similarly falls. Despite the difficulties in legally procuring human organs for transplant, there has been a rapid escalation in the number of transplants. As Harrison (1999, p. 2) notes, 'of 6,000 heart transplants performed worldwide by 1988, 80% had occurred after 1984' with the majority of these being carried out in technologically advanced Western countries.

The rescaling of blood and vital organ transplants from an extremely risky experimental procedure to become an applied and in some cases public medical provision that relies on the division of bio-material into ever-smaller components has been labelled *bio-medicalization* (Riska, 2010). Also, the rescaling of the organizational side of medicine includes the international networks of medical practitioners who share similar requirements and standards of practice and training; the global standardization of technologies and instruments; global drug firms – where drugs are developed out of and for global markets; medical research – including access to international data bases; and the digitalization of patient records (to enable the discussion of cases without meeting the patient) (Bilton *et al.*, 2002, p. 378).

All these technological and organizational factors have influenced medicine's domination of the social organization of dying and death. During the 1980s, orthodox medicine began to lose its ability to define and regulate areas of human life – those functions were increasingly taken over by state and federal bureaucracies as theirs were the policies and procedures that decide needs, how these needs should be met, and at what level. For example, it is political bureaucracies that developed policies of community care in the 1980s and 1990s which, by claiming to be progressive policies promoting de-institutionalization, shifted responsibility and costs on to communities.

Bio-medicalization and the increased managerialization of health care is linked to a shift in the organization of dying and death. Voiced through 'death with dignity debates', the shift is evident in the emergence of charity and community-based hospices in wealthy, centrally organized nations. The first hospice *homecare* programme in America was the

> Hospice of Marin, now called Hospice by the Bay, just north of San Francisco. It was founded by psychiatrist William Lamers ... and initially it relied entirely on volunteers to provide in-home support care. Lamers abandoned plans to build a freestanding hospice for financial reasons and instead incorporated it as a non-profit organisation and sought funding as a home healthcare agency (Fontana and Keene, 2009, p. 42).

It is also evidenced in the shift to palliative care *teams*, which are most usually the result of national health strategies. All European Union, American and Antipodean national health bodies have palliative care strategies which are deeply informed by the idea of multi-disciplinary palliative care teams. These teams ideally include consultants, social workers, nurse specialists or oncology nurse specialists and the patient, where 'the patient's subjectivity and the psychosocial context of illness are emphasised' (Lewis, 2007, p. 54). Over recent decades, the trajectory of palliative care initiatives around the world has been one of separation from, then re-incorporation within mainstream clinical services (that is, general hospitals): 'Palliative-care services are now seen as being in a continual dynamic state of development within healthcare systems that are themselves in a state of instability and rapid evolution' (Ashby, 2009, p. 85). Other crucial institutional changes include the wide promotion of patient choice in the ways that hospitals frame the doctor–patient relationship. Otherwise known as marketization, it surfaces in the inclusion of the wishes of the terminally ill person in the palliative care team discussion on the wards (McKinlay, 2001; Phipps *et al.* 2003; Morris and Thomas, 2005; Sinclair, 2007). The distinguishing feature of the process of dying today is that, to some degree, it can be negotiated and controlled depending on the preferences of the dying person, the goals of particular medical specializations, the organizational features of technology-intensive medical settings, and the presence and wishes of family members.

There are other ways that bio-medicine and the organization of death are increasingly at the mercy of state bureaucracies. For example, an economy that is increasingly invested in bio-technology deeply enmeshes the health of its elderly population with the fates of less fortunate others from elsewhere. This happens by way of, for example, the voluntary and involuntary investment strategies of national pension funds, where future pension income is tied to the success of the new medical technologies.

In the modern organization of death, the division between a beating, breathing, systemically sustainable body and an anoxic, irreversibly shut-down one was the division that marked a change in how medical professionals would 'treat' the person. What it means to be alive and what it means to be dead are no longer tied to a single bodily entity. Death in bio-tech times is no longer fully embodied. Technological advances are allowing the reversal of systemic breakdown/ failure and the boundary between being alive and being dead is permeable. Generalizations and experiments – focused on isolating and harnessing the life-giving capabilities of cells (for example, stem cells) – are not tied to particular kinds of bodies but rather to particular kinds of cellular capacities (the on/off switch). It is no longer understood through the dualism of a whole living material body and a whole dead material body. Death, as it disconnects from the idea of a lifetime and the human body as a whole entity, becomes an intermediate zone, where the boundary between being alive and being dead is permeable.

The new interpenetration of life and death also leads to the reformulation of human interrelations as they disturb the legitimacy of long-established symbolic referents. For example, organ recipients actively generate new relationships with their donor's families *and* claim a connection with the soul of the deceased donor (see Sharp, 2006). Does the meaningful body of a transplant donor reside in the coffin or in the host's body cavity? Is, then, the death certificate and funeral a fully legitimate symbolic marker? Also, the idea of a life-course becomes disrupted. When does one life begin and another end if biological birth and death are no longer clearly defined?

Contemporarily, death is understood as a condition to be managed in multiple and potentially lucrative ways rather than an irreversible or unstoppable biological process. We live in a time of great biological possibility; of hybrid humans and human cadavers. Many people are alive only because they have another person's vital organs, skin or bone inserted into their bodies. And these vital organs have remained usable through the process of extraction from those who are, to all intents and purposes, unrevivable, through their re-insertion into those who have tipped over the edge of systemic shut-down. This use of body components and fluids has become routine only because of the capabilities of global networks of bio-medical production and consumption. Not only does a truly global market for human organs and bio-products exist, but the directions in which such products move through these routes reveals a disturbing characteristic of contemporary global networks. Raw materials flow consistently from poorer countries and communities to highly technologized, Western nations. Typically, these latter nations contain a proportionately higher percentage of wealthy older people with degenerative medical conditions.

In cultural terms, there has been a shift to a new culture of death – one that is deeply embedded in a consumer-based culture of longevity. This trend can be paraphrased as *buying into Ever-Land* which makes direct reference to the desired outcome of practices designed to forestall ageing while suggesting that this hope is based on a fantasy world similar to the fairytale world of *neverland,* where children never grew up or old. Cultural attitudes to death, especially in the Western and Northern axes of nations, are transforming. While baby-boomer populations are ageing in a time of medical innovation, there is a growing expectation that ageing should no longer mean untreatable degeneration. When bits of the body wear out, they can be replaced with synthetic prosthetics, bio-products or other people's tissue. Successful organ transplants speak to a way of understanding life based on an expectation of physical health with longevity, underpinned by a belief in the acceptability of replaceable body parts and the presumption of limitless and accessible medical progress (Waldby and Mitchell, 2006). These new challenges and struggles dovetail neatly into cultural attitudes that see death as an option (at a price) rather than being inevitable. The cultural view that death is negotiable depending on the purchase of particular kinds of bio-products is associated with a broader shift towards what is called consumer capitalism. Consumer capitalism is based on a particular way of encouraging people to buy specific kinds of consumables. It is closely linked to the desire for affluent lifestyles (young, rich, healthy and famous). The markers for these lifestyles are the names and consumer goods with which they are associated – such as Gucci, Jimmy

Choo and Louis Vuitton. Youthful longevity is a marker for wealth in a global consumer society, and the bio-product industry has found a lucrative market for its various products, including new-for-you body parts, skin grafts, replacement organs and so on. Many consumers of bio-products associated with the dead are, it could be said, buying into the consumer concept of Ever-Land, as noted above, where it is possible to at least extend the quantity and quality of life by hiving-off and consuming products from the dead. It is not only wealthy individuals, however, but also wealthy nations that have succumbed to the beguiling call of extended living. The provision of vital organ transplants by national health care organizations is testament to the cultural acceptance of life extension through the death of another human being. Investment in cryotechnology is another, more extreme, example of a cultural sentiment of longevity for some, and health service industries are set up around a set of attitudes that favour long life even in the face of significant communal cost and underlining social inequalities.

The new trends in cultural attitudes toward death, of a consumer-based culture of longevity, have fuelled critical debates about the character of contemporary social relations within and between nations. Indicting current race relations in America, statistics on the sources of organs for transplants drew pointed comment. In 1991, in New York City one in four organs came from murder victims. In response, Louis Farrakhan, leader of the Nation of Islam, asserted that white authorities would not stop black-on-black violence because it provided organs for transplant.

In practice, there is a slow but steady incidence of transplant doctors falling foul of the indistinct boundary between legitimate and illegitimate organ harvesting; that is, between taking organs from the already dead and hastening death to procure the freshest organs. One of the critical factors in the success of vital organ transplants is the need to keep organs functioning as well as possible until the moment of removal. When shutting down, the body is flooded by a series of chemicals that severely damage the organs and radically reduce their successful use as transplant material. The most successful transplants occur when the organ has been sustained up until the moment of transfer. The best source of organs is from what were called living cadavers: 'Living cadavers, as they were known – now more commonly the 'brain dead' – have bodies that function close to 'normal', thanks to technological support, but their brains are permanently destroyed' (Lock, 2003, p. 167). San Francisco transplant surgeon Hootan Roozrokh was the first in the USA to stand trial for this, in December 2008. He allegedly prescribed excessive amounts of medication in an attempt to hasten the death of a disabled man, Ruben Navarro, in order to harvest his organs. Though found not guilty, the case became a symbol of problems facing national organ transplant programmes (McKinley, 2008).[5] Other problems that reveal interesting socio-economic and political dimensions of bio-medicine include directed donations and reimbursement.

Directed donations are when people who are giving permission for their organs to be used after their death imposes conditions on who can receive those organs. In 1998, a white British man stipulated that his organs could only be given to a non-ethnic – that is, white – recipient. With no template to follow, and with the person at the top of the donation list being white, an ethical dilemma was narrowly missed. However, the case was picked up by the media prompting public debate over who had the right to selecting recipients. In the ensuing public debate, many people believed that since they were prepared to donate *their* body parts, they should have some say in the criteria for selecting recipients, even if it appeared unfair. Others, including Harrison (1999) and Waldby and Mitchell (2006), point out that, as the transplant and tissue industry is seen to be making massive profits out of donated tissue without reciprocating to families of the donors, many people are no longer as willing to donate without being 'gifted' in some way.

The growing public concern raised by new ethical dilemmas over who has the right to say how a donor is to be selected (more of this in Chapter 9) and capitalistic exploitation of human tissue, coupled with ongoing contamination scares, such as the case of Alistair Cooke's bones detailed at the start of the chapter, have prompted formal initiatives at a level of national and global policy to curb the worst excesses and hazards. However, it is becoming clear that these attempts may be compounding rather than mitigating the problems.

Freeman and Cohen (2009, p. 23) suggest that 'recent cases of donor-transmitted diseases from donors labelled as being at 'high risk' have engendered concern, new policy proposals and attempts to employ additional testing of donors'. The World Health Assembly first expressed its concern in 1987 regarding trafficking in human organs and the need for global standards for transplantation, in response to the increasing awareness of the dangers and risks involved in transplantation. There was also to need to stop the prevalence of organ trafficking by introducing standards to be followed to reduce the risk of the spread of contaminated organs and to protect innocent people from being used for harvesting. However, this may have had a reverse effect to that intended, as a shortage of legally procured organs globally has occurred as a result of the increased regulation. The guidelines laid down by the World Health Assembly and other global platforms, including the World Health Organization, the World Medical Authority and the Council of Europe, have made their way into national law in most countries. Legal provisions against the sale of organs and against organ trafficking are now near enough global (Pearson, 2004).

The concern growing among those involved in the legal trade of organs, and the risks that have been identified in order to reduce them, are laudable in principle; however, these risks are not regulated in the ever-growing illegal organ trade. The restricted legal sources of vital organs, coupled with excess of demand over supply and the failure of non-market solutions to meet this demand, has provided the material basis for the emergence of a global trade in human body parts (Harrison, 1999). The Gurgaon organ theft scandal broke in January 2008, when police raided a private medical clinic in the wealthy city of Gurgaon, outside Delhi, India, to find day labourers, rickshaw drivers and impoverished farmers who had been picked up from the streets with the offer of work, driven to a well-equipped private clinic, and duped or forced at gunpoint to undergo operations to remove organs. During the raid, letters and email messages from 48 foreign citizens – among them, three from Greece and two Indian-born Americans – inquiring about transplants were discovered in one of the clinics (Kumar, 2008). Though kidney transplants do not automatically mean that the donor has died, because human beings have two kidneys and survival is possible with one, health status and life expectancy is compromised by living with only one kidney. Chinese authorities have also been accused of making executed prisoners' vital organs available on the global transplant market. In China, around 12,000 kidney and liver transplants were performed in 2005. While accusations are linked to circumstantial evidence, most of the transplanted organs were alleged to have been procured from executed prisoners. And even though the number of foreign recipients in China is difficult to estimate, media reports offer circumstantial evidence that over half of the 900 kidney and liver transplants performed in one major transplant centre in 2004 were for non-Chinese citizens from nineteen countries (Shimazono, 2007).

Transplant tourism is a parallel development in the international organ market. Geis and Brown (2008) explain that most dealings in body parts have been labelled transplant tourism, which typically involves purchasers from the USA and sellers from poverty-stricken areas in developing nations coming together in secluded, yet medically supported, contexts. The growth of transplant tourism when seen apart from the Indian and Chinese incidents, supports the claim for the existence of inter-continental organ farms, in practice if not in name (see Table 2.1).

These contemporary trends in the social organization of dying and death – in particular the organ trade and trafficking – highlight arguments present in broader sociological debates about the character of advanced modern risk society. The responses to the risks involved with organ transplants and trafficking, including the spread of disease and the exploitation of the vulnerable, highlight how sectors of the global community have responded to the downside of these technological and social advances. Yet even as global non-government organizations attempt to respond in ethically prudent ways, they should not be used to conceal interesting development with regard to the value of human life versus the values of human organs in a transcontinental network of buyers and sellers. It is increasingly apparent that organs are becoming more valuable than the people from whom they are harvested. The trend towards illegal organ and bio-product trafficking has increased the spread of infectious diseases such as HIV/AIDS and hepatitis. The unintended consequences of increasing regulation in the

Table 2.1   Transplant tourism web sites available
21 March 2007

Name of organizations, website	Location of transplantation	Transplant package
BEK-transplant (http://www.bek-transplant.com/ joomla/index.php	China	Kidney (US$70,000) Liver (US$120,000) Pancreas (US$110,000) Kidney and Pancreas (US$160,000)
China International Transplantation Network Assistance Center (http://en.zouklishoku.com/)	China	Kidney (US$65,000) Liver (US$130,000) Lung (US$150,000) Heart (US$130,00)
Yeson Healthcare Service Network (http://yeson.com/index.htm)	China	Kidney, liver, heart and lung
Aadil Hospital (http://www.aadilhospital.com/ index.html)	Pakistan	Kidney
Masood Hospital (http://www.masoodhospital.com/ services/surgery/ktp/kidney_ transplant.htm)	Pakistan	Kidney (US$14,000)
Renal Transplant Associates (http://www.renaltransplantsurgery. com/index.html)	Pakistan	Kidney €16,000 (US$20,500)
Kidney Transplant Associates (http://www.kidney.com.pk)	Pakistan	–
Liver4You (http://www.liver4you.org/)	Philippines	Kidney (US$85,000)

Source: Shimazono (2007).

legal supply of bio-products has merely pushed the trade underground, to where there are no regulations or overseeing bodies. The attempts to mitigate the new risks associated with this bio-medically and commercially oriented social organization of death and dying, and the escalated transfer of flesh from the dead to the living, has only generated new and more recalcitrant risks.

Global society, though it may set out to manage existing and newly manufactured risks, is, in the case of the social organization of death, inadvertently amplifying them. Perhaps it can be said that death wins out in global society's attempts to re-organize it.

Conclusion

'It matters not how man dies, but how he lives. The act of dying is not of importance, it lasts so short a time', *The Life of Samuel Johnson* (Boswell [1769]1952, p. 174). Johnston's proclamation that death is fleeting is far removed from contemporary experiences. Now, in the twenty-first century, not only has the boundary between life and death been extended almost indefinitely; it has also been breached and rendered porous.

The global rescaling of the social organization of death holds the possibility for a bright new future, free from ageing and decrepitude. It also threatens to re-inscribe the enduring unequal redistribution of scarce resources. The new social relations instigated by bio-medical technologies reveal a fresh paradigm of death for advanced modernity – one driven by a commodification and commercialization of death rather than a denial of it. Death is being put to good use by global bio-commerce to reap benefits from a cultural turn towards buying into Ever-Land. It is a time of living cadavers, hybrid humans and intercontinental organ farms. We are witness to, and participants in, global social relations and practices that have profoundly shifted the possibilities of what it means to die, and therefore also what it means to live.

Questions

This chapter discussed the death paradigm.

1. What is a death paradigm?
2. Explain how the modern death paradigm shapes modern death practices. Give some examples to illustrate this influence.
3. What current changes in death and dying challenge the 'modern' death-paradigm. Use the following exercise to investigate the links between contemporary technologies and the changing boundary between life and death. Get hold of a copy of a daily or Sunday national newspaper. Go through each section and identify any piece of copy that relates to death (this could be an editorial, a feature article, a letter, an advertisement and so on). You may be surprised to see how much material is linked to death and dying in our daily papers. Choose a piece that you think relates to this chapter's topic about new technology 'blurring' taken-for-granted boundaries between life and death. Make the following notes: take the details of where the copy came from (remember to include date, page number, the name of the source, the author/journalist and so on), and write a sentence or two on how this piece relates to the blurring of life/death boundaries.

Chapter 3

Patterns in Life and Death: Demographic Trends and Life Expectancies

Introduction

Mr José Luis Garza, a 47-year-old man from Juarez, Mexico, who weighed 70 stone 10lb (452 kg), died of heart failure during an attempt to take him to hospital. His bedroom wall had to be demolished to get him out of his house, before being taken to hospital on the back of a lorry, but he was pronounced dead on arrival. He had always had a weight problem but became depressed and began overeating excessively after both his parents died within a period of two weeks. He had been bedridden for four months at the time of the rescue attempt. His family wanted him to be cremated but there were no facilities to deal with someone as big as him. Eventually, carpenters built a special coffin and a large grave was dug. It took 20 people to lower the coffin into the grave (Associated Press, 2008).

As one of the world's heaviest people, Mr Garza suffered from the medical condition obesity, the outcome of an enduring imbalance in energy intake and expenditure, where more energy is consumed than is used up on a day-to-day basis. Over time, the body accumulates this excess energy in the form of fat deposits called *adipose tissue*. A diagnosis of obesity is made by using the body mass index (BMI). The BMI is used to categorize people in an approximate weight-to-height measure. Individuals are considered to be overweight when they have a BMI large than 25 kg/m^2 and are considered to be obese with a BMI larger than 30 kg/m^2 (World Health Organization, 2011).

Obesity in itself is not a mortal condition, but it certainly increases a person's chances of dying. It is not like an infection, where microbes overwhelm a person's antibodies and kill the host. Instead, it has effects on the body that prevent it from working to such a degree that normal functions collapse. This is called a degenerative disease. There are different types of degenerative disease and they are not all deadly. For example, arthritis debilitates but does not kill. However, the way that obesity debilitates does put it in the category of a killer degenerative disease because it tends to affect the vital or *life-giving* bodily functions, such as circulation and breathing. Most commonly, obesity has been linked to cardiovascular disease, Type 2 diabetes, a range of cancers, osteoarthritis and gallbladder disease, among others. A study conducted in the UK showed that obesity reduces individuals' life expectancy by nine years on average (Moon *et al.*, 2007). As a degenerative disease that is caused by consuming more energy than is spent, obesity can be *reversed* if treated in time. Obesity is therefore a preventable, non-communicable killer.

Since Mr Garza's MBI exceeded 40 kg/m^2, it was no surprise that he died. There was just too much of a strain on his body. And not only was his weight a mortal impediment, but it also fits with a new global pattern of death-dealing diseases. According to the World Health Organization (2011), being overweight and suffering from obesity are jointly the fifth leading cause of death globally. Once considered to be a problem only in high-income countries, overweight and obesity are now dramatically on the rise in low- and middle-income countries, particularly in urban settings (World Health Organization, 2011). Some populations seem particularly vulnerable to obesity, including Hispanics, Maori, Pacific peoples and African Americans (Swinburn *et al.*, 2011).

Obesity started to become a global problem around the start of the 1980s and has been increasing annually since then. Statistics show that, in 2008, about 1.5 billion of the world's adult population were overweight and more than 500 million of these people were obese (Swinburn *et al.*, 2011). Today, obesity is responsible for over 2.8 million adult deaths per year worldwide (World Health Organization, 2011).

The growing prevalence of obesity-related deaths nestles within a broader global trend. More people than ever before around the world are dying from what are called non-communicable diseases (NCDs). Life threatening NCDs are dominated by heart disease, stroke, cancer, diabetes and obesity, and NCDs dominate death in every continent in the world apart from Africa (Beaglehole and Yach, 2003, p. 903). In fact, NCDs are the most popular way to die in the world today, as they are ranked at number one in the World Health Organization's global causes of death (World Health Organization, 2008).

The *global obesity epidemic* is one of the distinctive features of the patterns of death and dying in the world today. Mr Garza fitted the profile. He was from a middle-income country, lived in an urban environment and led a sedentary lifestyle. His premature death from a non-communicable, preventable disease is, on reflection, hardly surprising.

If he had not died from overeating, it is quite likely that he might have fallen victim to a growing range of fatal infections circulating around the globe. Since they first walked the planet, human beings have been in a constantly shifting tussle with the various parasites that cause infectious disease (McNeill, 1998). Yet, at this point in time, the dynamic balance of this human encounter with infectious diseases is shaped by factors that are unique to contemporary ways of living, in particular the increasing intensity and mobility of people, money and products around the world. This has led the world's population into a particular set of infectious disease issues. The rates of newly emerging, resurgent and deliberately emerging infectious diseases are on the increase in the world. A *newly emerging disease* is a disease that has never been recognized before. Unknown before 1980, HIV/AIDS is a newly emerging disease, as is severe acute respiratory syndrome (SARS), Nipah virus encephalitis and variant Creutzfeldt-Jakob disease (vCJD). *Resurgent* diseases are those that have been known for decades or centuries but have come back in a different form or in a different location. For example, the West Nile virus is now present in the Western hemisphere, and monkey pox in the United States (this is directly related to the fashion for importing monkeys as pets into American urban domestic homes). Dengue fever, carried by infected mosquito vectors and originally from Indo-China, is now in Brazil and working its way into the Caribbean. *Deliberately emerging diseases* are those diseases intentionally introduced as agents of bio-terror. The most recent example was the dispersal of anthrax through the American postal service some weeks after 9/11 (Fauci, 2005).

Not all infectious diseases are fatal, but there are some well-known factors that prime populations in ways that make them massively susceptible to the rapid and devastating consequences of infectious disease. These include a lack of basic immunity. If there is no immunity in a community, infections quickly reach epidemic proportions: if an invading microorganism has no challenge, it can quickly overwhelm and kill its host. In the sixteenth and seventeenth centuries, the rapid capitulation of Mexican and Peruvian civilizations numbered in the millions to a motley band of fewer than 600 Spanish conquistadors with a base immunity to the smallpox they carried, testifies to the shocking power of an old infection finding fresh pastures (McNeill, 1998, p. 21).

The spread of new infections is also directly related to the confluence between the infectious period and the pace of movement of its host or carrier. Many infections last only a few days or weeks. If people are prevented from moving while they are infectious, infections can peter out as they run out of fresh susceptible hosts. Thus they become self-limiting. The quarantine of ships and cities during the bubonic plagues of the Middle Ages was a direct and effective social practice, or public health measure, to try to prevent the spread of this death-dealing infection. If a population has suffered significant privations or has come together in crowded and unhygienic conditions, through, for example, war or famine, general resistance is low and what would under normal conditions be a survivable infection, can also quite easily resurface and kill large numbers of people. The underlying principle to this ever-shifting relationship between humans and disease is, according to McNeill, all about reciprocity and equilibrium.

The reciprocity between food and parasite that has underpinned civilized history is matched by parallel reciprocities within each human body. The white corpuscles, which constitute a principal element in defence against infection, actually digest intruders. Organisms they are unable to digest become parasites, digesting in their turn whatever they find nourishing within the human body. At every level of organization – molecular, cellular, organismic and social – one confronts equilibrium patterns (McNeill, 1998, p. 25).

The sedentary, high-fat, high-sugar lifestyles of the urban poor; the high mobility and super-connected lifestyles of both the wealthy and poor in the chase for profit; the increasingly intensive interface between humans and animals as urban settlements encroach on new ecological habitats; the rapid reduction in travel times of humans, products and pathogens; the escalating displacement of people through armed conflict, poverty and ecological degradation; and the increasing polarization of social and economic relations across and within nations is having a cumulative effect on the finely-wrought balance between humans and disease. Combined, these factors bring the world's population into contact with new kinds of infections and non-contagious conditions that are only now becoming fully traced, understood and appreciated. The distribution and rates of both infectious diseases and NCDs are a cipher for health inequalities within and between countries as they affect poor populations, largely because of inequalities in the distribution of both risk factors and health care (Beaglehole and Yach, 2003, p. 903).

The overall effect is a pattern of life and death that is explicitly shaped by contemporary global relations. It is important to examine the chains of influence more closely, for two reasons. One is that it becomes possible to discern more clearly the connections between patterns in life and death and the uneven effects and cultural reception of the global spread of diseases. Another is that such an exercise draws attention to a significant aspect of sociological endeavour in general, and the sociology of death and dying in particular. It emphasizes why counting the dead matters.

It matters because patterns in life and death are context dependent. This may strike one as odd, because death is one of the true constants in life. Death is a constant in the obvious sense that it is ultimately unavoidable, but also because there are only a few ways of dying. All the millions of people who die every year, and the untold legions who have died over the millennia, do so for only a handful of immediate reasons: infection, disease, malfunction, starvation, dehydration and injury. Of course, these six ways of dying are caused by the interplay of a constantly expanding myriad of direct and indirect factors, including mechanized and self-inflicted injury (armed conflicts and suicide). Some of these new causes are linked directly to technological innovations. The capacity to harness nuclear fusion led to the invention and use of the nuclear bomb, and to radiation sickness. New farming practices encouraged innovation, and animals were given foodstuffs their digestion was not designed to cope with. Cows fed on pellets that contained animal remains developed mad cow disease, which jumped the species barrier as the deadly Creutzfeldt-Jakob disease (vCJD) when humans consumed the animals' carcasses.

It is the complex combination of circumstance and pathogen that helps to decide the particular form that our ultimate fate will take. Each constellation enables a particular kind of death. For example, a life replete with food, physical comfort and medical care is often long and ends with slow degeneration, whereas a life of hardship and deprivation is, as Thomas Hobbes famously put it, 'nasty, brutish and short' (Hobbes [1651] 1968). What a person dies of, when they die and how they experience dying are strongly influenced by the social contexts within which they live.

While death is a constant, a death pattern signifies a distinctive calibration between humans and the things that kill them (be they microbes, wear and tear, poison or violence) that endures because of the influence of a specific set of social conditions or events. For example, there is a pattern of high rates of meningococcal disease in young Pacific Island children who live in the poorer suburbs of Australian, New Zealand and American cities such as Sydney, West Auckland and Los Angeles. The pattern of this swift killer is closely linked to poor, damp, cramped living conditions that are the direct result of unequal social relations in these countries. Patterns in death are shaped by, and shape, social relations.

Why counting the dead matters

It is possible to see the broader patterns in individual deaths by gathering together and analysing information about people's lives. Working out the sheer numbers involved, and looking at trends in birth, death and migration rates over time, is known as *demography*. Measuring how many people die each year and why they have died is one of the most important means of understanding the causes and consequences of social change. Social change is an abstract concept. To make it more concrete, counting the dead helps to make connections between what is happening to the population and how the society organizes itself. If a country recognizes that many children are dying of malaria, but only a small portion of the health budget is dedicated to providing effective treatment, adjustments can be made in its health policy. If a country traces the escalation of tuberculosis rates to the rapid influx of migrants from nations with 'unfavourable sanitary-epidemiological profiles' then it may increase border surveillance and migrant screening, as has been the case between the United States and Mexico (Demin, 2006, p. 216).

Demographic information is useful because of its importance for organizational planning. Governments need to know how many schools to build, how many hospital beds will be needed, how much and what type of transport to develop for its ever-changing population, and so on. Sociologists are especially interested in life-course transitions. Such transitions are the essential signposts of life, and with them come enormous changes in peoples' activities, goals and priorities. Having accurate demographic data is invaluable for understanding how communities work and how they change.

Demographics deal in averages. Take, for example, the average life-course. This does not describe anyone exactly, but is a useful base line to compare different averages between groups and across time. For example, over the last 100 years or so, American women have gained approximately 31.8 years of life, while American men have gained 28.5 years (Shrestha, 2006, p.10). Sociologists are interested in *why* these averages change. Why are American women lasting longer than the average American man? The changing averages across the century and between women and men prompts questions about what has changed in American society.

Counting the dead can show how social values have a direct influence on birth and death rates, and also helps to identify and uncover social injustice. Through a comparative study of birth rates in India, epidemiologist Prabhat Jha suggests that selective abortion associated with prenatal sex determination 'may account for 500,000 missing girls every year – about 10 million missing girls from 1985 to 2005' (World Health Organization, 2010).

In the same interview, Jha explains the capacity of epidemiological analysis to reveal hidden links between consumption habits and non-contagious diseases. The *Million Death Study* (World Health Organization, 2010), the first nationally representative study of the effects of tobacco-smoking on health, examined illness and death rates for smokers in India. Prior to this study, the research literature argued that while the risks for smoking were well-known internationally, the risks in India were presumed to be less because of local conditions. People smoke locally manufactured cigarettes (*bidis*), which contained only a quarter of the tobacco of other commercially manufactured cigarettes. People took up smoking later, and fewer cigarettes were smoked per day compared to international rates. However, the study found that men who smoked *bidis* lost about six years of life, and women about eight years. Men who smoked commercial cigarettes lost 10 years. This surprising result is apparently because 'smoking appears to turn sub-clinical infection with tuberculosis (TB) bacillus into active disease ... the leading cause of smoking-related deaths in India was TB, and perhaps 40% of all TB deaths in Indian middle-aged males are due to smoking' (World Health Organization, 2010). We shall return to a further discussion of tobacco later in this chapter.

Demography relies on *vital statistics*, gathered by official bodies about key life events that relate to births (natality), deaths (mortality), marriages, health, disease (morbidity) and migration which occur in a given territory, as well as the principal characteristics related to these demographic phenomena. Vital statistics rely on the official registration of these events, and this first came about in London as a response to the plague. The London Bills of Mortality were designed to monitor deaths from the plague and other epidemics. They first appeared after an outbreak of plague in 1519 and were published weekly from information collected by parish priests (Porter, 1999). The idea was that, if an outbreak could be identified and tracked, measures such as quarantine could be put in place to try to curb the spread. Again, social attitudes of the time prevailed: 'During London's plagues, including that of 1665, causes of death were not certified medically, but by the "searchers of the dead",' typically 'impoverished, ignorant old women who trudged from house to house and examined corpses to certify the cause of death' (Orent, 2004, p. 150). And because the bills were based on parish records, they did not include the deaths of Jews and others outside the official faith (Koch, 2011, p. 64). By 1570, the bills included baptisms, and by 1692 the cause of death was also added. The Bills of Mortality were superseded by the Registrar General's returns under the Births and Deaths Registration Act of 1836.

When combined, vital statistics produce aggregate numerical descriptions or *rates* of birth, death and illness, often communicated in statistical tables. The *crude birth rate* (CBR) is the number of live births per 1,000 mean population at mid-year. It depends on both the level of fertility (the incidence of childbearing in a country's population, calculated by the number of births per woman) and the age structure of the population. During a woman's childbearing years, from the onset of menstruation to menopause, a woman is capable of bearing more than twenty children. *Fecundity*, or the maximum possible amount of childbearing, is sharply reduced by cultural norms, finances and personal choice. The *crude death rate* is calculated by taking the deaths in a particular year and dividing the number by the total mid-year population. *Morbidity rates* can mean either the incidence rate or the prevalence rate of a particular disease or disorder in a population, usually expressed as cases per 100,000 or per million in one year.

Demographic rates reveal how particular ways of living make certain ways of dying more prevalent. Allan Kellehear (2007) gives a useful example of using demographic and epidemiological material to find patterns in personal experiences of dying. He compresses the eons of human life into distinct styles of living that are linked explicitly to styles of dying, and hence to demographic rates. For example, in ancient times of hunter-gatherer living there would be many births but also many deaths, with the vast majority a result of infection or injury. The demographic rates of that time would have been of high birth and death rates – morbidity would have shown high rates of infection and trauma and lower rates of degenerative disease and famine. As ways of living transformed from hunter-gatherer to sedentary, agrarian-based living, there would have been a transformation in the demographic rates. High birth rates would have remained, but there would be lower death rates from infection and trauma from hunting, while death rates for degenerative diseases and famine would have increased. If it were possible to gather details about the numbers of people living and dying, and what they died of, it would have been possible to chart this transformation in ways of living in the demographic trends of the time. Another way to think about it is that when a population has high numbers of aged people, this means that they have survived childhood illnesses (which include infections and trauma) and have had effective treatment for infectious and curable diseases. As a consequence, they die from degenerative conditions such as circulatory diseases, cancers and dementias.

The *demographic profile* of a population represents a snapshot of that population. With respect to death, it captures the relative relationship between birth, death and morbidity rates, and the overall characteristic of the population at a given time. This might include the proportion of female to males, and young to old, and those suffering from infections or degenerative diseases.

A useful way of encapsulating the complex interplay of birth, death and illness rates as they change over time is *life expectancy*. Life expectancy is a statistical estimate of how long a person is likely to live. An increase in life expectancy suggests improvements in health and well-being, while a drop in life expectancy signals some significant change in living standards. Global life expectancy increased dramatically during the twentieth/twenty-first centuries. According to the World Health Organization, global life expectancy in 1900 was just 31 years. By the mid-twentieth century, average life expectancy had risen to 48 years, and in 2005 had reached 65.5 years, and over 80 in some countries (World Life Expectancy, 2009).

One of the most far-reaching population changes in a society is called the *demographic transition* (see Figure 3.1). This describes a shift in birth and death rates that leads to a rapid transformation in the size of the population, usually experienced as an escalation.

In stage one, pre-industrial society, death rates and birth rates are high and roughly in balance. In stage two, that of a developing country, the death rates drop rapidly due to improvements in food supply and sanitation, which increases life spans and reduces disease. In stage three, birth rates fall and population growth begins to level off. During stage four, there are low levels of birth rates and death rates. Birth rates may drop to well below replacement level. Originally, the demographic transition model only had four stages, however some theorists suggests the need for a fifth to represent countries with higher death rates than birth rates, leading to population aging and decline.

Demographic transitions rely on a change in the *epidemiological balance* of a population. From the Greek roots *epi* (upon) and *demos* (the people), epidemiology is the study of the causes, distribution and control of disease in populations (Morris 2007, p. 17). Epidemiological balance refers to a (theoretical) equilibrium between the resistance mechanisms of the host and the virulence of the agent. If an epidemiological balance is reached between diseases and people, this means that there is relative stability in the rates of disease and infection in a community. However, when the equilibrium

Figure 3.1   A graphic depiction of the demographic transition model

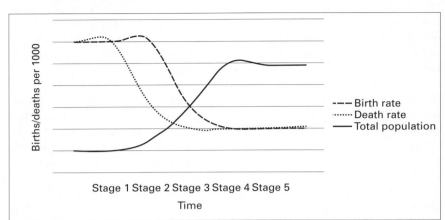

Notes: In Stage 1, pre-industrial society, death rates and birth rates are high and roughly in balance. In Stage 2, that of a developing country, the death rates drop rapidly because of improvements in food supplies and sanitation, which increase life spans and reduce disease. In Stage 3, birth rates fall and population growth begins to level off. During Stage 4 there are both low birth rates and low death rates. Birth rates may drop to well below replacement level. Originally, the demographic transition model only had four stages; however, some theorists suggest the need for a fifth stage to represent countries with higher death rates than birth rates, leading to population ageing and population decline.

between people and disease shifts, then the epidemiological balance is lost and rates of death begin to alter. This change is called an *epidemiological transition*.

Epidemiological transitions, like demographic transitions, describe changes in the causes from which people die. An epidemiological transition is linked to the idea of mortality substitution: namely that human beings have to die of something. If they are spared an early death from infections such as tuberculosis and typhoid, they fall prey instead to conditions such as heart disease, cancer or stroke (Kirkwood, 2001). The change from a pattern of mortality dominated by acute infectious disease to a pattern in which the chronic degenerative diseases play a major role is an example of such a transition.

The analysis of epidemiological transitions is an excellent means of examining how and why population profiles change. The British economist and clergyman, Thomas Robert Malthus (1766–1834), is often regarded as the father of modern demography. His *Essay on the principle of Population* (Malthus [1807] 1970) was the first treatise to note and express alarm about the potential for the numbers of people to grow more rapidly than the extent of the food supply necessary to support them. Though there are serious limitations to both Malthus's calculations and his theory of social change, he was one of the first to link the rates of change in populations with social conditions. And it was not until the mid-twentieth century that the connection between trends in death rates and changing social conditions could be established categorically (McLennan *et al.* 2009, p. 256). There is now well-documented research to show that the decrease in deaths from infectious diseases (such as cholera, typhoid, tuberculosis and plagues), that has occurred in industrialized nations from the end of the nineteenth century, was not a result of the role of medicine. Rather, it has been attributed to 'increased standards of sanitation, improved housing and better nutrition associated with the emergence of public health' (Powles, 1971; McKeown, 1976; Najman, 2000, p. 27). In general, demographic trends draw attention to the quality of and transformations in people's living circumstances.

Sociological debates about how best to interpret epidemiological transitions have had significant consequences for death studies. It is well known that the world's population has surged in different places at different times. European and North American populations escalated rapidly during the nineteenth century, and the late twentieth century saw a rapid population explosion in developing nations such as India and China. Until recently, theories that dominated discussion and policy interventions presumed that the cause of these increases in numbers was linked to the level of development of the population under examination. When a country industrialized, it was presumed that its population would benefit from new economic relations, better health care and education – that is, a general rise in the standard of living – and this would reduce death rates from infectious diseases and prompt a classic demographic transition. The different time scales for developed and developing nations was rooted in their historical experience of industrialization. However popular, this explanation has several problematic limitations. Beyond the unreliability of data, it presumes that industrialization equates to improved public health; and that all people living in industrial nations have the same experiences of good fortune. It also paints a dualistic picture of the pattern of death and dying in the world: First-World, industrialized countries are marked by old people dying of degenerative conditions, while Second- and Third-World (or developing) nations are marked by a relatively young population that suffers inordinately from infectious conditions (Howarth, 2009, p. 44).

This dualistic explanation is overly simplistic, misrepresenting the relationships between countries, because 'the picture thus created is of a dichotomy between modern industrial societies in which dying can be controlled and dying in poverty in developing countries with insufficient and inadequate medicine and healthcare' (Howarth, 2009, p. 99). Howarth suggests that it conceals the vast array of dying experiences, such as the slow deterioration of the body in old age, and dementia diseases, and that the implicit medical presumption is that, with enough resources and commitment, longevity can be extended and quality of life enhanced. This also hides non-illness dying, such as in armed conflict and through suicide, and precludes analysis of the political motivations of privation and the prevention of access to treatment through indirect means. In her critique of the epidemiological transition, Howarth argues that it is not modernization as such that leads to changes in the nature of dying from illness, but a change in the way that human populations are living and interacting. The intensification and mobilization of contemporary social interactions is a case in point.

In the early 1970s, it was thought that medicine had reached a tipping point in the battle against death-dealing infectious diseases. When smallpox was officially eradicated around the globe in 1976, it was thought that the world was stepping into a post-infectious age. However, such high hopes were soon dashed. The relationship between human beings and microbes took an insidious turn, as countries across the world shifted their gaze economically, politically and socially. Communicative technologies made some great leaps forward, and people and goods became *hyper-mobile*. Arguably, intensification and mobility are the defining features of living in a global age. Our lives are increasingly interconnected, integrated and transnational. This raises the question of what are the changes to human interaction embodied in this intensification and mobilization, and how do they shape death patterns and, in turn, personal experiences of dying and death?

The period since the 1980s has seen the return of age-old scourges in new, drug-resistant forms (such as TB); newly emerging and deliberately-induced diseases (such as HIV/AIDS, SARS and anthrax); the increasing presence of lifestyle-related and manufactured non-communicable diseases (diabetes, obesity, and smoking- and environmental-toxin-related conditions); and degenerative conditions, such as dementia, that are linked directly to the health successes of previous generations that have led to an ever-ageing global population.

The next section focuses on three case studies. Though each scenario contains a complex interplay of factors, global and otherwise, the case studies pay close attention to how and why global relations are so heavily implicated in global death patterns. This will develop a picture of what personal experiences of death tend to be in an intensified, hyper-mobile era.

Global flows of money and Russian life expectancy

The mobility of money can have a profound (and debilitating) impact on demographic trends. Up to the mid-1980s, Russia's population exhibited a demographic profile associated with developed nations: it had a low death and birth rates coupled with a relatively long life expectancy. Though never fully matching the high life expectancies of Western European countries, during the 1980s something profound happened that transformed this demographic profile in a startling way. Russia's life expectancy rates plummeted and its epidemiological trends showed a sharp reversal of fortunes.

More people were dying at younger ages of injury, infection and preventable diseases. This trend was so steep and so rapid that Russia quickly reached the point where the population was shrinking because the birth rate was not increasing in line with the increase in deaths. Not enough Russian babies were being born and surviving long enough to replace the dying populace.

Russia's plummeting life expectancy was a consequence of ideologically infused political responses to socio-economic circumstances. Best illustrated in the fall of the Berlin Wall in 1987, and *perestroika* (President Mikhail Gorbachev's programme of economic, political and social restructuring), Russia plunged into a rapid period of social and economic liberalization. With its intellectual origins in Milton Friedman's laissez-faire capitalism (Friedman, 1962), this brand of economic liberalization based itself on a central 'commitment to the policy trinity – the elimination of the public sphere, total liberation for corporations and skeletal social spending' (Klein, 2007, p. 15). Economic liberalization is seen as a means to encourage global markets as it pulls down institutional barriers to free trade.

Laissez-faire capitalism mobilizes money. Associated with labour market deregulation and public funding cuts to social welfare, health and education, economic liberalization habitually generates periods of instability experienced as high unemployment and a time of diminished welfare spending. As a result, people's living conditions tend to deteriorate rapidly.

Figure 3.2, depicting Russian male mortality rates, shows clear spikes in the death rates that link the socio-economic circumstances brought about by the mobilization of the Russian economy to three significant moments in Russia's recent past. Point 1 marks the beginning of the anti-alcohol campaign by Gorbachev; point 2 is the beginning of *perestroika;* and point 3, marks the 1998 financial crisis debt default that saw the rapid devaluation of the rouble, and in turn wiped out millions of Russians' life savings. It marked the culmination of privatization policies that led to the rapid escalation of unemployment rates (Lokiit, 2009). British researchers examined death rates among men of working age in the post-communist countries of Eastern Europe and the former Soviet Union between 1989 and 2002, and found that as many as one million working-age men had died as a result of the economic shock of mass privatization policies (Stuckler *et al.*, 2009). Following the break-up of the old Soviet regime, at least a quarter of large, state-owned enterprises were transferred to the private sector in just two years. This programme of mass privatization was associated with a 12.8 per cent increase in deaths (ibid., 2009, p. 400). Of significance, the study also found that some countries with robust social support networks withstood the turmoil better than others. Russia's post-Soviet demographic crisis up to and including its recovery to a growing population, and more specifically, rapidly falling mortality rates ties into the general point being made, given that the turnaround has coincided with increasing social stability (politics aside).

Figure 3.2   Russian male mortality rates, 1950–2008

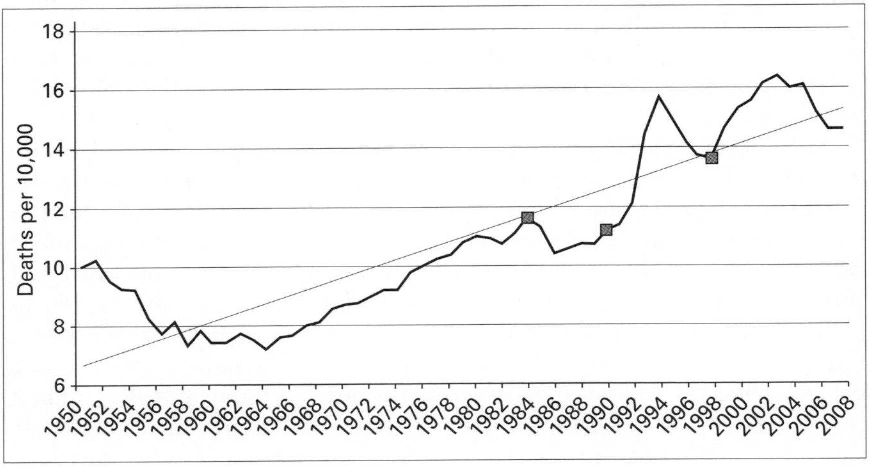

Notes: point 1, beginning of anti-alcohol campaign by Gorbachev; point 2, beginning of *perestroika*; point 3, beginning of privatization policies that led to unemployment.

Source: Lokiit (2009) *Russian Male Death Rates 1950-2008*, Wikipedia. Retrieved: 9 June 2012, from http://en.wikipedia.org/wiki/File:Russian_Male_Death_Rate_since_1950.PNG.

Researcher Martin McKee of the London School of Hygiene and Tropical Medicine (BBC News, 2009) said that the death rate was already high in the old Soviet Union, as the health care system was inadequate, rates of smoking and alcohol use were high, and diets were poor. These background susceptibilities were intensified by the place of Russia in the changing political and economic world order. At the time of the dissolution of the Soviet Union, according to Demin (2006), countries leading the neo-liberal market reform version of globalization, indifferent to the consequences of reform unless it threatened relevant interests, stood back and watched as Russia struggled with its shift from being a global superpower to becoming a vast country with a small share of global trade dominated by raw materials. As a result, Demin argues, a form of 'crony' or 'wild' capitalism developed in Russia that was different from the Western model as it lacked a labour basis or an ethic of entrepreneurialism, and put Russia on the periphery of the globalizing world as 'an object rather than subject of globalization' (Demin, 2006, p. 209).

Many of the critical global health concerns linked to increasing global interdependence began to present in Russia including:

Demographic destabilization; accelerating developmental disparities; health-in-development strains; health-in-prosperity strains; persistent underattention to the vulnerabilities and capabilities of girls and women; infrastructural inadequacy and inappropriateness; deficiencies of cooperation, coordination, and governance; facilitation of biomedical research; facilitation of clinical practice; microenvironmental problems; environmental degradation; demand for personally and socially harmful substances; violence (Demin, 2006, p. 208 referring to Koop *et al.*, 2000)

The intensive mobilization of people and of economic relations combined to the detriment of social welfare, health and education. Together these factors raised the risk of infectious and non-communicable diseases. Unchecked illegal migration brought in thousands of hosts and vectors of infection who went on to live impoverished lives in dense urban settlements.

Non-contagious diseases rose as background conditions began to align. Economic turmoil helped to fuel increasing rates of heart disease and stroke as well as mental illness. This was compounded by rising unemployment with workers suffering from uncertainty and stress. Not only does stress have a direct effect on health, but it is also closely associated with unhealthy lifestyles, such as alcoholism; 'The workplace also tended to provide what healthcare was available, along with social support. People got everything from work – and when they lost their jobs all that just went' (BBC News, 2009). Disenfranchised from what little social and health support remained after the liberalization of social and health policy, many people turned to the sex trade and intravenous drug use to survive. These conditions heightened the ease of viral transmission and host susceptibility to infections old and new. HIV/AIDS began to spread rapidly.

AIDS is now the leading cause of death among young adults, and the fourth-largest cause of mortality worldwide. First identified in the 1980s, though thought to have crossed the species barrier between primates and humans at some time in the past, the virus can only be transmitted through the exchange of bodily fluids – via unprotected sex, breast-feeding or the blood (through sharing intravenous needles, blood transfusions or via the umbilical cord). AIDS has spread rapidly and targets the traditionally least vulnerable sector of the population – young adults (compared to the very young and very old). In the years since its identification, 20 million people were estimated to have died of AIDS by 2002.

While two-thirds (63 per cent) of the world's adults and children with HIV live in Sub-Saharan Africa, recent increases have occurred in Eastern Europe, East Asia and Central Asia, where the number of people living with HIV in 2006 was over one-fifth (21 per cent) higher than in 2004. It mainly affects young people, particularly young women. In the Russian Federation, for example, some 80 per cent of people with HIV are under 30 years of age (UNAIDS, 2006, p. 7). While, by 2007, 93.19 per cent of adults and children with advanced HIV infection were receiving anti-retroviral therapy, a lack of financial commitment to sex and drugs education in schools is hindering effective prevention programmes (UNAIDS, 2006).

The reality of HIV/AIDS is that it is slow to develop, potentially painful and likely to be severely debilitating and extraordinarily demeaning. Death can occur from destruction of the central nervous system, in which case the person involved may become paraplegic or quadriplegic and may lose both their eyesight and mental faculties. It may also be associated with a variety of tumours and a range of severe and painful infections. As Najman (2000, p. 33) explains, 'an increasing proportion of patients are likely to be experiencing multiple symptoms, including pain, lethargy, as well as difficulties with their food intake and bowel functioning'. Though HIV is infectious, it takes some 10 years for the virus to shift from HIV to full blown AIDS, then a further number of years for the sufferer to die a lingering death.

The common understanding about the spread of HIV/AIDS is that it is contracted through unsafe sex and injected drug use. However, this view is tempered by persuasive arguments that the real cause of the epidemic is in fact poverty: 'Identifying a microbial agent does not itself constitute an explanation for the epidemic. Poverty causes AIDS, T.B., malaria, yellow fever or cholera epidemics because the infecting agent is a necessary but not sufficient condition to explain its spread' (Kellehear, 2007, p. 205). The economic transformations associated with the spread of the free market ethos impacts upon poverty levels that in turn escalate the rates of infectious diseases, including HIV/AIDS (Altman, 1999, p. 574). Ironically, economic liberalization also generates new pockets of extreme wealth. At the same time as Russian men were dying in unprecedented numbers, Russia's personal wealth reached new heights (Guriev and Rachinsky, 2009, p. 136).

Russia's dramatic drop in life expectancy shows that no nation, however technically and socially developed, is immune from the direct, troubling and polarized impact of this kind of social change. This is as true for our contemporary era of globalization as it was for former times. When social support (broadly understood) is treated with indifference, people pay the price in increased infectious and preventable diseases and lowered life expectancy. Their encounters with death have become more 'nasty, brutish and short' in times of untold personal wealth and personal liberty. Russia's AIDS profile reveals specific connections between sexual behaviours, age and poverty, which also signal it is not infection as such, but rather socioeconomic conditions that drive patterns of epidemiology.

Trading death: the tobacco industry

Mr Garza's death, discussed at the start of this chapter, was caused by eating too much over a considerable period of time. As with a gun, it is not food *per se* that kills people, but it is what people do with food that causes the damage. More insidious are the products that are known to do irreparable damage. Tobacco is one such substance. Much about contemporary globality is not so different from previous phases of socio-economic global-ity; the story of tobacco consumption, in the West at least, is familiar from mercantile capitalism/slavery stories onwards. Even so, it serves to highlight how non-communicable conditions are explicitly linked to global economic relations.

Tobacco is a global product. According to Liemt (2002), tobacco is grown in more than 100 countries, with China being the world's leading producer. Other principal suppliers are the USA, India, Brazil, Turkey, Zimbabwe and Malawi. Tobacco products are consumed all over the world and most tobacco is used for smoking – the essential ingredient for ciga-rettes, pipes, and cigars. Tobacco is also used for such items as snuff and chewing tobacco.

Tobacco has addictive properties and poor health outcomes for smokers and non-smokers alike. Although nicotine is what gets (and keeps) people addicted to tobacco, other substances in tobacco are also responsible for its illness-causing effects. For example, there is evidence that smoking contributes to many types of cancer. Tobacco use accounts for at least 30 per cent of all cancer deaths in the USA, and smoking causes about 87 per cent of lung cancer deaths. Smoking also causes cancers of the larynx (voice box), mouth, pharynx (throat), oesophagus (gullet) and bladder. It also has been linked to the development of cancers of the pancreas, cervix, kidney and stomach, and some types of leukaemia. Cancers account for only about half of the deaths linked to smoking, however. Long-term, smoking is also a major cause of heart disease, aneurysms, bronchitis, emphysema and stroke. It also makes pneumonia and asthma worse. Wounds take longer to heal and the immune system may not work as well in smokers as in non-smokers. According to a study done in the late 1990s by the US Center for Disease Control and Prevention (CDC), smoking shortened male smokers' lives by 13.2 years and female smokers' lives by 14.5 years. Men and women who smoke are much more likely to die during middle age (between the ages of 35 and 69) than those who have never smoked.

There are also indirect health consequences of tobacco smoke. Each year about 49,400 non-smoking adults die of lung cancer or heart disease as a result of breathing second-hand environmental tobacco smoke (ETS). Babies of parents who smoke have a greater chance of dying of sudden infant death syndrome (SIDS). Pregnant women exposed to ETS are at risk of having a low birth weight baby and may also be at risk for pre-term delivery and miscarriage (American Cancer Society, 2008).

Though it is a lucrative business, the costs of smoking are far higher than the income from cigarette sales. According to the CDC, in the USA, smok-ing incurs more than US$193 billion each year in health-related costs. Smoking-related medical costs averaged more than US$97 billion each year between 2000 and 2004. This translates to US$2,197 in extra medical expenses for each adult smoker per year as of 2004. Death-related produc-tivity losses from smoking among workers cost the US economy more than

US$96 billion yearly (average for 2000–4). Of the 1.3 billion smokers alive today, 650 million will eventually be killed by tobacco, and of these, 325 million will die between the ages of 35 and 69 (CDC, 2009).

According to the WHO's global assessment of the distribution of the effects of tobacco consumption, in 2002 about one-third of the global adult male population smoked, and smoking-related diseases were killing one in ten adults globally (four million deaths annually). The distribution of smoking deaths is not even, as smoking is on the rise in the developing world but falling in developed nations. Nine hundred million smokers, or 84 per cent of the world total, live in developing and transitional economy countries. If current trends continue, by 2030, 70 per cent of deaths attributable to tobacco will occur in the developing world.

The tobacco industry is a most profitable business, making billions of dollars every year (Yach and Bettcher, 2000). The tobacco industry promulgates tobacco consumption as a source of revenue on a global scale, though the economic importance of tobacco-growing and processing differs from country to country. At the national level, cigarette (sales and import) tax can be a substantial source of government revenue and profit, when governments own the companies. For example, according to Liemt (2002, p. 22), in Russia cigarette tax revenue contributes around 8 per cent to the state budget. In China, profits from state-owned China National Tobacco Corporation (CNTC) amounted to the equivalent of US$11,000 million in 1999. CNTC has been the Chinese state's top revenue generator for years. Japan Tobacco earned more than US$400 million for the Japanese state in the fiscal year ending March 2000. As these companies control the market, they are state-run monopolies, and as monopolies they also have a socioeconomic function. In Italy, several of the state monopoly's factories are placed in areas of high unemployment.

As Yach and Bettcher (2000) suggest, by being so large the tobacco industry is a global force in its own right in the sense that its sphere of influence and the extent of its market and circulation routes span the globe in intricate networks of production, distribution, consumption, prevention, treatment and death. The tobacco industry's actions are seen as a vector of the global tobacco epidemic of costly non-contagious death-dealing conditions.

Tobacco and food are products that can cause cancer and obesity when taken in harmful quantities. The global chains of consumption, distribution and production of goods clearly have harmful consequences for the life chances of many millions of people in the world today. However, the separation of economic systems from their health consequences means that the true cost of these products is not acknowledged or dealt with by producers and distributors. Instead, the burdens of non-contagious, though life-shattering, conditions are carried by individuals, families and national governments. The next section focuses on the intensification of global flows of people – how very rapid geographical mobility raises the stakes in an unprecedented way when it comes to the spread of hyper-infectious pathogens.

Global flows of people: SARS and H1N1

If they get the chance, or when they are forced, people move to get out of poverty and away from limited life chances. The Highland Clearances from the Scottish Highlands in the eighteenth and nineteenth centuries are a historical case of a forced removal of people, and the contemporary influx of migrants from various countries – such as Mexico to the USA, and Indonesia to Australia – are examples of voluntary movements. We live in a time of population flux and mobility. Even though human beings have always migrated, people are on the move now more than ever. Despite the Scottish saying that as a people we are made for export, more people travel further and faster than has ever before been the case. As Urry (2007) points out, the scale of current mobility is unprecedented in sheer numbers, distance and speed. At the turn of the millennium

> there were at least one billion legal international arrivals each year (compared with 25 million in 1950). There are four million air passengers each day; at any one time 360,000 passengers are in flight above the United States, equivalent to a substantial city; 31 million refugees roam the globe (Papastergiadis 2000: 10, 41, 54) and there were 552 million cars in 1998 with a projected 730 million in 2020. (Urry, 2007, p. 3)

One consequence of people's newfound mobility is that, as they move about, new patterns of concentrated living emerge. In 1950, only 30 per cent of the world's population was urban. More than 50 per cent were living in urban areas by 2008, and it is expected that 60 per cent will be living in cities by 2030. The number and size of mega-cities is growing as people flock from other countries and rural areas. It is estimated that of the almost 1 billion poor people in the world, over 750 million live in urban areas without adequate shelter and basic services (Urry, 2007, p. 3).

When combined with rapid travel over long distances, intensive urbanization produces a unique effect: the spread of old diseases and the emergence of new infections. The more we come into close contact with one another, and the more stressed our living environments, the greater the likelihood that infections and diseases will take hold and spread rapidly. This is because warm, living bodies are a preferred host and vector for spreading infection. In the 1990s the World Health Organization proclaimed that the world was facing a 'global crisis with respect to pathogenic microbes' (Fidler, 2004, p. 2). In a study of the location and incidence of new diseases, Jones *et al.* (2008) found that 335 new or emergent infectious diseases (EIDs) appeared between 1940 and 2004 in the global human population.

Most of these have emerged more rather than less recently, with 'their peak incidence (in the 1980s) concomitant with the HIV pandemic' (Jones *et al.* 2008, p. 990). The global hotspots for EIDs are the north-eastern USA, Western Europe, Japan and south-eastern Australia. The reasons for these being hotspots are linked to 'socio-economic drivers such as human popu- lation density, anti-biotic drug use and agricultural practices because these are major determinants of the spatial distribution of EID events' (ibid., p. 991).

The SARS (severe acute respiratory syndrome) and H1N1 swine flu viruses are a good case in point because the way in which they emerged, spread and were ultimately brought under control demonstrates the opera- tion of global infection and prevention networks. SARS was a new pathogen that reached its *epidemiological tipping point*[1] in the summer of 2003 to become a new global pandemic. The SARS epidemiological tipping point occurred when Dr Liu Jianlun went to stay at the Metropole Hotel in Hong Kong for a family wedding. Dr Liu passed the contagious SARS virus to fellow travellers, who dispersed the syndrome around the world and trig- gered a global public health crisis (Fidler, 2004, p. 187).

We now also live in a time of rapid and widespread global infectious disease *surveillance*. Customs officials and airline staff are duty bound to report any signs of illness on flights and at border crossings, as they are one vanguard of global infection disease control. In March 2009, an outbreak of the new H1N1 'swine flu' pathogen was upgraded from Level 3 to Level 4 pandemic status by the WHO. The rapid global spread of swine flu out of Mexico, through a handful of international flights via Los Angeles, was charted through hourly bulletins and warnings from the WHO. By the end of April 2009, the vast majority of about 2,000 cases had been identified in Mexico, with 51 in the USA and 15 in total across the UK, Canada, New Zealand, Spain and Israel.

All the 150-plus deaths from the swine flu were recorded in Mexico, with patients in other countries experiencing far less severe symptoms. Keiji Fukuda, the deputy head of the WHO at the time, made the global links and disparities between nations in connection with swine flu explicit as he called for special efforts to be made towards less rich nations which are hit disproportionately hard by pandemics (Walker and Williams, 2009).

The significance of SARS, especially its containment, alongside other rapidly spreading infections, such as the H1N1 flu, serves to highlight how rapidly and how far people travel around the world. It also points to the distinctively global health surveillance measures that are now in place. As noted by Knobler *et al.* (2006), academic scientists, public health officials and pharmaceutical companies acted together in a way that was unprece- dented. The co-ordination across research, commerce and government for a global public health end can be seen as an attempt to re-scale public health strategies from the national to the global. The move beyond tradi- tional public health perimeters is because national public health strategies are no longer effective against the specific health risks associated with global movements of people and illnesses.

Global trends in death and dying

We have seen the ways that population mobility redistributes people and infectious diseases, how economic mobility redistributes wealth, and death-inducing poverty and product mobility redistribute dangerous goods and the consequences of their consumption in particular ways. The question to ask now is how do global intensifications and mobilities such as these impact on global demographic trends, and what is the ensuing global death profile for life in a global age?

One of the most striking global trends since the early 1960s has been the unprecedented increase in population. According to the CIA's estimates, as of July 2009, the world population stood at 6,790,062,216 and is growing by about 80 million people per year. World births have levelled off at about 137 million per year, from their peak at 163 million in the late 1990s, and are expected to remain constant. As of 2008, deaths stand at only around 56 million per year, though they are expected to increase to 90 million by the year 2050 (CIA, 2009). Reasons for the escalation in the world's population are that people in more countries around the world have been living healthier lives.[2] The world's population growth has a significant impact on death because it signals that the world's population is ageing. A century ago, just 1 per cent of the world's population was aged 65 and above. This figure has already risen seven-fold and will rise to around 20 per cent of the population by the middle of the twenty-first century. In the UK at the time of writing, 85 per cent of newborns can expect to celebrate their 65th birthday. And those reaching 65 now can expect to survive for 16 more years if they are male, or 19 years if they are female. Since the 1960s, life expectancy has continued to increase steadily, by two years each decade. It is almost as if for every decade modern humans have lived, we have gained an extra 20 per cent free (Kirkwood, 2001). The death rates of the older age groups are showing the greatest decline at present. It is these older age groups – those aged over 85 years – who now constitute the fastest-growing segment of the population: 'In 1960 Japan, there were 144 people who reached the age of 100 years; by 1997 Japan, 8,500 people became centenarians. In the UK in 1900 (Siddell and Komaromy 2003: 44) twenty four per cent of all deaths occurred to people over 65. In 1999, this figure rose to 83 per cent' (Kellehear, 2007, p. 202).

During 2004, an estimated 59 million people died around the world, with the number one cause of death being cardiovascular disease. However, as treatment improves and more people survive cardiovascular illness and crises, so rates of dementia-related deaths are on the increase (Brayne *et al.*, 2006). Even so, as the century comes to its close, it seems sure that infections are coming back, regaining their old importance for human life; and medical men have begun to recognise how their increasingly powerful interventions had the unexpected effect of accelerating the biological evolution of disease germs, making them impervious to one after another chemical attack. (McNeill, 1998, p. 10)

The first case study of Russian life expectancy revealed the links between economic liberalization and the spread of AIDS. As medical knowledge of HIV/AIDS increases, it is now understood as a *resurging* rather than a *new* disease (McNeill, 1998). HIV/AIDS is beginning to shift from being a rare and highly contagious killer disease to an endemic, ever-present background infection in many populations round the world: 'Overall and in the long run, the familiar ecological pattern of mutual accommodation between host and parasite is almost sure to prevail. That means endemic will tend to replace epidemic infections while less lethal strains and chronic infections gain in importance against more virulent germs' (McNeill, 1998, p. 15).

But, what is the more general interplay between official responses to infectious diseases and non-contagious diseases? The World Bank and donor countries use structural adjustment policies (SAPs) to increase recipient countries' dependency on the global market by increasing privatization and trade liberalization while at the same time decreasing government subsidies for such things as health care and education. Loans made by the World Bank and other global financial institutions are usually conditional on a country's adherence to SAPs. Paradoxically, the World Bank is putting large amounts of money into countering AIDS in states where its own SAPs served to sabotage the health institutions that could have prevented the spread to begin with (Altman, 1999).

Also, because of growing economic interdependency and the ease of travel thanks to new technologies, the powerful actors that have been the propelling force of neo-liberalism are no longer safe from the detrimental effects of their own policies. HIV/AIDS could not be kept out of state borders, yet high-income countries still have relatively low rates in comparison to middle- and low-income states. In a study of intellectual property rights and access to AIDs drugs, Lisk (2010) claims that the high cost of anti-retroviral drugs for treating HIV/AIDS has kept treatment out of the reach of millions who need it. This leaves the battle between the pharmaceutical companies and developing countries that cannot afford the medicine or, as Lisk puts it, ' patient rights versus patent rights', with some poor countries accusing Western pharmaceutical companies of profiting from the disease and putting profit before life (Lisk, 2010, p. 119).

It is worthwhile stating that non-contagious diseases attract a fraction of research, policy and political attention compared to infections, despite being the number one cause of death worldwide. At the same time, the ongoing burden of the direct care needed for those with non-contagious diseases devolves in the main to families and national governments. These same families and governments must also face up to the social and economic lost opportunity costs associated with people with debilitating conditions. Why are non-contagious diseases not an equal priority with infections? NCDs are notoriously hard to tackle because they are often linked to intractable human behaviours rather than the eradication of a particular microbe, and that requires a different kind of social and political intervention with which medical science is not quite as adept. Though conjecture, responses may suggest the relative power of economic and health policy agendas worldwide. Global trade in food and tobacco, for example, feed off and profit from the behaviours and consumption patterns that cause NCDs. Global health policies are, for reasons that say a lot about human interrelations, not willing or able to interfere with neo-liberal free market economic policies which generate the profit and tax returns that finance their policy objectives and infrastructure: 'No amount of drugs and doctors can create health if essentials are becoming more scarce due to ecological erosion, and non-essentials more pervasive due to consumerist lifestyles, environmental pollution and the accumulation of waste' (Shiva, 1994, p. 4).

A message to take from the experience of infectious diseases in today's intensified and highly mobile times is that organic evolution is operating in a higher gear now, largely because of human intervention in natural ecosystems and bacteriology. For non-contagious diseases, it is the invidious spread of death-dealing conditions and diseases, where the vector is not a human body fluid or a flea but the neo-liberal forms of free market economics. That they foster the specialization, fragmentation and interdependence of global food production and consumption which distributes nutritionally variable food to more-or-less wealth populations across and within nations, or distributes addictive and debilitating products such as tobacco to the same effect, is great cause for political and health policy reflection. The ways in which non-contagious diseases are spread nowadays is deeply embedded in social relations that foster the invidious mix of interdependence and polarization between people, products and wealth.

The three case studies of Russian life expectancy, tobacco and SARS/H1N1 show to good effect how global relations shape contemporary demographic and epidemic profiles of the world in significant ways. They have shown how these three aspects influence changes in infections and non-contagious diseases that alter the epidemic balance and demographic patterns of the world's population. The characteristic way of death in contemporary times can now also be given substance.

The rapid mobility of people brings a different set of risks where new infections emerge that the global population has never encountered before, as there could be very rapid and large-scale die-offs. These two opposing trends – of battle-scarred urban populations and sudden population die-offs – inform ongoing attempts by humans to manage their health. Infectious diseases such as SARS easily fall under the mandate of WHO and the health administration attempts that can be very imposing, but also effective. However, tobacco and other addictions that are death-dealing are under much less direct control. Financial interests and the implicit notion that people make some sort of choice to consume/participate in addictive behaviours means that there is not the same ability, political will or institutional capacity for health organizations and governments to put populations on lock-down when a tobacco company begins to encroach into new populations' territories in the search for new markets. The balance between profit and cost still wins out in favour of profit, even as the tobacco business is moving out of its original host populations (Europe, America) into the Chinese and Indian markets. The limitations of public health in relation to profit factors raises the point of acute health issues – those that kill many very quickly are paid more attention than those that kill slowly through 'side-lined' populations.

An examination of global demographic and epidemiological trends reveals the distinctive marker of death in a global age – there has been a move towards slower, degenerative dying, whether caused by age-related dementias or infection-laden viruses such as HIV/AIDS. At the same time, social attitudes and practices of caring for types of dying (that is, existing institutions and social practices) are not designed to cope with the sheer scale and impact of these changing ways of dying.

This is linked to another population trend: a drop in the world's fertility rates. Worldwide, the fertility rate (children per woman of child-bearing age) has fallen from 5.0 to 2.7 since the 1980s. Coupled with reducing death rates in the older population, the decline in fertility is turning the traditional population pyramid on its head. It also means that, without massive immigration from developing countries, the population of the developed world will soon peak and begin to decline. There are proportionally more people dying when they are older, of slow or degenerative and epidemic diseases, and fewer younger people around to provide care and support.

Dying slowly places a large demand on nursing skills, time and resources from any community. The term 'global burden of disease' is used to describe the rates of illness that a given country carries. When calculated globally, an interesting feature emerges. Developed countries make up 16 per cent of the global population; they suffer only 10 per cent of the global burden of disease but account for 80 per cent of the total amount spent on health care globally (World Bank Organization, 2008).

Contemporary global distributions of infectious and degenerative illnesses reveal divides between the richer developed and poorer developing nations. They also reveal continuing divisions in wealth within nations (Castells, 2011). As the world's population is ageing, more people than ever before in human history will die of age-related, degenerative conditions in situations of reduced social, family and personal support. We are now more aware than ever of our own, and others', mortality. As the decades go on, we are less likely to give the dying support and care as they approach death.

Conclusion

The three case studies discussed go some way to demonstrate that global relations do shape contemporary encounters with death. The exploration of the impact of neo-liberal economics on national health policies in Russia, the impact of globally co-ordinated responses to emergent infections (such as SARS), and the account of the more insidious chains of non-communicable diseases that rise out of new dangerous consumption patterns (food and tobacco) deliberately progressed by transnational companies and quietly overlooked by global health non-governmental organizations all reveal ways in which global geo-politics inform mortality and morbidity rates.

Our personal encounters with death are connected through the deliberate global mobility of people, money and things. Deliberate or forced decisions to move people, money or goods profoundly shape how people live and how they die. Old inequalities are still prevalent in different forms as they directly shape the patterns of life and death, solutions to disease and their uneven cultural reception and effect. This reveals an unpleasant irony. The intensive, mobile world of globalization produces slow, debilitating, degenerative deaths for those in rich and poor populations alike.

Questions

This chapter was all about patterns in death. As a way to engage with the topic, use the exercise below to identify the death patterns in the society in which you live.

1. Look up your government's website for deaths caused by degenerative conditions, infection and violence. Write a short paragraph that describes this death profile. Go on to discuss how contemporary global economic relations may be shaping these demographic patterns. Draw on ideas about global epidemics such as AIDS, obesity and tobacco consumption, to help your discussion.
2. Do you think that these global epidemics are unique to current times? Why?/Why not?

Chapter 4

The Death Industries: Bespoke My Death

Introduction

Since 1998, the Swiss Dignitas clinic has arranged for 5,989 people to die. The top eight countries seeking help to die are Germany (2,971), Switzerland (834), UK (694), France (471), Italy (146), the Netherlands (125) and Austria (102). Dignitas clearly serves a need in Western European communities. When the countries of origin of the 5,989 dead are plotted across the world, it is apparent that the need to travel for assisted dying spans the globe.

As care for the dying is managed by independent organizations (such as Dignitas) which draw their client base from around the world, so care for the recently dead is optimized through customized and personalized services. The following is a list of theme funerals compiled by the National Funeral Directors and Morticians Association, and taken from *Harper's Magazine* (2002):

Airport: If the loved one was a pilot, rent a hanger at the local airport. Local pilots would fly out of the hanger, land and line up their aircraft in order of age of craft.

Aquarium: Rent the local aquarium after hour of closing. Excellent viewing environment.

Banker: Rent a local bank or use your local branch. Set up on the officers' side of the building, and make sure that the window blinds are closed. Still gives the family some privacy.

Boat cruise: Rent a three-hour boat cruise. An environment for viewing and also for cremation service.

Family reunion: Loved one is placed in the living room of host family as the family celebrates annual family reunion.

Go-kart racing: Only during the spring and summer, after closing hours. Excellent viewing location. The visiting family and friends use go-karts. Dress the loved one in a car-racing suit.

Horse racing: Rent the track during off-season. Viewing in the horse stables, and jockey uniform on the deceased. Use racing tickets and racing booklet as program, with obituary included within.

Living room: Loved one is laid out near a La-Z-Boy lounger, with television, remote control, and faux cigar in the ashtray.

New Orleans jazz funeral: Two-horse-drawn hearse with jazz band leading to cemetery. Along with two dozen doves released.

Shopping mall spree: Some malls have rental space available for meetings. Use this area for viewing. Funerals cannot be held during the day due to poor taste for shoppers.

Toy land: Excellent for the kid in all of us. Use all the favourite toys, TV shows, and records, as well as movies. Posters and banners are extra touches.

Train: Old train museum for viewing and funeral. Before leaving for cemetery, put family and body on a three-mile train ride (returns back to the museum). Then to the cemetery.

Walmart (or special store of choice): Have the viewing room in a store. Use signs, discounts, and items most purchased by the deceased.

Working man: All the working tools of the person's profession or trade. Dress in work clothes; if not, have the clothing on a plastic adult doll. A 4x4 will be used as the hearse to the cemetery.

Zoo keeper: Rent the local zoo, after closing, for a private viewing. Note: the location would be where the deceased visited often. In a recent case, it was the elephant area.

What do these new organizational forms of personalized care for the dying and recently dead signify about contemporary death practices? And how have these hyper-individualized services come about? Do they mark over-commercialization and reduced professionalized standards, or do they attest to new ways of acknowledging one of life's most profound rites of passage?

This chapter focuses on the changing material and ideological basis for death management and is concerned with the organization of the dying and the recently dead. Tasks associated with tending the terminally ill through the ultimate rite of passage have long been conducted by specially designated people. The skills they employ and the institutions that support them in their duties together generate an archetype for managing death. Such archetypes vary across cultures and historical timeframes. Therefore, as whole societies transform, the experts and the attendant skills and institutional infrastructure that supports them as they guide the dying and dead also reconfigure, and new death archetypes appear.

A focus on the changing archetypes of death management is useful soci-ologically because it brings together values and expectations about care for the dying and recently dead with the actual social practices and the substan-tive conditions that limit them. As it focuses attention on the conceptual bases through which society's members embrace changing material realities, it is an example of cultural sociology, It pays attention to socio-cultural forces, phenomena, institutions and contexts.

To distinguish the contemporary archetype, the first section of this chap-ter gives a historical account of medical doctors and funeral directors, as they have come to be the ritual experts for managing death in twentieth-century Western societies. It outlines the form that the rite of passage has taken; including what was paid attention to, the social infrastructure that supported it, and the implied relationship between the expert and the initi-ate before the transforming effects of globalization gained a foothold in the management of death.

A central aspect of professions is that they are a means to make a living that is self-regulated through a professional code of ethics. Professions are also part of the institutional infrastructure of modern societies (Outhwaite *et al.*, 1996, p. 513). One feature of living in a global age is the significance and widespread change in the way that many professional institutions conduct their practice. This broader social change has helped to transform the symbolic management of death, and suggests the presence of a new, globally infused archetype for managing death. The aim of this chapter is to outline this shift in the death arche-type. For heuristic reasons, the account is organized into two case stud-ies, one focused on those who manage the dying, and the other on those who manage the recently dead. Each case study begins with a brief overview of the profession's rise to ritual authority over managing death. It then outlines how a professional transformation linked to globaliza-tion, rewrites the rules of ritual engagement between these professionals and their charges. Each concludes with a surprising response to the effects of this global turn.

The modern death care archetype

Cicely Saunders, palliative care pioneer and founder of Saint Christopher's Hospice in London in 1967 wrote:

> It appears to me that many patients feel deserted by their doctors at the end. Ideally the doctor should remain the centre of a team who work together to relieve where they cannot heal, to keep the patient's own struggle within his compass and to bring hope and consolation to the end. (Saunders,1958, in Clark, 2005, p. 7)

And Jessica Mitford, critic of the American funeral industry's pricing and sales strategies, voiced her opinion:

> Is the funeral inflation bubble ripe for bursting? A few years ago, the United States public suddenly rebelled against the trend in the auto industry towards ever more showy cars, with their ostentatious and non-functional fins, and a demand was created for compact cars patterned after European models. The all-powerful auto industry, accustomed to *telling* the customer what sort of car he wanted, was suddenly forced to *listen* for a change. Overnight, the little cars became for millions a new kind of status symbol. Could it be that the same cycle is working itself out in the attitude towards the final return of dust to dust, that the American public is becoming sickened by ever more ornate and costly funerals, and that a status symbol of the future may indeed be the simplest kind of 'funerals without fins'? (Mitford, 1963, p. 22)

To relieve where they cannot heal and to provide funerals without fins, these are the clarion-calls of the twentieth century's most vocal and effective advocates for death care reform. Saunders' and Mitford's significant talents and energies profoundly changed the professional management of the dying and the recently dead over the second half of the twentieth century. Now best practice for the dying is holistic palliative care that attends to the physical, psychological, spiritual and even social aspects of a person's singularly unique dying. Best practice for the recently dead is customized disposal by way of a life-centred ritual of recognition that neither anonymizes the dead nor pauperizes the bereaved.

Saunders' and Mitford's iconic efforts at social change are often told as if their successes were solely the outcome of personal courage and sheer tenacity. And contemporary death management is often judged in the light of their role as a moral compass. Yet this personification of social transformation is misleading. Changed ways of caring for the dying and recently dead do not come solely from such Herculean efforts to challenge deeply institutionalized convention. With the benefit of hindsight, their labours (though significant) were just one aspect of a multi-dimensional period of social change. Together with a general dissatisfaction with the status quo and a broader transformation in the place of professions in contemporary society, the iconic pronouncements of Saunders and Mitford reconfigured the management of death. The form it now takes is deeply informed by global social relations.

Death professionals

In recent centuries, care of the dying and the recently dead has spanned private commercial (private hospitals and hospices), religious voluntary (for example, the Jewish Chevra Kadisha), charity, co-operative and (local and national) authorities. None the less, and despite this spread, professions have come to control the provision of care for the dying and the recently dead in modern societies. There are a number of occupations associated with dying and death that carry the professional mantle. These include medical doctors, the military, law enforcement, funeral directors and professional care givers such as nurses. Not all of these professions share the same status or institutional role within a given country, and they also vary markedly between countries.

The two areas most overtly associated with death are the medical and funeral professions. The medical professional is most associated with the lead up to death, while the funeral director is the professional who manages the recently dead. Both professions can be taken as the ritual experts who manage death as a rite of passage in modern Western societies. The medical profession deals with the transition from living to dying. The funeral professional then takes over and continues to manage the initiate through to the rite of interment, which marks the completion of the symbolic transition from life to death.

Experts for the dying

The medical profession came to monopolize the management of dying by way of its quest to secure a central role in the provision of health care. This took place over the course of some centuries. Some argue that medicine's power began to build once England's King Henry VIII granted a Royal Charter to the Company of Barber-Surgeons of London in 1540. By gaining this Royal Charter, medicine was able to exercise control over the entry and delivery of its expert body of knowledge and services. In terms of dying, it *also* represented the beginning of a gradual shift in symbolic authority from the priest to the medic that culminated in 1879, when it became mandatory that a doctor should certify death before a death certificate could be issued (Jackson, 2011).

Institutional arrangements within the medical profession altered over the centuries. For example, medicine in the Middle Ages was the preserve of the religious sphere. Christian concern for the sick and injured, as well as contact with the Arab world during the Crusades, led to the creation of many large hospitals built and run by monastic orders. However, as the role of institutional religion gave way to secular systems, as Jackson puts it, from

> the end of the eighteenth to the end of the nineteenth century, Western Europe was transformed by urbanization, industrialization, and colonialism, and from the later nineteenth onwards by nation-states that offered material benefits to large segments of the citizenry, including

medical services ... medical relationships themselves came to depend increasingly on the provision and regulation of public services, from hospitals to health insurance. Informal medical relationships persisted, of course, but the redistribution of wealth through taxation, and the control of medical licensing and reimbursement through bureaucratic mechanisms, gave national governments large powers and responsibilities. (Jackson, 2011, p. 200)

Significant to this discussion, the state came to be the keeper of access to markets and monopolies during the early decades of the twentieth century by way of social insurance. Otherwise known as welfare states, they organized for the institutional provision of health care. Medicine secured its central place in the provision of nationalized health care and the care of the dying by becoming the designated provider of health expertise.

Britain, New Zealand, Australia and Sweden's universal and comprehensive coverage of state-delivered services offered nationalized health care. France, Germany and Japan's combined social insurance principle alongside a private sector offered a regulated mixed model of health provision. Communist countries also put medicine at the centre of their nationalized health care systems. In countries that preferred market-based models of social welfare organization, medicine also dominated the market place (Lewis, 2007).

Regarding medicine's search for legitimacy in an era when its therapies often did more than cure, Mohr (1984) noted how the mid-nineteenth-century anti-abortion movement of physicians stemmed not so much from concerns about morality but rather from elitist fears of a drop in the birth rate of society's better classes. This was at a time when approximately one in five pregnancies was deliberately aborted, according to an 1871 American Medical Association committee estimate (O'Donnell, 1871) and from physicians' attempts to enhance their professional recognition. Mohr comments that 'persuading the public that embryos were human lives then persuading state legislatures to protect these lives by outlawing abortion may have been one of the few life-saving projects actually available to physicians' (Mohr, 1984, p. 31).

Medicine's preferred approach to dying is through the bio-medical model of disease discussed in Chapter 2. There are some very positive consequences of the bio-medical approach. Often people are cured of their ailments or receive treatment that reduces the risk of dying from specific conditions. However, because the overriding focus is on curative treatments, this has tended to preclude and exclude the practice of palliative care (treatment to relieve suffering and pain for those who are dying) within medical environments. The bio-medical approach generated gaps in the provision of palliative pain relief within medical procedures. It also generated gaps in the provision of palliative or hospice services within the institutional provision of health care.

Hospice care is a concept of care that incorporates different models and systems of palliative care of patients with advanced or terminal disease. Keeping in mind that a hospice is primarily a concept of care, and not a specific place of care, different types of hospices exist that include, for example, home care teams, hospices themselves and palliative care units (PCUs) (Milicevic, 2002, p. 30). With the benefit of hindsight, the rise in the medical profession's monopoly of health care, especially in the twentieth century, meant that even though medicine held the symbolic authority over the process, dying was paid scant attention. Palliative knowledge and technical expertise were not highly regarded, so remained underdeveloped as a specialist area (see Lewis (2007) for an extended account of the relegation of palliation in the medical profession). The archetypal patterns to the medical profession's care of the dying took the form of an autonomous and authoritative division between the specialist doctor and the dying patient, where dying is located in hospitals and medical intervention is focused on using technologies to prolong life rather than to offer palliative or hospice support.

The nation-state protected professional titles and markets, while, in turn, the professions undertook the provision of welfare state services for citizens. In the wake of globalization and nation-state transformation, new patterns of governing the professions, more flexible markets and new demands on professional practice as well as new forms of professionalism emerge (Kuhlmann, 2006). Called the 'Washington Consensus' (Townsend and Gordon, 2002, part 1), the main sweeps of this moment in world relations capture the sense of how a response to the perceived world economic crisis prompted by the 1970s oil shock took hold in ways that have come to deeply influence death practices, particularly in wealthy nations.

In the 1970s, the rise in the price of oil from the Gulf crisis and the growing costs of servicing the fully-fledged welfare systems were seen to push many hitherto wealthy welfare state nations into a state of near if not actual bankruptcy. The first major check was seen in the adoption of Washington Consensus directives by countries having to tangle with the World Trade Organization and the World Bank. Countries needing support were encouraged to adopt free-market policies and to curb social assistance spending. The term Washington Consensus was coined in 1989 by the economist John Williamson to describe a set of ten relatively specific economic policy prescriptions that he considered constituted the standard reform package promoted for crisis-wracked developing countries. These policies were advocated by institutions based in Washington, DC, such as the International Monetary Fund (IMF), the World Bank and the US Treasury Department. The prescriptions encompassed policies in such areas as macro-economic stabilization, economic opening with respect to both trade and investment, and the expansion of market forces within the domestic economy (Williamson, 1989).

The change in relationship between professionals, the state and business has had a significant effect on the death professions. In the case of those who care for the dying (for example, those working in the health sector) it took place through public-sector institutions and as new public management (NPM). NPM is based on fiscal accountability achieved by contracting-out services. The turn to NPM represents a significant loss of professional autonomy and the handing over of authority regarding treatment decisions to cost-conscious institutional managers, and the emphasis of professional credibility shifts from secrecy to transparency.

In essence, the globalization of these neo-liberal economic policies represents a very real threat to and erosion of professional status. In the prevailing academic discussion about the global dimensions of death professions there is deep pessimism for the future of institutionalized professional care arrangements for the dying. For medicine, this would be represented in the expansion of bio-medical models of health and their familiar, Western-style hospitals around the world, leading to the universalization of bio-medicine. The space for alternative health practices, including the holistic palliative approach, would always be on the margins of medicine and health care provision. Kellehear (2007) offers a gruelling glimpse into such a scenario of hospital-located, bio-medically-oriented care for the dying:

> Dying from old age with an assortment of serious, disabling and chronic disease seems to be a difficult affair across all cultures (Shih *et al.*, 2000), and dying in hospital and nursing home settings is a formidable and separate picture even today. A third to a half of all nursing home residents die in 'moderate' to 'excruciating' episodic, daily pain (Last Acts, 2002: 79). Aminoff and Adunsky (2004), in a study of seventy-one inpatients in a geriatric department of a large American hospital found that 70 per cent of dying elderly admissions did not die calm; 70 per cent had pressure sores; 90 per cent were in an unstable medical condition; and 94 per cent were malnourished. Furthermore, 15 per cent were screaming and 90 per cent endured an invasive medical procedure one week before their death. Not surprisingly, 75 per cent of the medical staff thought these elderly people had 'suffered' (!) (Kellehear, 2007, p. 208)

Kellehear's account paints a fearful picture of bio-medicine and Western hospitals are able to expand their influence and presence *ad infinitum*, aided and abetted by ever-deepening global relations. These pronouncements presume that bio-medicine and hospitals are taken up in different places with no appreciable alterations in their organizational practices or ethics of care.

The presumption of unfettered expansion is not borne out by the historical record. Instead, something much more interesting has taken place. Implemented by such inspirational health professionals as Cicely Saunders, Elisabeth Kübler-Ross and Colin Murray Parkes, the holistic palliative care approach, though already present, positively flourished as it coincided with the social movements for de-institutionalization and the governmental responses to the consequences of the 1970s oil shock. In the USA, the National Center for Complementary and Alternative Medicine became part of the National Institutes of Health (NIH) when it was established in 1991. According to Slater, (2005), in 1996, for the first time, there were more visits by Americans to alternative practitioners than to traditional Western physicians.

In addition, the realization was dawning that existing systems of care, especially those based on the universal provision of institutionally based services, were no longer ideologically or economically viable. As Papadatou (2009) notes: 'this approach turned into a social movement that spread around the world. The response was so impressive that within only 30 years, approximately 5,000 hospice, palliative, and bereavement care services were developed in several countries across all continents' (Clark, 2002, cited in Papadatou, 2009, p. 7). As Lewis's study of the development of palliative care services indicates: 'between the 1970s and the 1990s, palliative care services grew considerably in Britain, North America, and Australasia. In Britain, the numbers of hospices increased to about 7,000, and in the United States to 1,500' (Lewis, 2007, p. 121).

To get a sense of the timing and rate of growth, 'in 1969 Saint Christopher's introduced a home nursing service, and in 1975 the Macmillan nurses began to work with primary care teams. By the mid-1990s there were 1,200 Macmillan nurses, 384 home care teams, and 5,000 Marie Curie nurses providing 24-hour home care (Lewis, 2007, p. 127). This rate of expansion is startling, given that the institutional organization of terminal care had languished outside the mainstream and 'remained in the hands of a small number of homes and hospices inspired by older traditions of Christian charity' since the late nineteenth century (ibid., p. 125).

In Papadatou's (2009) book, she calls for a reworked ethic of care for death professionals, based on a relational rather than a bio-medical or bio-psychosocial model. Papadatou's professional handbook represents shifts in the medical discourses of what care means and how it is best achieved. It tips the balance away from existing attitudes and organizational ethos and offers a means to re-articulate medicine by framing past bio-psychosocial and medical models of care within a new and purportedly better relationship-centred approach. One of the interesting aspects of Papadatou's work is that it represents a move away from professional authority towards practices that foster collaboration and negotiation. It can be taken as a significant inroad of already existing alternative discourses into the centre ground of the mainstream bio-medical approach to dying and death. The medical professions' response to the impact of globalization has been to re-incorporate and rewrite relations between professionals and bureaucracy (institutional management) and recipients. Patients or clients have more say in the process of dying.

A surprising feature of this shift is the way that recipients are instigating novel ways to experience dying. This is seen in the rise of death tourism – the practice of travelling to a destination with the intention of gaining access to medical support to die. As a barely legal enterprise, it is the terminal version of medical tourism, itself a growing global phenomenon. The Asian economic crisis of 1997–8 and the global financial debt crisis of 2008–9 are seen to have had a profound consequences on the particular ways that medical services are organized, delivered and paid for, 'as hospitals sought overseas patients to maintain revenue arising from the short-fall in local patients' (Pope, 2008, p. 15). In reverse, many smaller nations make use of larger neighbours' greater capacity, expertise and economies of scale to provide research and teaching hospitals, and expensive and innovative treatments, to export patients: 'Currently the international trade in health services is estimated to be worth around US$30 billion globally (WHO estimate, 2004)' (Pope, 2008, p. 15).

Death tourism, though hard to track because of its marginal legal status, is also beginning to emerge as a new global medical service. For example, Switzerland has gained a reputation as a death tourism destination. Globally networked groups such as Exit and Dignitas advise on and facilitate assisted suicide.[1] As described in the introduction to this chapter, this has led to increasing numbers of foreigners coming to Switzerland specifically to die. A recent study (Fischer, 2008) sought to determine whether differences exist between the members who received assistance in committing suicide from Exit Deutsche Schweiz and Dignitas. Second, to investigate whether the practices of Exit Deutsche Schweiz have changed since the 1990s. Results suggest that more women than men were assisted by both organizations, and that Dignitas provided more assistance to non-residents, younger people and those suffering from fatal diseases such as multiple sclerosis and amyotrophic lateral sclerosis. Furthermore, the number of women and the proportion of older people suffering from non-fatal diseases among suicides assisted by Exit Deutsche Schweiz has increased since the 1990s.

As Fischer's examination suggests, euthanasia support is offered to non-residents. This is corroborated by Hurst and Mauron (2003), who suggested that one Zurich-based right-to-die society (which offers assisted suicide to non-resident foreigners) has attracted a great deal of media attention and concern, including the case of Craig Ewert, who travelled to Switzerland to commit suicide in 2008:

Mr Ewert, a retired university professor and father of two was struck down by motor neurone disease at 59. Within five months it had left him unable even to breathe unaided, so he paid £3,000 for an assisted suicide with the Swiss-based Dignitas euthanasia organization. Film cameras followed him during his final days in a Dignitas-owned apartment in Zurich. The resulting documentary – *Right To Die?* – shows him passing away with Mary, his wife of 37 years, at his side. In law,

Dignitas can only assist suicide and cannot carry out the final act. So, with his body barely functioning, Craig is given a timer to bite on which turns off his ventilator. Retired social worker Arthur Bernard, who has acted as an 'escort' in more than 100 assisted suicides for Dignitas, also mixes a lethal dose of barbiturate and pours it into a glass. He says: 'Mr Ewert, if you drink this you are going to die.' Craig drinks through a pink straw, then says: 'Give me some apple juice. Please can I have some music?' Moments before his eyes close for the final time he says: 'Thank you.' His wife then says: 'Safe journey. Have a good sleep.' After 45 minutes he is pronounced dead. (Coles, 2008)

In these ways we can see how the provision of medical, and especially palliative care and access to euthanasia, is becoming re-ordered as a consequence of economic decisions made in response to perceived global trends. The symbolic role of the medical professional has shifted from the 'sage on the state' who has full autonomy and authority over the dying to a 'guide on the side' who negotiates with the dying regarding the manner in which they can best bring about the kind of death the dying regard as appropriate.

It should be noted that this transformation in the death archetype is not yet fully complete. Despite emancipatory aims and innovative practices, the realities of managing dying within palliative care movements abutted to bio-medically oriented health care systems mean that life-sustaining interventions remain excessive, and physical pain is largely mismanaged; palliative services are offered only to limited populations and particularly to those with conditions with predictable trajectories (for example, cancers and AIDS); the elderly and chronically ill are deprived of palliative care because they are not recognized as officially dying; and access to end-of-life care is very limited for people from minority ethnic backgrounds. In the first decade of the twenty-first century, the majority of people in Western societies die in intensive care wards in hospitals, and the majority in non-Western societies die with drastically limited facilities of any sort.

Experts for the recently dead

The historical trajectory of funeral directors has been slightly different. In a parallel move to medicine, funeral directors (or undertakers as they used to be known), wrestled control over burials of members of the aristocracy from the College of Arms in medieval times, later coming to supply burial rituals to all classes during the rapidly industrializing nineteenth century. Howarth (1996) describes it as a shift from community and craft-based tasks, where local women would lay out the dead, and local builders and carpenters would make coffins and help local clergy undertake the necessary rites and bury the dead, to a more institutionalized set of occupations.

Funeral directors gained a professional mandate over possession of the body, the science of humanization (embalming and dressing the body/casket) and control of the funeral ceremony.

The capacity for funeral directors to take over tasks previously done in the community sprang from an urge to improve sanitation. The late-nineteenth-century grand projects for separating potable water and sewage are one of the long-standing successes of this era. One aspect of this sanitation was the need to prevent cross-infection from the dead and decomposing to the living. Achieved in multiple ways, it included physically sanitizing and separating dead bodies using the rapidly progressing science of embalming, and by making new out-of-town municipal cemeteries (see, for example, Laderman, 2003; Querioz and Rugg, 2003; Rugg, 2006).

The need to transport the dead over much longer distances and the Victorian cult of elaborate funerary arrangements and mourning procedures goes a long way to explain the emergence of the funeral director as a choreographer of funerary ceremonies during the latter half of the nineteenth century, when each aspect of the service became heavily commodified and commercialized. The boom was short-lived, however, and the funeral industry came under significant threat with the Edwardian eschewal of elaborate funerary protocol. The need to form associations and to take on a professional identity was seen as vital to combat the slump in the industry. One of the professionalizing strategies was to take on form filling; that is, bureaucratic responsibilities that linked the profession to already well-established medical and legislative institutions. Another was business investment in buildings, vehicles and services to provide those facilities once available in the home. These strategies further cemented the professional and institutional position of funeral directors.

By the 1890s, state registration of morticians was well under way in the US *New Deal* environment of voluntary charity or privatized insurance systems of social and health provision (see, for example, Laderman, 2003; Harrington, 2007). The UK and the Antipodes trailed somewhat, though the reason for the lag remains unclear, given the particular influence of the American funeral industry in the Antipodes. By 1940, British practitioners had followed their American colleagues and relinquished the professional title of undertaker for funeral director, adopted the newly scientized art of embalming, emphasized education and training, and set up a national professional association and in-house journal by 1953 (see also Parsons, 1999). This pattern and timeline was repeated in other closely allied, British settler nations such as New Zealand (Schafer, 2007) and Australia (Jalland, 2006, p. 30).

Though the funeral profession did not gain the same institutional foothold as medicine right across Western nations, funeral directors became thoroughly embedded as the first port of call to manage the recently deceased. They liaised between the bereaved, the medical establishment and legislature, and the clergy and local authorities, which provided both cemetery space and often cremation facilities. Through this process of professionalization, mourners came to rely on funeral directors as a source of expertise similar to the ways in which the sick and dying rely on doctors as a source of expertise and succour.

For the management of the recently dead, the professional engagement is between the funeral director, the deceased's body (centred on the preparation of the body) and the bereaved (centred on collating official documents and the preparation of the funeral rituals). Again, the professional relationship is a hierarchical one, based on the delivery of expert knowledge and services. The care of the recently dead takes place in a specialized location (the funeral home/embalming room/morgue) and expertise is focused on the commercial provision of scientific treatment of the body, and specialized services and goods such as hearses, caskets and trims. This arrangement ensures that the recently dead are rendered hygienic, legal requirements are met and the funeral ritual is organized by people who have made it their business to carry out the disposal of the recently dead.

This form of professional practice also has problematic consequences: standardized services allow little room for difference, and by maintaining professional control over who has access to funerary knowledge and expertise means that people have little option but to use these professional services. Funeral directors' care is centred on the scientized preparation of the recently dead body that takes place in an institutionalized and legally controlled environment (the embalming room) in specially designated premises (the funeral parlour or funeral home). Once prepared, care is also achieved through the organization of the legally required documentation and the execution of the funeral ceremony according to accepted convention.

The funeral industry has also been transformed under the global shift in professional relationships. For funeral directors, the emphasis on financial transparency of NPM was enforced through legislation. In the UK, the 1977 study of funeral charges by the Price Commission made a number of recommendations to tilt the balance in favour of the client, including the provision of a written estimate, the prominent display of price lists on the funeral director's premises, the itemization of prices, and a widening of the complaints procedure of the National Association of Funeral Directors (NAFD). Following this report, and in consultation with the Office of Fair Trading, the NAFD introduced a code of practice for its members (Secretary of State for Trade and Industry, 1987). The effectiveness of the code of practice has undergone periodic review by independent ombudsmen (see, for example, Vickers, 2001). In a similar vein, in 1984, the US Federal Trade Commission (FTC) began to regulate the funeral home industry in order to protect consumers from deceptive practices. The FTC Funeral Rule requires funeral homes to provide all customers (and potential customers) with a General Price List specifically outlining goods and services in the funeral industry, as defined by the FTC. Seen as the outcome of severe criticism by Mitford (1963) and various pricing scandals, the funeral rule requires a funeral director to give consumers accurate, itemized price information and various other disclosures about funeral goods and services. The FTC Funeral Rule, among other things, also requires the equivalent display of the most and least expensive casket.

Funeral industries have also transformed their labour practices in ways that maintain their professional status in the new era. At one level, the industry is becoming legitimated as a profession as it engages with labour regulation laws. At another level, the occupation is gaining professional credibility by taking on a corporate culture. According to Whittaker (2005), the funeral industry has gained formal categorization as professional as a consequence of the corporatization of the industry in the USA.

The rise in corporate culture in the funeral industry has led to widespread shifts in the type and expectations of the labour force working in this occupation. Harrington (2007) outlines the changing environment within which funeral directors operate. He outlines four key changes shaking up the USA market (and by extension other developed funeral markets). These are: the emergence of larger, corporate style funeral businesses; the growing presence of internet retailers; the increased rates of cremation; and the rise in migration that increases the demand for non-standard services and for migrants' rights to work in the funeral trade.

These four contextual considerations are greatly altering the landscape of funeral directing these days. For example, growing global corporatization of the funeral industry is forcing up costs and potentially threatening variability. There has been a great growth in the corporate organization of funeral businesses, where companies buy up the production and consumption chains and so control as many aspects of the service as possible. This works best through a take-over and conglomeration strategy, which has led to the rapid global expansion of a limited number of corporate funeral companies. Whittaker captures the speed and extent of global corporate momentum:

> Growth had been rapid. For example, with the aid of venture capital, Tom Johnson, once associated with Pierce Brothers (funeral homes) in California, struck out on his own in the early 1990s and, in slightly over four years, he had acquired over 160 operating units with a market value, by some estimates, in the $295 million range ... The Loewen Group went public in 1987: a firm with 47 funeral homes and one cemetery. Within a decade, it could boast 950 funeral homes and 289 cemeteries throughout Canada, the United States and Puerto Rico. Service Corporation International, the world's largest operator of funeral homes, cemeteries, and crematoria, started with a single mortuary in 1951. It went public in 1969. In 1993, SCI expanded its operation into Australia and, during the same period, acquired properties in the United Kingdom where it quickly became the largest funeral services provider. In 1995, it purchased the funeral operations of the French conglomerate, Lyonnaise des Eaux. (Whittaker, 2005, p. 13)

The successful expansion and conglomeration of multinational funeral companies is being repeated elsewhere in the world. For example, Australia (Jalland, 2006, p. 300) and New Zealand (Schafer, 2007), have both experienced multi-national take-overs of many locally-owned funeral businesses. As Jalland notes, corporatization can escalate funeral costs as more services and products are made available. In Sydney, Australia, 'the average price of a funeral in 1990–1991 was $3012, which was 10.3 per cent more than the previous year and due to increased levels of service: these included grief counselling, preparation of bodies for viewing, chapels in the funeral directors' premises, better quality premises and refreshments after the funeral' (Jalland, 2006, p. 300).

As with the pessimistic literature on the care of the dying, there is a similar gloom associated with the new global management of the recently dead. This negativity is articulated in ways that parallel broader arguments in the globalization literature. One argument is that, with the spread of global economic practices associated with freer trade and movement, corporate capitalism will expand exponentially and have dire consequences for death care. The worst case scenario in terms of funeral professions is often referred to as the 'McDonaldization' of funerals (Howarth, 2007, p. 247). This term, often attributed to Ritzer (1993), but in fact in use a decade earlier in Tom Fisher's 'There Could Be a McDonald's in Funeral Service' (1983) is the process by which the organizing principles of the fast food industry (efficiency, calculability, predictability and control, and the economies of scale) which are also the basis of corporate business culture, come to dominate other sectors of society, including the funeral industry.

Some of the perceived drawbacks are associated with the corporate practice of *conglomeration* (a strategy where production and consumptions chains are bought up to ensures the supply of goods and potentially push out competition). The combined effect of McDonaldization and conglomeration is the homogenization of goods and services. The quality and ingredients of McFunerals in Rome are identical to those in Los Angeles, Auckland and Tokyo. Though standardized quality controls are not, by definition, a bad thing, the perceived social and cultural consequences are problematic because there is 'the risk that funerals will become less personalized, and less culturally distinct' (Howarth, 2007, p. 247). One funeral would become very much like another, regardless of the global location of the burial.

The corporate takeover and conglomeration of funeral services do offer particular kinds of streamlined and consistent funeral packages much like their global fast-food counterparts. Yet, despite the predictions of cultural flattening, the expansion into local markets has *not* continued unabated. It has been relatively short-lived, as multi-national companies have found it harder to maintain their profit margins in countries where incomes are lower and people's funerary practices are less attuned to extravagance. They also fail where people's increasingly multi-cultural expectations cannot be met within the standardized provision of services that McFunerals offer. At the same time, local companies have reworked their professional practices to be more fluid and responsive to both the market and their customers' increasingly varied needs (see, for example, Suzuki, 2003; Cottle and Keys, 2004). The funeral industry makes the shift from mass production to increasingly customized products and services.

This shift is not the only new and surprising global networking strategy that has emerged. More recently, and perhaps in the face of corporatization, many funeral businesses and organizations are engaging with the possibilities that internet retail allow. The growing influence of internet retailers who offer the purchase of, for example, low-priced caskets, also puts pressure on conventional funeral homes as more customers want to use their premises but not to buy their stock merchandise. More funeral homes are now working in conjunction with internet retailers to offer component services (Harrington, 2007).

Among the successes of global economic expansion is the realization that funeral directors' practices are changing in response to peoples' newly emerging desires and expectations. One way that this new global networking is surfacing is that long-standing community strategies are having a new lease of life as people galvanize to move against the perceived consequences of corporatized funerals. For example, in Quebec, Canada, co-operative networks have taken on and won business from corporate giants.

Lefebvre (2006) examined local co-operative funeral societies' responses in Quebec to the presence of international funeral conglomerates in their area:

> Economic globalization and the search for profitable activity sectors linked to the aging population phenomenon have attracted new foreign players looking to invest in the large-scale purchasing of Quebec funeral companies. The arrival of multinationals on the Quebec funeral market in 1993 generated a shock wave that hit private (mum & dad) funeral companies and cooperatives hard. Following that wave of acquisitions, non-Quebec companies controlled a total of thirty funeral companies in Quebec, handling nearly two fifths of the 55,000 deaths in the province each year. The effect was to drain communities' capital toward shareholders outside Quebec and local communities began to respond in productive and successful ways. Funeral cooperatives developed new strategies that focused on strengthening existing and building new cooperative networks. These cooperatives successfully regained and expanded market control while offering competitively priced services according to a study by the Quebec Department of Industry and Trade, the average funeral cost was higher in Quebec than elsewhere in Canada before the emergence of cooperatives at $794 for Quebec in 1972 compared with $665 for Canada as a whole. That gap of almost 20% was bad news for

Quebec consumers. In 2000, the average funeral cost was $5,723 in Canada, $5,250 in Quebec and $3,163 in the cooperatives network. Community mobilization, pooling resources in a consolidated network and rapid reaction and decision-making have enabled funeral cooperatives to gain ground in all markets occupied by U.S. multinationals. (Lefebvre, 2006)

Another study by McManus and Schafer (2009) examined attitudes to the cost of funerals in New Zealand, drawing attention to the increasing diversification of funeral provision. They argued that ways of managing the costs of funerals are changing, as are ways of thinking about and organizing funerals arrangements. There is a clear turn towards secular, personalized funerals that focus on a celebration of the individual's life. At the same time, this does not mean that people are willing to forgo funerals or eschew the services and expertise of funeral professionals, for which Mitford campaigned. Rather, it is experienced as people making more and varied demands on funeral professionals. In turn, funeral directors become more networked and proactive in meeting people's perceived needs for support and succour. McManus and Schafer's (2009) research corroborates earlier trends identified by Parsons (1999), who suggested a backlash against 1980s multi-national funeral conglomerates in his accounts of the niche marketing of smaller boutique funeral firms in the 1990s. He stresses that funeral businesses have shifted from big to small, readily adaptable businesses that also see their work and present themselves in a new light.

Cottle and Keys (2004) discussed the global corporatization of funerals and, after a close look at Australia, concluded that 'the dominance of American companies in the Australian funeral market cannot simply be interpreted as the "McDonaldisation" of Australian funerals because instead of *standardising* its products, it has done the opposite and offers an abundance of different funeral products' (Cottle and Keys, 2004, ibid., p. 41). Similarly, Suzuki's (2003) account of contemporary Japanese funerals explores a complex interplay of custom, innovation, professionalism and standardization. New consumer-driven funeral practices are becoming more popular – these are 'living funerals' (*seizensō*, which literally means a funeral while still alive, with a fun-loving and joyous atmosphere) and 'non-religious funerals' (*mushūkyōsō*, a funeral conducted without priests of religious practices. In Japan, the majority of funerals are Buddhist and have Buddhist priests present to chant the sutras). According to Suzuki, 'these innovative funeral practices reflect the fact that some Japanese have come to desire funerals that celebrate their own lives more than funeral practices that focus on the deceased as ancestors of the household' (Suzuki, 2003, p. 69). These new ceremonies do not imply that Japanese consumers are opposed to the commercialization of funerals. They are willing to pay as long as it is a meaningful ceremony, and it is this changing 'meaningfulness' to which the funeral industry makes adjustments (Suzuki, 2003, p. 70).

Bremborg's Swedish study (2006) interprets the shift as a mode of professionalization by broadening work tasks in different fields. Similarly, Grossberg (2004) tells of how a small company (All Nations Society – ANS) applied an American approach to outsourcing, pricing and service bundling in the very traditional industry of Japanese funeral services so as to create a competitive advantage for itself against companies that practise opaque pricing and with high overheads. Although an example of business practice transfer in a global age, the following account is of explicit costings, highly tailored products and bespoke services rather than conglomeration and opaque and routine business dealings.

'All Nations Society is a tiny newcomer in a $30 billion industry that consist of about 4,000 Japanese companies, with about half of that number active in the Tokyo metropolitan area. Roughly 600 people die every day in Tokyo and a typical Japanese funeral is made up of three components: (1) the funeral ceremony itself; (2) the monk and temple; and (3) the headstone and grave. According to the Ministry of Economics, Trade and Industry, the average price of the ceremony is between ¥1,500,000 and ¥3,000,000 (approximately US $14,000–$28,000). While no official estimates exist, the other components average about ¥3,000,000 ($28,000) together, so a funeral can cost anywhere between $15,000 and $50,000 or more' (Grossberg, 2004, p. 38). The proprietor of ANS, John Kamm, has capitalized on funeral trends. In 1993, only 5 per cent of the representatives of the 600 people who die each day did not order a room for the ceremony from a funeral company. By 2003, this had reached 35 per cent (Grossberg, 2004, p. 37). As most funeral companies maintain large bricks and mortar facilities to accommodate cremations and funeral ceremonies, they are compelled to offer full service funerals to cover their running costs. However, fewer people are willing to pay the very high cost of a full service. John Kamm obtained a business licence and in 2003, while studying for an MBA in Japan, set up ANS, offering cremation and ceremony-only facilities to the recently bereaved, the terminally ill who wanted to arrange their own funerals, and people interested in pre-planning their funerals. Kamm offered cut-rate, no-frills funerals, emphasized the transparency of its pricing strategy and, unlike traditional Japanese operators, 'tried to encourage the consumer to pick and choose only those elements that he or she wanted' (Grossberg, 2004, p. 38). He used available funeral parlours to outsource ANS clients' service, and since most of the funeral businesses in Japan had no more than one funeral or so a week there was plenty of excess capacity that ANS could utilize. This new, networked model broke into the lucrative Japanese funeral market successfully by offering cheaper, client-driven services. These examples serve to illustrate that consumers are given a sense of control over the ritual. The industry has shifted the ceremony away from a religious discourse toward more therapeutic ones. Traditional emphasis on the virtues of an afterlife has shifted towards celebrations of life. Humour increasingly occupies the spaces left by the theological account of death.

The rise in bespoke or customized funerals raises a parallel point to death tourism discussed earlier: local consumer-driven responses to global trends in the organization of the funeral industry highlight a growing attention to the person rather than an exclusive focus on the body.

Across rich nation-states around the world, the global funeral industry is reshaping professional practice in multiple ways, including a proliferation of tasks and responsibilities that are more in tune with the perceived needs of their consumers. The funeral industry has been transformed under global practices: there has been a significant realignment in institutional practice and a proliferation in the ways of organizing funerals professionally. At the same time, funerary ethics of care have shifted from a concern with the scientific preparations of the body to a concern with the celebration of the life lived and care of the bereaved. The bereaved, as buyers and consumers of funerals, are more likely to ask for different and more specialized services that fit the needs and expectations of a contemporary life-centred funeral.

A new, advanced modern archetype for managing death

As a consequence of seeking recognition and the right to earn a living from specialized occupations, medicine and funeral directing have become pivotal death professions. Particularly during the middle course of the twentieth century, they came to dictate ways of understanding and managing the care of the dying and the recently dead. Their particular sets of medical and funerary expertise (knowledge, techniques and instruments, sites) formed the crucible of the twentieth-century professional management of the dying and dead.

As Saunders, Mitford and many other observers have commented in a similar vein, 'this medicalisation (and commercialisation) have increased the marginalization of people and have served as a form of social control over death and suffering' (Papadatou, 2009, p. 6). Indeed, the twentieth-century death-management archetype is a set of professional relationships based on the provision of heavily protected expert knowledge and services, decided on and controlled by the professionals. Those in receipt of the professional services must accept what is given with little question or challenge to either their ethics of care or the system of occupational organization. One way to encapsulate this is to see that the archetype for the modern, professional management of death that underpinned both approaches is a concern with autonomous and authoritative management of the rite of passage.

The advanced modern archetype for death is no longer grounded in professional practices dominated by expert concerns that pay technical attention to processing the dying or recently dead body. Instead, we can see that a different archetype for managing death has taken shape. It has transformed into an archetype marked by collaboration between specialists who pay attention to the concerns of the dying or recently dead person. The new archetype is deeply embedded in global social relations. Death tourism and bespoke funerals are the new traditions of a global age. They host the enduring rites of passage that signal the transition from a living to a dead person. The experts are no longer in a hierarchical relationship where professional dominion over the body dominates the proceedings. Instead, professionals have become the specialists who help to solve the problem of negotiating the symbolic transition, and they do so alongside and with attention to the person. The professional, the dying, the dead and the bereaved come together to negotiate the symbolic content, the meaning and the terms-of-passage for those who are transitioning from life to death. The negotiation highlights how these new customs are underpinned by a shared, collective understanding of the social circumstances (tortuous dying and meaningless funerals) and modes of organizing action in terms of contemporary concerns (death tourism and customized funerals). This is the archetype for managing death in a global age.

Conclusion

If we survey the multiple ways in which care for the dying and the recently dead has been transformed, it over-simplifies things to say that globalization has brought reduced professional standards and lack of care. Currently, countries, people, governments and professions are all engaged with the thorny issues of caring for the dying and the dead in different ways certainly, but within those differences, continuities of care are clearly present. Death professionals are more than ever marked by new networks of practice that are highly attuned to consumer needs and expectations, and more than ever responsive to the plans of the recently deceased and the expectations of the recently bereaved. A new archetype of death management has emerged. It is one based on professional ethics of care that pivot on negotiation and collaboration with the dying and the recently dead on their projects of the self.

Questions

Chapter 5, on changes to the institutional organization of dying and the recently dead, examined the recent reorganization of death professions.

1.   What does new public management (NPM) mean, and how does it change people's experience of dying?

2. Compare Stannard's Puritan funeral embellishment (see Chapter 1) with new trends in personalized funerals outlined in Chapter 4.
3. If the chapter is about change in the death professions, can they *both* be read as examples of the 'modern' death contradiction that Stannard talks about? Why?/Why not?

Funerary Rites: Give Me a Decent Send-off

Introduction

What do a tartan coffin and resomator remains[1] (see Figures 5.1 and 5.2) have in common? They are both forms of bodily disposal in accord with contemporary technologies and values. The tartan coffin, as an emblem of Scottish identity, speaks to an explicit sense of vulnerability of, as well as pride in, the cultural identity of the deceased person. This goes hand in hand with individuals and populations that constantly mix with those from other cultural backgrounds. The chalky 'ash' and bio-liquid remains of a resomated corpse is also a thematic response to the sense of ecological

Figure 5.1   Tartan coffin

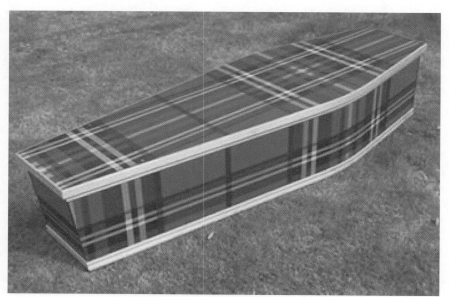

Source: JFunerals www.jfunerals.com/coffins.htm.

Figure 5.2   Resomator with bag of ashes

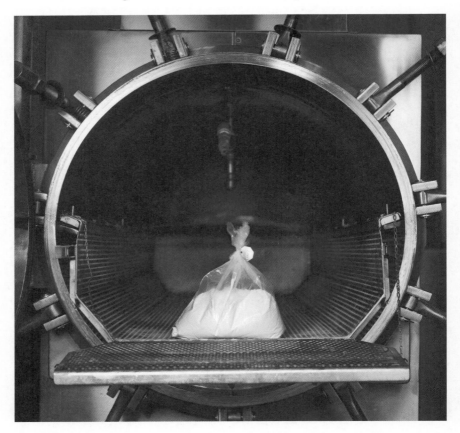

Source: Photographer Finn O'Hara / Gallery Stock / Snapper Media.

vulnerability that pervades much discourse about the contemporary relationship of humans with the planet. A fear of cultural and ecological
collapse skulks within novel forms of bodily disposal. This sense of susceptibility and the need to respond to contemporary cultural and ecological
pressures is, it is argued by many sociologists of our time, a predominant
feature of living in a world that emphasizes connections between different
people and places.

Chapter 4 focused on the personalized services rendered for the dying
and the recently dead. This chapter examines more closely the nature of
contemporary funerary rites in terms of their changing traditions, rituals
and symbolic content. It is concerned with how current global trends in
interment practices manifest particular kinds of symbolic connections to
people and places. The first section begins with a general discussion of how

living in a global age may decouple long-standing connections between interment, belonging, people and place. It then compares and contrasts customary ways of interring the dead at two different periods – the mid-twentieth century and the twenty-first century, and across two similar countries – Scotland and New Zealand. This two-by-two strategy is used as a way to explore how contemporary trends in bodily interment are a means of expressing unique cultural identities through a global sensibility.

Interment rites as practices of belonging

The form, content and location of funeral rites are significant. They are an ancient means of forging significant connections between people and places. Another way to say this is that the connections made manifest in the manner of interment are an expression of belonging and cultural identity. Interment is an expression of cultural belonging, and involves ideas about the ways that people experience life and death. We begin with the concept of *belonging*.

Belonging is a 'complex mesh of material, social and emotional factors' that engender a sense of connection to people and places (Jones, 2007, p. 54). Many people have sought to unravel the whys and wherefores of belonging, including sociologists. A personal *and* communal sense of connection is the basis of any society or culture. But there is a gnarly conundrum at the centre of all of this: people are born and they die. There is a perpetual need to welcome and send off new and departing individual members in ways that maintain the overall sense of belonging of the group. Rituals associated with membership of sports teams are a version of this. New members are inducted into the team through (sometimes humiliating or degrading) rituals. By going through such a ritual they are recognized as members of the group and their identity becomes associated with it. When they leave, their exit ceremony often involves being inducted into a hall of fame – very much like an ancestral line-up. As members come and go, the group identity also has to be maintained. The group has to be more than the collection of individuals in it at any one time: the history of a football team is more than the individual histories of its team players. It includes events, places and relationships that transcend individuals as they are important to the group as a whole. A sense of belonging is achieved through the practice of *traditions*, as these foster continuity despite the changes among members.

Traditions are made up of rituals. Observing rituals, such as, for example, Thanksgiving or Christmas, reinforces connections between the people who observe them. The rituals that make up traditions are heavily symbolic. They are taken to mean important things for the members of group. While I am not an American, I am aware of the significance of Thanksgiving to American collective sensibility as a nation, but also at the micro level of family engagement. To participate or not in Thanksgiving has more meaning to an American than a person brought up in any other culture. It is an important way to embody, acknowledge and display one's membership of that culture.

Framing this multi-layered sense of belonging at the level of culture, Daniel Bell (1976, p. xv), for example, notes that 'tradition becomes essential to the vitality of a culture, for it provides the continuity of memory that teaches how one's forebears met the same existential predicaments'. Traditions are made up of ritual behaviours that are re-enacted time and again in response to specific events. Participation in rituals, it is argued, creates a sense of communion between those involved, and it is this sense of close association that offers a feeling of connection and belonging despite the turnover of members and the passage of time.

Durkheim, not surprisingly, thought deeply about the role of funerary rituals in society. Aware that death rips the social fabric because a member is lost, he argued that, for example, the expectation to cry at a funeral is more related to reasserting the social bond than the actual feelings one might have about the deceased: 'One weeps, not simply because he is sad, but because he is forced to weep. It is a ritual attitude which he is forced to adopt out of respect for custom, [people] cry together because they continue to be precious to one another and because, regardless of the blow that has fallen upon it, the collectivity is not breached' (Durkheim, [1912]1995, p. 405). By taking part in funeral rites, one recognizes personal loss and the loss of others in the community, and one comes to feel the sentiments of connection. In this *functional* approach to funeral rites, the emotional effect of the ritual is to bond the community into a shared sense of belonging.

While Durkheim's interest is in repairing the social bond through shared emotions, other social commentators see that rituals play a significant role in creating belonging because they are the means through which people *imagine* their communities. According to Anderson (1991, p. 6), a sense of belonging 'is *imagined* because the members of even the smallest nation will never know most of their fellow-members, meet them, or even hear of them, yet in the minds of each lives the image of their communion'.

Rituals achieve this imagined community because they aim for what Victor Turner has called *symbolic communitas*, which is the feeling of connectedness to a larger imagined community (Turner, [1969]1995). This feeling of connectedness is achieved through expressions of intense emotion.

Traditions help to define the specific character of that imagined community, or culture, as they express the unique and specific 'wisdom of generations' that provide the living with 'ready building-blocks for shaping their world' (Sztompka, 1994, p. 64). Traditions also assure the identity of a society through time, because they enrol current generations into the past. This is not achieved by blindly enforcing old ways, but by current generations having to grapple with their own identity as it connects to their past.

As Misztal (2003, p. 95) puts it 'this continuation is achieved due to a consensus between living generations and generations of the dead (where) the consensus changes through interpretation by a new generation, whose reinterpretation, actions and beliefs [in turn] enter into memory'.

Interment rites are able to carry a sense of belonging because they connect people and places. When a person dies, the manner in which his or her remains are interred symbolically denotes a claim to a cultural connection with specific people and specific places. Tibetan sky burials are a good example of this. A sky burial is when the deceased's body is ritually dissected under the guidance of Tibetan monks then placed in charnel grounds, often high up in the mountains, for predatory birds, such a vultures, to feed on. Sky burials were first recorded in the *Tibetan Book of the Dead* in the twelfth century. Materially, the ritual dissection is practised in a way that places the living who undertake the ritual and the dead person within Tibetan culture. Symbolically, this ritual represents the impermanence of life and rebirth which denote the core values and beliefs of Tibetan Buddhist culture (Goss and Klass, 1997).

As a central part of any culture, funeral rites are extremely diverse, and there are thousands of different funeral rites used around the world. Even so, there are some significant trends in bodily disposal and funerary rites that are connected with globalization. Previous chapters have discussed the move towards tailored death care as a response to global relations. This chapter looks at how rituals and symbols associated with saying farewell to the dead are also transforming in the light of globalization. The next section explores interment customs of the mid-twentieth century and the early twenty-first century from two examples of modern Western society: Scotland and New Zealand's settler society. This is a means of seeing how two societies, located on different sides of the earth, have transformed their interment rites in their response to cultural globalization.

Taking belonging for granted

This section examines mid-twentieth-century Scotland and New Zealand. The aim is to give an account of how cultural identities were articulated through the conventional interment practices of two modern nations prior to the shift towards a global sensibility associated with advanced modernity.

It is argued in the sociological literature that societies such as New Zealand, Australia, the UK, North America and Western Europe are a distinctive group because they have all gone through and emerged from a transition to modernity. The centrality of modernization processes is well recognized in the literature of death. Its development throughout the nineteenth century saw a dramatic shift in modern Western countries' funeral and burial practices in response to industrialization and the urbanization of populations. Walter (2005) succinctly describes this period of change:

Religious concerns were eroded in the face of public health requirements, though not always without a struggle. Further, mobility from country to town, or from Europe to America, detached mourners from traditional funeral customs, leading them to become more reliant on experts to tell them what to do. Everywhere, we find two linked innovations. One is increasing use of technical, especially medical, rationality. The other is the rise of new specialists: registrars, pathologists, funeral directors, cemetery entrepreneurs and managers. (p. 176)

In terms of interment in Western society, this shift is often associated with the rapid and widespread uptake of cremation. This is a method of bodily disposal that is organized in the West in such a way that it relies on the technologies of industrialized society: fossil fuels and furnaces in municipally regulated, purpose-built buildings (Jupp, 2005). The key to understanding how the disposal method gained momentum, despite a very slow start in the 1870s, was the idea of hygiene. To be specific, hygienic practices came to embody the interconnected fear of contagion, infection and miasmic disease from the stench of rotting corpses from overfull burial yards, and the belief in the revitalizing capabilities of the modern world of science and technology (Prothero, 2001). Yet, even as the material practices of bodily disposal accommodated themselves to new authority vested in the power of science, at the same time, cultural conventions continued to rearticulate symbolic connections to people and places.

A country comparison of interment practices

Scotland and New Zealand are very similar despite their geographical separation, and they share a similar death profile in terms of population size and density. New Zealand had a population of 4,315,800 people in 2009 (World Bank, 2010) and Scotland's population that same year was 5,194,000 (Scottish Government, 2010). In New Zealand, more than 85 per cent of the population live in urban areas, and 81.3 per cent of Scots are urbanized. The majority of residents live in large cities, particularly Glasgow, Edinburgh and Aberdeen in Scotland, and Auckland, Wellington and Christchurch in New Zealand. The majority of both countries' land area is sparsely populated rural areas, used for farming and agriculture.

New Zealand's population is slightly more ethnically diverse than Scotland's: 30 per cent are of non-white European descent; Maori, 8 per cent; East Asian, 5.7 per cent; Pacific Islander, 4.4 per cent; other, 0.5 per cent; mixed, 7.8 per cent; unspecified, 3.8 per cent (World Bank, 2010). Though not tallied in terms of indigenous ethnic identity, Scots have a non-European ethnic diversity of 8 per cent. In both countries, the dominant religious affiliation is Christianity. Life expectancy in Scotland is 75.0 years for men and 79.9 years for women (General Register Office for Scotland,

2009). In New Zealand, life expectancy is slightly higher at 78.0 years for men and 82.2 years women (Statistics New Zealand, 2009). In Scotland, 16 per cent of the population is over 65, while in New Zealand, they represent 9.8 per cent. The proportions of the elderly are growing in both countries. Both countries have seen similar developments and effects of globalization.

Both experienced a significant decline in major industries during the late 1970s and 1980s – mainly heavy industry, such as shipyards and mining in Scotland and agri-industry including freezing-works and timber-processing in New Zealand. Both weathered an enduring social decline during the 1980s, seen in diminished welfare provision at a time of high unemployment. Both overshadowed by an economic big brother (England/ Australia), they are now heavily involved in global and transnational networks. Each has invested heavily in information and communication technologies to remain competitive and advance their populations through increased access and interaction, and to overcome the limitations of physical isolation. Though the land mass differs considerably, the terrain is comparable – vast tracts of Scotland and New Zealand are mountainous, with much smaller areas of highly concentrated urban living (in the 3–4 main cities).

Scotland and New Zealand share a similar death profile across the population: most people die of slow, degenerative diseases such as cancers, heart disease and organ failure rather than infection and accident. The countries also share habits of body disposal. The dominant form of body disposal is cremation, but only just (approximately 57 per cent cremation). Both have a mixed economy of body disposal – organized through networks that span the commercial, municipal and ecclesiastical domains of funeral directors, local authorities and religious organizations. All 72 New Zealand and 32 Scottish municipal authorities are the primary providers of body disposal services under state authority, responsible for the effective management, maintenance, community consultation and planning of body disposal needs within their jurisdictions.

Scottish interment conventions of the mid-twentieth century

Scots tend to regard themselves as a distinct cultural group that are in an historically and politically interesting relationship with other nations of the British Isles, most notably England. Scottishness, like any other sense of cultural identity, is always in the making through people's everyday habits, practices and institutions – and this is never more so than in death.

Studies of Scottish culture suggest a distinctly Scottish set of interment rituals and institutions.[2] By the start of the twentieth century, common practices found across Scotland mixed custom and regulation in particular ways. After centuries of wavering between allowing and banning various elements of the burial service, the dominant Church of Scotland had settled into a pattern of at least some kind of religious ceremony (Raeburn, 2010). This was interlaced with customary rituals of, for example, the bell-ringer

announcing the death, the *lykewake* (viewing of the body), a few words
from man of the cloth, *kisting/chesting* (closing the coffin), men going with
the body to the place of interment, and women staying in the home and
preparing the post-funeral meal. After the interment, it was the customary
practice in the West of Scotland to have a 'big scoff and a wee dram'. As
my mother put it, until fairly recently (the mid-1970s):

> The body would be in the good room – but you wouldn't light a fire, and
> you'd be organizing like mad to get the funeral arranged – like today,
> getting the forms from the doctor, contacting the council and the
> gravediggers, and getting the minister sorted for when you could do the
> funeral and figuring out when to shut the coffin. The house would be
> packed to the gunnels and there'd be lots to do feeding everybody and
> keeping the place tidy – folk staying over would sometimes make the
> most of it. On the day, everybody would be at the house and the minis-
> ter would do the service there. Then the men would go off with the
> hearse – not many had cars back then, and the women would set to
> making a big steak pie for them coming back for a wee drink or two. In
> the winter it would be bitter and some of the men would aye come back
> with the flu! (McManus, 2008)

According to McFarland (2010), these rituals made for a decent send-
off because they bestowed dignity and a sense of belonging to both the
deceased and the bereaved. What made these decent send-offs Scottish was
deeply embedded but not necessarily made explicit in these rituals. For
example, the steak pie is a customary meal associated with funerals and
Hogmanay (New Year observance), especially in the West of Scotland.
Also the full event, from death to disposal of the body, would be conducted
through the auspices of Scots law, municipal regulations and church
canon.

These comforting, familiar and reassuring rituals endured across the
twentieth century, even as death became more professionalized and secular-
ized in Scotland. As McFarland (2010) notes, during the middle decades of
twentieth-century Scotland, the location of services, viewings and feastings
shifted to funeral directors/funeral parlours from family, home, ministers
and undertakers. It also included a shift to women's involvement in the
whole process, from organizing and attending interments to being undertakers themselves. The underlying balance of institutional power also
shifted to favour the regional authority over the church, and interment
options opened up to include cremation as well as burial. Though the site
for organizing a decent send-off shifted, the basic components remained
intact (Spence, 1998). A recognizably Scottish send-off endured until the
latter stages of the twentieth century. Non-Scots who died in Scotland were
subject to the same regulations and facilities as indigenous Scots. Cultural
assimilation was presumed so therefore practised and achieved.

Kiwi internment conventions of the mid twentieth century

Turning to the New Zealand context, historically, there are strong connections between Scottish and New Zealand internment practices of the late nineteenth and up to the mid-twentieth century. Historical research on Scots migration to the colonies, including New Zealand, reveals the presence of connections to people and land in early settler internment rites. Powell's (2007) *Death, Grief and Mourning Among Scottish Migrants to New Zealand, 1840–1890* charts the emotional pull of the land they called home. As migrants interred their children and partners who died on the crossing and in the new land in the early years of settlement, Powell documents how in grief, the significance of connection to people and homeland was a fundamental enactment of identity.

In the diaries of the bereaved, Gaelic, although forbidden as a medium of education since the 1872 Education (Scotland) Act (1872), was used to bring a measure of comfort in telegrams and in spoken word. Many headstones in settler New Zealand bear the weight of Scottish-ness in their inscriptions. For instance, 'James McGeoch's headstone, which can be seen at the Presbyterian cemetery in Symonds Street Auckland, carries a simple sentiment in the Scottish dialect that resonates with first generation migrants everywhere "It was hard to die frae hame"' (Powell, 2007: ii)

Mid-twentieth century New Zealand internment rites share the secularization, professionalization and rationalization experienced across the whole of the Western nations including Scotland, UK, Europe, USA and Australia during the twentieth century. For instance, in the 1930s funeral directors organized themselves into an occupational group with responsibility for bodies, funerals, burials and cremations (Schafer, 2007). Buchanan's (2005) accounts of Pakeha (New Zealand settler) funerals just after the Second World War reveal perhaps unsurprising similarities with their counterparts in other modern nations. According to Buchanan, internment rites involved laying out the bodies. They were washed, dressed, put in a coffin or wrapped in a shroud. On the day of the funeral, men would 'stand almost to attention with hats removed as a mark of respect as the funeral cortege passed whether or not they knew the deceased. Women or children were not expected to attend funerals, the woman's task was to prepare food for the men's arrival back at the house' (Buchanan, 2005). The manner of preparing food followed local custom where women would 'bring a plate', which is the Kiwi settler practice where those who attend a gathering each contribute a dish of previously prepared food and usually a woman's signature dish, for instance baked goods such as Pavlova, cold cuts, salads (Johnston, 2008).

Schafer notes a significant and enduring ambivalence in the uptake of funerary practices as 'New Zealand funeral director discourse, however, consistently demonstrated a degree of ambivalence about American practices and ostensibly aimed to distance New Zealand funeral practices from

American rituals that were often considered excessive and extravagant. Grief counselling and grief therapy, for example, were represented as being stereotypically American, and incongruous with the New Zealand way of life ... In contrast, New Zealand funeral director rhetoric focused instead on the sincere and honest personalization of post-mortem practices together with the need to ritually mark death and provide meaning in an increasingly secular society' (Schafer, 2007: 7). This cultural ambivalence may go some way to explain the delay in professionalization between the United States (circa 1890s) and New Zealand (circa 1930s).

Maori communities of the twentieth century were subject to the inter-connected pressures of cultural assimilation or separation. Maori who died were either subject to and absorbed without distinction into the dominating settler society. Or their internment unfolded as an entirely separated social space. For example, when New Zealand burial laws and regulations were set up in the nineteen thirties, Maori *urupu* (burial grounds) were excluded from New Zealand municipal authority jurisdiction (Searle and Heremaia, 2007).

Many commentators conclude that the ways modern societies dispose of their dead help constitute the marks of modernity, and so constitute modern notions of belonging. Scotland and New Zealand internment practices of the twentieth century share a common approach to enacting connections to people and place. Modern regulations that emphasize efficiency, rationality, secularization and bureaucracy, combine with modern customs that take place in local communities and draw upon local custom, the steak pie for West of Scotland and the 'plate' for New Zealand, bring forth cultural identities interpreted as reserved or even stoic (McFarland, 2010). Those outside of these dominating cultural spaces were expected to either assimilate or make their own arrangements outside of any institutional umbrella. This particularly *modern* constellation of interment regulation and custom presumes and so un-assumedly enacts relations to place and people because they are always already embedded in practices that are only recognizable as local.

These institutional and symbolic interment practices constitute belonging in the imagined communities of the modern, secular nations of twentieth-century Scotland and New Zealand. Decent Scottish and New Zealand send-offs were characterized by subtly enacted rituals that presumed, and bestowed, a sense of belonging to places and people.

Belonging in a global age

Recently, a shift in interment culture has made itself felt not only in Scotland but throughout other Western nations, including New Zealand. This coincides with much wider social transformation, including a shift from industrial to knowledge-based economies, from welfare to post-welfare states struggling with low tax revenue and ageing populations, flagging economic performances and a growing realization of the down-sides of global connectedness. An unforeseen consequence of living as one world is a growing sense of unease. This unease takes, for death studies anyway, a very interesting form. There is a palpable sense of risk in the world today, which shapes up as a fear about the loss of belonging. It is embodied in two distinct yet interconnected threads of personal separation from, and material destruction of, culturally significant people and places.

For personal separation, it is argued that people's personal connection to communities and places is challenged by living in a global age. One aspect of contemporary living is that we are all more aware that we belong to the globe. We all share the *same* natural habitat of humankind. Our awareness of this shared belonging comes sharply into focus when we perceive things going awry because of the concerted activity of human beings around the globe. The issue of global warming is a good example of this sense of unease. At the same time, as this sense of shared connec-tion to the Earth becomes harder to ignore, the ways in which people live on Earth seems more disconnected than for previous generations. Humans are more peripatetic than at any other time in human history. People migrate in greater numbers, and global communications make it easier to keep in touch with friends and family anywhere in the world, almost instantaneously. We can now engage with each other in everyday ways without, it seems, the tyranny of distance. This sense of living globally denotes a qualitative change in human relations. We now have the capac-ity to move while still being present in our different and dispersed networks of relations (through, for example, electronic connection such as Skype). Consequently, social linkages are at the same time spread *and* intensified. Giddens (2004) calls it a change in time–space distanciation. These new global sensibilities present unique challenges to the long-stand-ing ways in which people have embodied their connections to other people and places. And this is never more evident than when it comes to the final exercise in belonging: interment.

For material destruction, 'as contemporary life is characterized by increasingly intense industrialization, urbanization and globalization, these processes together produce a complex web of hazards. The dominant risks affecting communities are global and wide-reaching in their effects, and they are regarded as the product of human endeavour' (Lupton, 2006, p. 12). This global perception prompts particular kinds of responses that Giddens (1999) and others such as Beck (1992; 2006a) have labelled a *risk society*. The term risk society is not intended to imply an increase of risk within society, but rather a society that is organized in response to risks: administrative procedures and bureaucratic protocols are geared towards reducing or avoiding unacceptable risk.

One set of risk-reducing responses are global treaties and agreements that seek to manage the perceived dangers associated with the intensification of industrialization, urbanization and the like. The two most significant ones for our discussion of interment are the United Nations Agenda 21 and the Kyoto Protocol:

> An international commitment was made at the Rio Earth Summit [organized by the United Nations] in 1992 to develop an Agenda 21 in the UK. A local Agenda 21 is the strategy and action programme for implementing sustainable development at a local level. The local Agenda 21 should be developed in close liaison with local communities and organisations. Sustainable development is based on the idea that the quality of people's lives, and the state of our communities, is affected by a combination of economic, social and environmental factors. (Aberdeen City Council, 2009)

The Kyoto Protocol focuses on ecological sustainability in a similar way. A protocol to the United Nations Framework Convention on Climate Change (UNFCCC or FCCC), it is aimed at 'combating global warming with the goal of achieving stabilization of greenhouse gas concentrations in the atmosphere at a level that would prevent dangerous anthropogenic interference with the climate system' (United Nations, 2005).

As preventative measures, both initiatives presume and presuppose the profound risk of ecological and social collapse in the contemporary world. This discourse also shapes how they are to be implemented: through local authorities' assessment of their services and delivery using a process focused on both environmental impact and community consultation.

When considered as rituals, risk-averse institutional practices become the means through which late-modern *symbolic communitas* is achieved. If risk has become a central way of defining society's relationships with the contemporary world, it also means that a risk society is the means through which people come to imagine their communities and their connection to people and places.

Initial discussions on the effects of this risk society sensibility on belonging focus on how fragmented, increasingly mobile, fluid and globally oriented societies have lost the capacity to anchor belonging (see, for example, Mellor, 1993; Mellor and Shilling, 1993; Misztal, 2003). Sometimes called cultural homogenization, the concern is that indigenous cultures will be cast adrift and lost to posterity when potential members move away in the global drift of people. Or that a place will become swamped by the material culture of other, more economically dominant, places. This fills local markets and entertainments with objects that do not foster that same sense of connection or carry the symbolic meanings specific to that culture and or that culture's sacred places. The extreme form of this is called *cultural colonialism*, where existing cultures disappear because people have become assimilated into the new, dominant culture. The fear of homogenization and assimilation populate many debates about the effects of globalization on culture.

More recent and less millenarian approaches frame the debate over how contemporary societies may be in the process of articulating new ways to anchor belonging and what these new ways might be (Moran, 2004; Walter, 2005). Even though death rituals are driven by the twin purposes of providing social solidarity as well as regulating the strong personal emotions associated with loss, up to now the details for risk societies have yet to be specified.

In terms of death and dying, many researchers and commentators have pointed to the growing interest over recent decades in sustainable interment and disposal, both by official authorities *and* clients (see, for example, Clayden, 2004; Howarth, 2007; Kellehear, 2007). The question remains open as to what this shift in interest might signify.

This is the point at which some original research on trends in contemporary interment practices across Scotland and New Zealand is discussed, and recent changes in the way that Scottish and New Zealand local authorities approach the management of interment in an age of risk are examined. These findings are coupled with a study of new trends in how people symbolically denote their identity through interment.

Twenty-first-century interment concerns

The common ground for new patterns of interment by both Scottish and New Zealand local authorities is the fear of ecological and social collapse that stems from the careless destruction of unique places and the ties of belonging. This common ground comes from implementing the Kyoto Protocol and the UN Agenda 21 as international attempts to rein in the consequences of greenhouse gases on environment (therefore the economy and also society). The Kyoto Protocol and Agenda 21 both predict ecological and social collapse if recognized risks are not managed. When countries sign up to them, they are required to undertake a risk analysis of all local authority services, including bodily disposal and interment. When studied across New Zealand (NZ) and Scotland, what is striking is that, in both countries, risks to the environment and risks to the community have been spelt out; for example, environmental risks are linked to a common way of talking about places and spaces as being *vulnerable* or *fragile*. Each country implemented the Kyoto Protocol and Agenda 21 through local government acts (Local Government Act New Zealand 2002; Local Government in Scotland Act 2003).

One recurring theme was the struggle to sustain interment space. This is framed in concerns over the *availability*, *suitability* and *viability* of existing spaces. Many council cemeteries in both NZ and Scotland are nearing capacity. This is a problem. Not only will the demise of the baby-boomers outstrip available space, but the existing space can't be filled completely to capacity because both countries practice in-perpetuity interment rights.

Existing spaces are also often environmentally toxic, unkempt and dangerous because of falling masonry caused by erosion or plant, animal or geological destruction (in particular, moles in Scotland and earthquakes in NZ).

All councils expressed a concern with the difficulties involved in maintaining sites. These difficulties include the running costs of ongoing maintenance. This is an issue in particular for interment grounds that are closed as they no longer generate any income (from the sale of plots) to pay for their upkeep. A related problem is deciding who is responsible for maintenance, and who has rights and responsibilities over the kinds of repairs and maintenance that is done. Those who purchase burial plots are responsible for their upkeep. However, owners rarely maintain headstones and gravesites for more than a few years as family move away or themselves die.

Another theme was the struggle to sustain relationships with the dead despite, for example, the loss of headstones and genealogical knowledge more generally. This theme, of the fragility and need to preserve social relations with the dead, was most evident when councils talked of their attempts to meet the provision of recently recognized communities of bereavement. Both sets of councils also had to accommodate the increasing requests, and in some cases demands, for different kinds of interment facilities – for example, 'alternative green burials' and various (for example, Islamic) cultural practices. A good example is the situation of stillborn babies. A hitherto under-acknowledged group that suffered exclusion, stillborn deaths tended to be unrecognized in any way until social attitudes towards women's experiences shifted. As community consultation procedures demanded by the Kyoto Protocol and Agenda 21 forced many councils to provide multi-cultural services and facilities, they were also required to respond to women's request to have these births and deaths acknowledged through special sites, often near children's sections of cemeteries. In response to the risk society, Scottish and New Zealand local authorities are putting more and explicit emphasis on the significance of protecting place and belonging in their dealings with the dead and the bereaved.

This shift in the emphasis of regulation is coupled with changes in the tone of everyday symbolism of Scottish and New Zealand interment. There are new trends in how people are symbolically committing and commemorating their dead.

Acknowledging special places for the dead

In recent years, particularly in the popular press, the literary world and commercial services, there is an increase in the self-conscious use of Scotland and New Zealand as special, placed in relation to interment. People are more commonly acknowledging what, for them, were special places in their lives. New digital precision stone engraving allows recognizable views and vistas to adorn headstones in ways that were never before possible. Recent ash-scattering services are designed to place people's remains in sites of personal significance. Informal shrines are a known current practice that causes distress, both when they are put there and when they are removed. Councils have had to intervene to find acceptable compromises. As more people are having their remains placed in the land-scape, with the effect that one person's shrine is experienced as another person's litter, it is becoming a public issue that authorities have had to adjudicate upon and regulate. This involves, for example, people spreading ashes in council-owned public spaces, such as recreation parks. It also involves leaving wreaths and markers at fatal crash sites, and mementos in sites of cultural significance or natural beauty spots such as the tops of mountains or waterways. Since many of those sites are linked to, for exam-ple, mountains and water, they are often also significant landmarks associ-ated with strong connections to place.

Protecting special places from the dead

How best to deal with the large number of plaques and other memorials that have been placed on a mountain to commemorate someone's loss is a sensitive and delicate issue for both Scotland and New Zealand. The Nevis Partnership (2007), for example, was set up to clear litter from the track and summit of Ben Nevis, Britain's highest mountain. After much debate and consultation it was decided to remove all existing memorials from the summit of Ben Nevis and to discourage new ones from being placed there. Existing plaques are disposed of only after a concerted effort has been made to contact those responsible for placing them on the mountain. In their place, a collective memorial in the form of a curved stone seat and cairn has been constructed in a wooded area close to the visitor centre in Glen Nevis. This has been designated a Site for Contemplation, where those wishing to do so can sit and reflect in peace and quiet. It is situated close to the River Nevis and offers a view towards the mountain. In addition, interested parties have the opportunity of adding a page of their own design to a virtual Book of Remembrance (accessible at : http://www.nevispartnership. co.uk/memorials.asp).

While unique places are getting special attention, cultural references are also becoming more evident in interment rites. This can be traced through the kinds of images made commercially available (see Figure 5.1). There is no mistaking the sense of belonging that is claimed explicitly through their use.

Cultural icons for the dead

Commentary on Scottish society has tended to view this call to the home-land as overly-romanticized and mawkish. Others consider it to be a spuri-ous fabrication of Scottishness by the English nobility (Hobsbawm and

Ranger, [1983]2008). It is famously referred to as 'tartanry and kailyard' kitsch (McCrone, 1992). Similarly, 'Kiwiana' is often decried as being déclassé (Bell and Matthewman, 2004). This recent turn to Scottish and NZ kitsch in fact signals neither sentimentality nor disconnection from important people and places. Rather, it should be read as a newly synthesized and important expression of unique cultural identities in death that make sense in an institutional context of global risk and vulnerability.

Local articulations of global policies on ecological and community sustainability embody Beck (2006a, 2006b), Giddens (1999, 2004) and Lupton's (2006) notion of risk society. Their implementation had a profound effect on how local authorities and everyday people symbolically conceptualize and manage bodily disposal. There has been a change in the decent Scottish and NZ send-off. In the first two decades of the twenty-first century, discourses regarding the fear of environmental disaster and social breakdown are underpinning local authority attention to ecological sustainability and social inclusion. This gives space for unique Scots and Kiwi cultural scripts framed through the twin heads of unique lands and unique peoples. Such a distinctive call is a means through which Scots and NZ identities are forged in the crucible of death. Giving it a label, this self-conscious use of cultural iconography for a new emphasis on land and human connection is usefully labelled as secular spirituality. We are all bound up in the same broad economic, political, post-colonial, globalized, technologized social context, yet, there is none the less a distinctive cultural send-off, heavy with specific emblems of place and people, and sustained by new obsessions with ecological and social vulnerability.

Conclusion

Cultural identity is always in the making through people's everyday habits, practices and institutions. This is never more so than in death. The distinctive features of a culture can best show themselves in death, because the ways that people bid farewell to and inter their dead are a well-worn path for asserting what is held dear to the departed and their nearest and dearest. The photographs of tartan coffins and resomators placed at the start of the chapter remind us that, across cultures, individuals hold connections to people and place very dearly. When vulnerable or contested people take it on themselves to assert explicitly those connections visibly and publically, be this through disposing of their remains in an ecologically conscious manner, or adorning caskets with especially significant icons. This sense of vulnerability is experienced in particular ways in a global age. And, as shown, is manifest in a transition from *presuming* to *emphasizing*, belonging through explicit performances of identity in interment rites. There is also a more self-conscious use of real places and cultural iconography that emphasize land and human connection.

Using globally recognizable cultural icons allows people to make profound emotional connections with their dead through the form and accoutrements of their interment. These icons also allow people to constitute their dead as repositories of unique traditions and history. These solutions enable enduring connections to be made between the living and the dead, and so engender a sense of belonging in a fragmented, mobile, risk-oriented world.

Questions

This chapter was about funeral rites, mourning and memorialization. It was also about social identity.

1. Thinking about your own demise, write a list of the ambience/location/objects/images you would want for your own funeral. Write a few words on how each item signifies an aspect of your personal identity and your cultural identity/identities.
2. A core debate is that of the effects of globalization on cultural practices. For death studies, it is focused on the concept of McFunerals. In a group, compare your lists made for Question 1 and identify the patterns in the kinds of things you want (for example, music/casket/order of service), and in the specific form these things take (for example, Sid Vicious singing *My Way*, biodegradable cardboard coffin, friends and family reading tributes to your life as the service and so on).
3. What could these patterns tell you about cultural globalization and the debate about McFunerals?

Chapter 6

Grief: Solace in a Global Age

Introduction

> For William Uzenski, the father of Nicholas Uzenski, a Marine serving in Afghanistan who was killed on Jan. 11, 2010, live Web-streaming has provided much comfort ... William Uzenski, himself a former Marine, said he wanted Nicholas's military colleagues in Afghanistan to be able to watch the funeral ... Nicholas Uzenski's funeral had three separate Webcasts and was invitation-only. The Webcasts included the arrival of his coffin at a local airport, the funeral and a graveside ceremony that his family said included a 21-gun salute. The funeral home tracked virtual attendees. The funeral and the graveside ceremony were watched by 124 and 39 people, respectively, with the funeral viewed in 80 cities and 4 countries, including Afghanistan. (Holson, 2011)

The funeral home owner Ms Irene Dahl, 'said that nearly one-third of the ceremonies arranged by her funeral home last year – about 60 – were streamed live, at no extra charge ... "Being a funeral director is about helping people with their grief," she said' (Holson, 2011).

To consider grief in a global age requires a sense of if and how instant communication and digital communities may have an impact on ways of grieving. The body of the chapter focuses on some of the ways that, in general terms, relations between the living and the dead are culturally understood and socially organized. It then gives an overview of contemporary literature on loss to outline one dominant cultural understanding of grieving that has emerged in advanced modern societies in recent years. Embedded in the notion of individualism, the recent accord approaches grief as loss-adjustment achieved by re-storying one's personal narrative through shared conversations with others. However, as a distinctive feature of global living, virtual communication potentially undermines the capacity to connect at this kind of interpersonal level. It also threatens people's capacity to grieve healthily and productively. The last section in the chapter looks at three examples of new virtual-grief practices as a means of exploring the impact of new communicative technologies on ways of grieving, and outlines the kinds of solace they might bring.

What is grief?

Grief is regarded as the overarching human response to loss. At a personal level, grief is linked to a wide array of emotions and sensations that can include anger, guilt, anxiety, sadness, relief and despair; crying, sleep disturbances, appetite changes and outright illness (National Cancer Institute USA, 2005). These emotions and sensations suggest that grief, as a response to loss, is synonymous with inner turmoil. Yet it is not just a turbulent internal experience of change: the external world of grief exists in equal measure. The personal relationships which joined the living and the deceased shift, and these shifts involve personal adjustments to new inner and outer environments. The shift is seen in the ways that, as existing relationships alter, they are also often renamed. A wife becomes a widow; a child becomes an orphan. The different entitlements and changed social locations that attach to these new statuses become apparent too – a widow's pension; a move to an orphanage. Those who are in this shift even have their own designated title and category: they are the *bereaved*, and are in *mourning*.

While grief, mourning and bereavement are often experienced together they are not one and the same thing, and it is important to be able to distinguish between them. Grief is the complex experience of loss-adjustment; while mourning refers to the socially prescribed practices that are activated by bereavement. Mourning may be more-or-less formalized into symbolic rituals. Bereavement refers to the time period immediately after the loss. Bereavement and mourning are the cultural referents for grief in that they are the means through which the objective event (a death) is socially noted and acknowledged. Bereavement is a social status allocated to those experiencing legitimate loss; this is a significant demarcation because, for example, there are many losses that are not given legitimate status or recognition. Called *disenfranchised grief* (Doka, 1989), it is experienced by those whose relationship with the deceased was not socially recognized. This can include, for example, the ex-wives or ex-husbands of the deceased, or the survivors of same-sex relationships. Those who are bereaved are often given temporary exemption from everyday expectations. The cultural expression of bereavement is seen in, for example, wearing distinctive mourning clothes and avoiding certain activities.

Grief is a form of loss-adjustment because it is the experience of reckoning with the shift in personal relationships and social location. As those who are grieving negotiate their changed relationships, so their relationships with the living also alter. They too are required to adjust to the loss by being called to recognize and act on someone's change in social designation. In the most general of ways, because grief involves a re-comprehension of oneself, experiences of grief are a significant component of personal identity. This loss-adjustment can be intense and demanding, and people experience it as a more or less disturbing and difficult transformation.

While loss-adjustment implies necessary shifts in self-perception, it also suggests that these shifts are worthwhile. Solace is a common way to approach the adjustments and transitions of grief. As Klass (1992, p. 157) put it: 'the defining characteristic of solace is the sense of soothing. The word means to comfort, to alleviate sorrow or distress. It is that which brings pleasure, enjoyment, or delight in the face of hopelessness and despair'.

When in grief, the known world of a person is rapidly changing. S/he is confronted with loss and change at many different levels, and the world may become an unrecognizable place that has to be newly explored and adjusted to. The symbolic realm plays a significant role in these adjustments, because it is in this realm that already existing culturally prescribed meanings and symbols provide some sense of security at a time of flux. As Victor Turner reminded us in Chapter 5, rituals are powerful events that move people formally through the liminal transition between different social states. Mourning rituals create a symbolic liminal state of being *betwixt and between*. The symbolic realm also gives the bereaved guidance and direction as they explore and adjust to their new situations, because these rituals make use of images, symbols and metaphors from the known world to make sense of the unknown. This translation is only possible when participants are willing to submit to the authority represented by ritual specialists (Turner, [1969]1995).

Religious beliefs are a significant source of solace in times of loss, because they involve explanations that are bigger than the situation at hand, and which refer to the meaning of life and death. For example, some Christianity-based religions teach that when a person physically dies, their soul lives on in a better spiritual place – heaven – and that this journey to heaven is prescribed for all the faithful. Such a belief can offer solace to the bereaved as it is a comforting guide through the tempestuous alterations that death brings.

The social context and personal experience of grieving

Whether in response to the death of a loved one, to the loss of a treasured possession, or to a significant life change, grief is a universal occurrence that crosses all ages and cultures. However, individual experiences of grief and solace are tempered through culturally specific attitudes, beliefs and practices regarding death, mourning and bereavement. Grief is culturally differentiated. Though each person will experience grief differently, there are similarities in the culturally prescribed way of understanding what grief means, what one should do in the face of grief, and how solace is offered. All societies have rules about how grief is be displayed and handled (Rosenblatt *et al.*, 1976). In some cultures, for example, those who grieve should talk of the dead, while in others the names of the dead should never be spoken. Anthropologist Unni Wikan compared the rules (or norms) in Egypt and Bali, both Islamic cultures. She found that in Bali, women were strongly discouraged from crying, while in Egypt they were considered abnormal if they did not incapacitate themselves in demonstrative weeping (Klass, 2007).

Specific grief rules are shaped through the way that relations between the living and the dead are culturally understood and socially organized, and these relations embody the cosmology (the way of understanding the world). Grief rules make sense in terms of these relations. For example, in Tonga, a grief rule is that only one person, the chief mourner, is permitted to cry in the presence of the deceased. This rule is built on the premise that once a person is dead, the soul or spirit of the deceased has to journey from the land of the living to *Pulotu* (the land underneath the land/the under-world/heaven). If everyone who felt upset showed their emotions, and if the deceased was to hear much wailing and crying, this could divert the spirit from the task of journeying to *Pulotu*. If the deceased's spirit is held back by the anguish of the mourners, it cannot then become an ancestor and fulfil its new duties to watch over and guide the living in their earthly endeavours (Arbeit, 1994). While emotional expression may be curtailed, painful self-mutilating rituals of flesh-cutting and blood-letting are seen as a mark of sincerity across many Pacific Island cultures. In Tonga, this can take the form of amputating a joint from the little finger (Smith, 2010, p. 142). The relationship between the living and the dead is cast as a close one between mortals and ancestors; death begins the journey to becoming an ancestor, and grief, appropriately observed, enables that change.

Grief is historically specific. In her exploration of some of the conventions and societal expectations that structured and guided the expression of grief in ancient Rome, Valerie Hope tells of how the bereaved were identified and in some sense separated from the rest of the community for a prescribed length of time: 'A cypress branch was placed outside of the house of the deceased; the mourners wore dark clothing [*toga pulla*] and might have a dishevelled appearance ... On the ninth day after the funeral the house and family were purified and the bereaved could resume their normal roles within the community (Hope, 2007, p. 173).

Hope's description of how Romans separated the bereaved highlights their liminal status. They are deliberately placed out of phase with their community for a specified length of time. They are to behave differently in this phase as the deceased transitions from the land of the living to the land of the dead. It is interesting to note how formalized Roman grieving conventions were. They had codified laws that detailed the length and manner of mourning; legal edicts allowed mourning to extend beyond the regulation nine days. Numa, the second king of Rome, specified the periods of mourning according to age and time: 'there was to be no mourning at all for a child of less than one year; for a child older than that, up to ten years old, the mourning was not to last more months than it had lived years, and the longest time of mourning for any person was not to exceed 10 months' (Hope, 2007, p. 174).

In ancient Roman times, grief was gendered, in that the expression of sadness and tears over a loved one was 'womanly', unbecoming and weakening for men to exhibit. Public eulogies, laments and letters of consolation were to make the point that 'grief accomplishes nothing and should not be indulged in' (Hope, 2007, p. 196). Even Cicero, who had waxed lyrical about stoicism in the face of bereavement, got into trouble from a friend when his own adult daughter died:

> If on the other hand, as before you left, you have abandoned yourself to weeping and sorrow, I am sad for your distress; but, if you will let me speak my mind freely, I will criticise you. For will you, whose intelligence penetrates the most difficult issues, be blind to the obvious? Do you not understand that your behaviour and complaining gain nothing; that you double your suffering when good sense demands that you reduce it? (Letter from Lucius Lucceius to Cicero, May 45 BC) (Hope, 2007, p. 196)

The vagaries of life in ancient Rome shaped the public articulation of grief and mourning in the same way that Pacific Island cosmology influences contemporary grieving practices in Tongan communities today. The social context within which we grieve profoundly defines the personal experience of grieving.

The forms that grief, bereavement and mourning take are under constant alteration as successive generations shape the existing rules, values and practices to their specific predicaments and predilections. For example, during the great influenza epidemic of 1918, many traditional New Zealand Maori grieving practices were brought to an abrupt halt as circumstances dictated that people should not gather to mourn and give solace, and so spread the lethal infection (Rice, 2005).

Remaining in the southern hemisphere, Pat Jalland's history of Australian death ways tells how, through the devastation of the two world wars and the great depression, emotional and expressive grieving became less common than it had been in the nineteenth century; ritual was minimized and sorrow became a private matter (Jalland, 2006). Waves of migration from southern Europe and Asia to Australia encouraged a growing diversity in death rituals and behaviour. This helped to spread the view that the open expression of grief could be healing, and from the 1980s, loss and grief again became topics of intense public concern and altered everyday practices in Australia.

The culturally and historically specific nature of grief in no way lessens the intensity of what it may mean to grieve. Rather, it helps to distinguish between the personal shifts within society that death dictates, and the broader alterations in grieving practices that social change brings. These dimensions are important because they allow us to appreciate grief as historically specific and socially patterned, even as it is experienced uniquely and intensely by each individual within a given culture. It also links to the theme of this chapter, a discussion of how broad social changes associated with living in a global age have affected people's grief, mourning and bereavement practices.

The next section gives an overview of the contemporary literature on grieving to outline one dominant cultural understanding of grieving that has emerged in modern, Western societies.

The scientization of grief

There have been dramatic historical alterations in the practice and symbolic understanding of grief, and these have coincided with the social transformation from traditional to modern Western society. This is usefully understood as a shift from a religiously based understanding of grief, as a condition of the human spirit, to a scientized understanding of grief.

Before the twentieth century, religious dogma had a pivotal influence on Western societies. Though grief was sometimes seen to cause insanity (people went mad with it), it was never in itself a pathology or illness. It was a condition of the human spirit or soul. Heavily influenced by the popularity of romanticism, grief, although heart-wrenching, was seen as a true source of creativity. The Romantic poets of the eighteenth and nineteenth centuries saw the torment and anguish of grief as a revered wellspring of creative genius. Literary examples include Werther's suicide resulting from unrequited love in the wildly popular 1779 English translation of Johann Wolfgang von Goethe's novel, *The Sorrows of Young Werther*; the death of Manfred, the tortured melancholic of Lord Byron's poem *Manfred*, later adapted as a play; and the ultimately redeeming melancholia in William Wordsworth's *The Prelude*; Samuel Taylor Coleridge's '*Dejection: An Ode*'; and John Keats' '*Ode on Melancholy*' (Dolan, 2003, p. 237). The influence of these literary works cannot be understated as they gave shape to and made meaningful a *Zeitgeist* of Romanticism in literature and poetry of the eighteenth century that came to influence generations of people in their romantic endeavours *and* their approach to death.

The Romantic era's understanding that grief was the wellspring of human creativity was underpinned by a particular way of understanding subjectivity. Regarded as both a continuation of and a rebellion against the Enlightenment, the Romantic Movement of eighteenth-century European privileged society involved placing the emotions and intuition alongside or above rationality. The Movement recognized that there are aspects of human experience that are neglected or unavailable to the rational mind, and encouraged a belief in the general importance of the individual, the personal and the subjective. As such, it was a cultural critique of blind faith in scientific progress. It challenged belief in a universal human nature, instead emphasizing the specificity and creativity of each unique individual. Rebelling against the order and balance that typified classicism, and against the rationalism and physical materialism of the enlightenment, the Romantic Movement emphasized a heightened interest in nature, the individual expression of emotion and imagination, and rebellion against established social rules and conventions.

With the emergence of scientific approaches to the human world, and the attendant shift to rational secularism, grief was altered from being a romantic, creative and truly human impulse to being a transitional state of repairing bonds (emotional, psychological and social) broken by death. The scientization of grief is associated with Anglo-American social science literature. Social science disciplines all share the understanding that grief is a form of repair work.

Within the scientization of grief, experiencing loss has been distinguished from expressing loss by means of the concepts of grief and mourning. Grief has become identified as an internal individual state or process and mourning as external, socially prescribed practices. This has produced a 'conceptual and disciplinary split in which grief, or the private, internal emotional state has become the province of psychology, and mourning, or outer observable behaviour that of anthropology' (Valentine, 2008, p. 92).

Social science approaches to grief are concerned with explaining people's experiences and their responses to loss. They offer social support and direction when the discomfiture of grief is oppressive and stultifying. Focused almost exclusively on a person's inner world, psychologically oriented theories have dominated the academic account. Psychological perspectives draw heavily on Sigmund Freud's theory of human relations. The starting point was Freud's 1917 essay on mourning and melancholia which detailed his theory of grief as a response to loss (Freud, [1917]1949). Freud's theory of grief was that the world the bereaved had known was shattered by death, and the task was to rebuild relations with others. This involved demanding emotional labour, labelled *grief-work*. For relations to be rebuilt, the bereaved must undertake a series of tasks that allows them to detach themselves emotionally from the deceased. These tasks are to recognize and accept the loss; to mourn the loss, giving expression to the grief; to perform the new tasks of life that the loss obliges individuals to take on; and to look to a new kind of future. As a job of work, each aspect is a stage with a specific task that should be finished before the next task begins.

It is useful to note that Freud's theory of grief-work was underpinned by a particular understanding of modern civilization and subjectivity. In itself open to much criticism and ideological contestation, it sought a synthesis of the deep antipathies embodied by the tense relationship between Romanticism and scientific rationality. Heaphy (2007) explains how, for Freud, the energy and creativity of modern culture were rooted in such a way that they promoted the repression of basic human instincts for aggression and pleasure. On the one hand, this enabled the realization of the most noble and creative cultural achievements, but on the other hand, such achievements could not wholly compensate for the thwarting of a basic human orientation towards pleasure.

One of Freud's most radical insights (highly influential in debates about modern and post-modern subjectivities) is that the subjective culture of modernity is defined by tensions and contradictions. This is related to how the human psyche is inherently split or divided (Heaphy, 2007, p. 25). He focuses on the splits in the human psyche (which he referred to as the id, ego and super-ego); how natural human desires must be repressed for the sake of civilized social order and his use of family relations (for example, the Oedipus and Electra complexes) as being central to his analysis of how subjectivity, identity and human psychology were structured, laid the foundations for social explanations of the psychological.

It is worth noting that Freud's use of the concept of melancholia not only forms the basis for the subject's relationship to grief but also as the foundational condition of subjectivity itself. The Freudian view of mourning is quintessentially modern in that, for Freud and his followers, mourning refers to one person's inner experience of the loss of the loved other through death. It does not have public significance (Freud does not in fact mention mourning practices). The burden of loss, once supported by the community, is now carried by the individual alone. Freud also considered that the psychical working out, in which painful memories of the deceased are repeatedly recalled till the energies of attachment neutralize, to be a form of challenging psychological labour. He also linked the inability to mourn to depression, thus paving the way for the pathologization of grief and, more broadly, a psychology of disillusionment to match the disappointments of modernity. In sum, Freud's theory of grief-work and its attendant understanding of modern civilization and subjectivity rendered mourning private and nothing more than just one more human psychological process.

Freud's notion of grief-work as a series of stages or processes has been extended and adapted to such an extent that stages-of-grief theories abound. Depending on the writer, 4 to 12 stages of grief are described. Elizabeth Kübler-Ross defined five overlapping and sequential stages: denial, anger, bargaining, depression and acceptance (Kübler-Ross, 1969). John Bowlby (Bowlby, 1980) and Colin Murray Parkes (Parkes, 1972) prefer to use Kübler-Ross's model of grief in terms of phases that can occur in any particular order rather than a series of sequential stages. J. W. Worden refers to four tasks of mourning: accepting the reality of the loss, experiencing the pain, adjusting to a life without the loved one, and finally being able to invest ones emotional energy into a new life (Worden, 2009). People are supposed to progress through each stage and emerge out of their grief with a feeling of having left the deceased behind and able to get on with one's life without the dead person.

From the psychological point of view, grief is a unique inner progress of emotional states. Mourning is the manifestation of these internal phenomena. This model of understanding grief is still extremely influential in the helping professions, popular culture and everyday Western life. In particular, Kübler-Ross's model has become the predominant way for counsellors and professionals to approach grief, loss, tragedy and traumatic experiences.

Despite their popularity, these stage or process models have suffered from their limited capacity to explain differences in grieving between cultures and across individual's own experiences. The dual-process model (DPM) was developed by Stroebe and Schut (1999) to engage with the dynamic and at times contradictory nature of grief, as it promotes a coping process of oscillation between loss-orientation and restoration-orientation by which bereaved people at times confront and at other times avoid their loss. Yet, despite offering a flexible approach that allows to some extent for individual, social and cultural differences, the inner psychological world still dominates. And this inner psychological world is in turn dominated by a particular concept of personhood rooted in a rational, embodied, material subject.

Psychological approaches to grief dominate, it is argued, because the culturally prevailing script for contemporary Western sensibilities of the twentieth and twenty-first centuries is of an internal emotional state that is linked to modern Western societies' individualistic orientation and approach to understanding, and the experience of selfhood (Hockey, 1994, p. 128). As twentieth- and twenty-first-century modern society is about individualism, so grieving and solace are experienced individualistically.

Narrating continuous bonds

Repair is the pivot of social science theories of grief. However, there were significant sea-changes over the latter decades of the twentieth century in how that repair is achieved: from making a break from the past, to re-incorporating the past into the ongoing lives of the living. For psychology, this transition is usefully described as a shift in the understanding of how adjustment is achieved. In essence, as Parkes puts it, grieving is a psycho-social transition where, through time, the 'bereaved person discovers that there is much in their past relationship which continues to have relevance in planning for the future' (Parkes, 2006, p. 35).

Walter's work on grief and bereavement makes an equivalent claim for sociology. He builds on a conceptual shift grounded in the recognition that sociologists accepted somewhat less than critically the psychologically dominated pathologization of the symptoms of grief to a more inclusive focus and socially engaged stance in *The Revival of Death* (Walter, 1994) and *On Bereavement: The Culture of Grief* (Walter, 1999). For Walter, speaking and listening that focused on the continuous construction of durable biographies came to dominate academic thinking and the everyday experiences of grief in the twilight decades of the twentieth century. Grief is the articulation of personal biographical narratives which incorporate rather than jettison the deceased. This shift emphasizes the ongoing relationships between the living and the dead that may survive the life–death boundary, and examines and promotes the stance of bereavement as an ongoing process of negotiation and meaning-making. Sociologically, this represents a change in emphasis towards interpretative, subjectively oriented accounts of loss and grief that encompass both letting go and keeping hold of the dead, and how people try to manage that paradox.

In *Death, Memory and Material Culture*, Hallam and Hockey (2001) develop a rich account of this narrative practice as they explore the ways in which memories and material objects are brought together in the remaking of autobiographical narratives. Their account is based on the idea that people know themselves and others through material memory-making. Day-to-day activities generate associations that form the basis of our social bonds (relationships) and our sense of self. With death, those day-to-day activities continually incite troubling memories. They are troubling because they bring the tension between continuity and change to the fore. To remember is to recall people as they were in the past and never to be experienced in embodied form again. These troubling memories require management by the bereaved. Essentially, as the bereaved go about their day-to-day tasks, they recalibrate troubling memories, and this is grieving. Through this activity, recollections become memories of never to be re-enacted experiences and associations. The qualitative shift of memories to *never-again* events also constitutes those memories as part of the personal history of the griever. The memories of the dead become re-incorporated into the ongoing biographies of the living, and the bond between the living and the dead continues through and by means of this cognitive re-association.

More recently, Valentine (2008) took the dominant model of personhood as a rational, embodied, material subject to task in her study of the complex narratives recounted by a varied collection of bereaved people. Valentine's attention to the diverse, contradictory and contingent constructions of people's experience of bereavement 'conveyed how the experience of loss is intimately linked to the extent to which we are interactive, social beings' (Valentine, 2008, p. 93). Experiences of loss are exercises in interpersonal meaning-making through the construction of narratives. These bereavement narratives serve to emphasize a relational, inter-subjective understanding of personhood, and the contingent and potentially contradictory nature of social relations.

There has been a confluence of ideas in bereavement studies around the role of narrative in reconstructing and maintaining durable biographies that maintain active relationships with the dead. As most contemporary writing about grief and mourning is based on research with people living in twentieth-century North America and Western Europe, the growing significance of narrative in these accounts is telling. We can see that autobiographical narrative is a significant and growing cultural script of contemporary times. It makes sense too, because autobiographical narrative speaks to the individualization that is seen as the crucible of contemporary modern societies. The construction of a durable biography built on ongoing relationships with the dead is as much a cultural as an individual project and it has come to dominate modern Western societies over recent decades. In this new narrative approach, grief is 'more than the intense immediate response to a death. We understand that death can be an interruption in an individual's or a community's narrative and the goal of grief is to reconstruct the narrative in a way that includes both the fact of death and how the bond with the dead will continue'(Goss and Klass, 2005, p. ix).

Grieving scripts have shifted from breaking bonds with the dead to finding personal ways to 'live easily with our active memory of the deceased' (Anderson, 2009), and re-telling and re-working one's life story is the dominant cultural strategy with which to do it. It is through re-telling our lives that we grieve, and find solace and support. To do this effectively, we must in some way join time and space, and connect the private and public as narrator and audience as we re-build our biographies on loss. Though a somewhat technical point, getting a handle on what makes for an *effective* or *successful* grief narrative is crucial, because the next section of the chapter asks whether durable grief autobiographies can be achieved at a time when face-to face interactions are increasingly sidelined by online engagements in almost every facet of contemporary life.

A key component of narrative is the effective production and consumption of some kind of narrative or story, whether that is as a conversation, a play or a published diary. This involves the author and the audience being able to connect and share the story, either through a face-to-face encounter or through some kind of enduring text medium such as a book or film and so on. Effective storytelling needs four things to make it work: a presence (narrator and audience); a connection between narrator and audience (through a shared set of meanings); a performance (where narrator and audience come together); and a sense of community (where the narrator and the audience share a sense of cohesion and co-operation in telling and listening to the story).

Joan Didion's *The Year of Magical Thinking* ([2005] 2006) was recognized as exemplary in the genre of mourning literature and won the 2005 National Book Award for Non-Fiction. It is a grieving ritual for the sudden death of her husband. She writes of her loss as an educated, middle-class woman living in the city of New York. As a professional writer, she uses her craft as a means to make sense of and respond to her loss. She does so in terms of her own life story. In listening to Didion's expertly-crafted narration of loss, her readers are cajoled into reflecting on their own journeys through bereavement. As they engage with her trials and ruminations, both

Didion and her reading public are in the act of re-storying the narratives of their lives.

Didion's account is an effective grief narrative because as she articulates the changes and shifts in her sense of self that her grief demands, she shares her lament with a wider community, who respond by reading her words and so acknowledging her grief. This public or interpersonal acknowledgement of her losses and shifts is the act of social repair, because it is the act of re-incorporating her dead husband into her life. In other words, writing and reading *The Year of Magical Thinking* brings solace.

To review, grief is a social affair. We are taught the cultural scripts through which we grieve, and our experiences of grief are predicated on relationships with others (or else there would be no experience of loss). To be effective, it is generally understood that grieving and solace come together when there is a connection between private and public, and over time and space. A well-rehearsed aspect of global living is that these two aspects of life have changed irrevocably. As people live much more dispersed lives and communicate more online, the private and public are seen to be almost separate, free-floating spheres, and the connection between time and space has *distanciated* because the flow of information and communication between different places and people has become to all intents and purposes instantaneous. This would suggest that grieving in an era of global communication and dispersed lives is almost bound to be at least ineffective and possibly problematic for those who grieve.

The contexts and tools for grieving have changed in recent decades. Online tools are unique to the contemporary era and have been incorporated rapidly into almost all aspects of daily living and dying. It is within the virtual that emergent, new grief practices are appearing. The next section examines some of the ways that everyday experiences of grief engage with the tools and technologies unique to this global age.

Grieving online

'Hitherto unimaginable technologies for mourning have begun to alter our procedures for grieving' (Gilbert, 2006, p. 245). A dystopic view of online grief practices would suggest that advances in online communication undermine the task of effective grief narratives because online activity disperses, isolates and disembodies people from each other. In this way, the capacity for presence, connection, performance and community is lost between those who grieve and those who would be a source of solace. The presumption is that it would be less likely to garner solace online because of the ways that people's virtual interactions are set up. However, the internet lends itself to grief support. It is used widely to provide information regarding health-related issues and is seen as an 'effective medium for promoting behaviour change' (Dominick *et al.*, 2009, p. 74). People are willing to behave and think differently online. There are different kinds of online grief support available. Communication technology has developed rapidly since the late 1980s saw the earliest forms of bulletin-board online support (Skinner and Zak, 2004). The amount and diversity of support, whether self-help, professional for-profit or state-subsidized, has grown exponentially in the late twentieth and early twenty-first century. This includes emails between clients and counsellors, blogs, information portals, video-conferencing, private online-based grief counselling practices, You-Tube videos, memorial web pages, online clairvoyant readings, Wikipedia entries, and the list goes on. Among this explosion of commentary and support is the realization that people have responded with alacrity and enthusiasm to grief on the internet. A Google search for 'grief' gave an instant count of about 95,200,000 results (0.22 seconds) in June 2012. According to Dominick *et al.* (2009), many websites offer grief support through text-based information, message boards, online resources and online support groups.

Given the dizzying amount of online grief activity, it is important to consider how online grieving works as a social practice of finding solace, and whether it is a help or a hindrance to those who grieve. In the next section, three examples of online grieving are examined. They are interapy, grief blogs and web memorials. Each is looked at in the light of their ability to foster presence, connection, performance and community between those who grieve and those offering solace.

Interapy

Interapy is internet-based professionalized counselling and psychological treatment. As with all such therapy, the aim of interapy is some form of emotional or behavioural modification. This is done through indirect or distance interventions. Indirect interventions have been in use for some decades (for example, by telephone and video links), especially where clients are unwilling or unable to go to the therapist's office. Interapy's roots are in online support groups and electronic bulletin boards, established in 1995 by a practitioner called Sommers:

> More than answering a single question, he sought to establish longer term, ongoing, helping relationships, communicating only via the Internet. From 1995 through 1998, Sommers worked with more than 300 persons on his on-line practice, spanning the globe from the Arctic Circle to Kuwait. Sommers employed several consumer-level internet technologies for e-therapy, primarily e-mail with encryption but also real-time chat and video-conferencing. (Skinner and Zak, 2004, p. 436)

Interapy is a significant source of professional online grief support. As the aim of interapy is to promote behaviour change, grief interapy involves interventions that support a change in a person's perception of their experience of grieving.

A study by Dominick (2009) offers a good explanation of how grief interapy can intervene and modify people's experiences. Dominick's study evaluated a 'prototype browser-based internet intervention designed for uncomplicated grievers who were bereaved within the last 6 months' (Dominick *et al.*, 2009, p. 75). *Making Sense of Grief*, the online intervention tool, had three different modules that participants could work their way through. The aim of each module was to help the bereaved feel comfortable and accept their way of coping with loss. To give a flavour of the tool, the first module, *My grieving style*, helps users to identify how they understand their own grieving style (whether they are instrumental or intuitive grievers, or some combination of these). Through affirmative video clips, it encourages users to accept their style as being personally appropriate. The module '*Who am I?*' asks users to think about how their loss has affected their life. Checklists are then made available to help users compare their roles and personal qualities before and after the death. The '*How am I doing?*' helps users to consider whether anything has changed in a positive way since the death of their loved one: 'it is designed to help grievers recognize that, despite the feelings of loss, they can survive and perhaps even benefit from their grief experience' (Dominick *et al.*, 2009, p. 75). Each module is designed to be reviewed on screen and allows users to complete the modules in any order and return as often as they wish. Dominick's study found medium to large positive effects. It seems that the people who used grief interapy found it personally beneficial.

Grief interapy is seen to help, but it is also important to consider it in terms of its ability to foster presence, connection, performance and community between those who grieve and those offering solace. How does this example of grief interapy measure up against narrative based scripts for solace? *Making Sense of Grief* is an effective narrative strategy for solace because it fulfils the four conditions of an effective narrative: it achieves presence because it has both narrator (the user) and audience (the people who have developed the online materials); user and audience share a set of meanings about grief that it involves loss; and a coming to terms with this loss in ways that alter a person's view on life and themselves. It also generates a sense of community. The user and the developers co-operate with each other to tell and listen to the story unfolding in the responses. Also, when a user works his or her way through the modules, the responses are tailored to the answers given – both are responding to each other's input. Though not the most personable online interchange imaginable, *Making Sense of Grief* offers a form of solace because it is a way to reflect on and re-evaluate one's life with other people's input, ideas and suggestions. Going through the modules involves personal self-reflection and reappraisal – in effect, a re-storying of one's own life in ways that may bring about a sense of personal change and growth.

Grief blogs

A blog is a type of website, usually maintained by an individual, with regular entries of commentary, descriptions of events, or other material such as graphics or video. Entries are commonly displayed in reverse chronological order. The word blog can also be used as a verb, meaning adding content to a blog. Many blogs provide commentary or news on a particular subject; others function as more personal online diaries. Also, many blogs allow readers to leave interactive comments.

Grief blogs are when people blog on their ongoing experiences of a journey through their own or someone else's death, usually someone close to them, such as a family member. Though grief blog entries vary from short, simple entries to complex textual constructions, they are constantly altering texts of the author's own thoughts, emotions and experiences. As vehicles for online solace, grief blogs operate as personal living histories of the blogger. Those who read and comment on blogs are like an audience for a live performance, in that bloggers interact and make comments that can shape the narrative as it develops. It is a form of real-time sequential interaction. Blogs have presence. Through entry and reply, author and audience engage with each other in ways that share a sense of community in their acknowledgement of both the death and the grief.

Grief blog entries work as a barometer of mood. They are a way to position and recreate a particular online self. In a grief-blog for his daughter, a father intersperses the itinerary plan for his daughter's interment with a call for information on other's experiences of his daughter life and a reflection on his own emotional state. 'Tentative plan: Memorial services in Winnipeg and Riverton/ Mennville possibly Saturday and Sunday... if you have stories, pictures, incidents, to share... that will help honour her memory, we'd love to hear from you ... we cry – we don't understand – we already miss her excruciatingly – I don't know what to write' as a means to communicate his emotional turmoil at his daughter's recent death (Dueck 2008). The immediate responses to this entry guide the father to recall warming memories of his daughter as a child, as they acknowledge his immensely deep emotional loss while telling him they are giving emotional support through prayer: ' I heard about the death of your daughter from ... thank you for sharing a piece of her with us. Our prayers are with you while you mourn the loss of your daughter' (Dueck 2008).

Sometimes referred to as a scrapbooking journey through loss, grief blogging is a multivalent activity. It can fulfil multiple functions for those writing and those reading and responding to the blogs. In an interview with a young widow who blogged as *A widow for one year*, after her husband's unexpected death from pancreatic cancer, reporter Kelly Heyboer asked Duffy, the widow, why she started the blog and what she got out of it. She said 'while he was alive and I was caring for him, I shut my emotions away so that I could be strong for him. Once he was gone, I had no outlet for them, so I started blogging... it is very therapeutic' (Heyboer, 2008). Blogging was also a means to raise public awareness about pancreatic cancer. The support role of the bloggers who read and post responses was also recognized. Responding to a question of what surprised her about this blogging, Duffy noted not only how therapeutic it had been, but also how much of that comfort had come from the support from people she never personally met, comments that speak to the succour of such cyber interactions.

According to Heyboer, a reason for *A widow for one year's* popularity, and hence her interest in it as a reporter was its good writing. This proficiency was explained through Duffy's background as an English major in college, former English teacher and a school librarian, as well as her comfort and in the blogosphere. It also suggests that blogs which gain public recognition may be those that successfully transpose the genre of mourning literature from book to webpage.

Grief blogs are a space for people to ask serious questions, of themselves and others. 'Who am I now?' and 'What am I to do in the face of this loss?' are common themes in grief blogs. They are also a means for people to figure themselves out while they and others engage with their loss. Grief blogs construct virtual communities of interest, brought together through engaging with a person's grief. As a form of peer-support, they enable people to reflect on their lives as they re-write them through bereavement. In these ways grief blogs do give solace.

Virtual memorials

Virtual memorials allow people to share their feelings and information about the deceased in a public environment. Many casual readers leave messages of condolence to those that upload their memorials. These sites reinforce as they alter existing grief and mourning practices. On the one hand, these virtual memorials are framed around traditional funerary practices. For example, it is possible to give virtual flowers, erect virtual monuments and offer condolences. Virtual memorials also extend conventional practices. For example, there are now many online Shinto shrines that allow practising Buddhists (if they are also Shinto) to conduct annual memorial ceremonies virtually, when they are unable to visit the tangible shrine in person. Virtual memorials also allow for less traditional memorials to become normalized. Virtual pet memorials are a case in point.

Despite the potential of online grieving, interapy, blogs and virtual memorial websites are as open to abuse as they are able to facilitate comforting support. This may be through unscrupulous online marketing practices, ill-considered advice and suggestions, and vindictive or abusive interventions. However, it is important to note that these mis-uses are as possible and common offline as they are online. It is people's engagement with each other rather than the technology as such that raises the negative and the positive possibilities of grieving online. Grief interapy, grief blogs and virtual memorials, though not exhaustive or fully representative, do indicate the kinds of ways in which people are finding cyber-solace. They offer the means of narrating one's own biography of loss through engaging with others online.

Cyber-solace

Interapy, grief blogs and web memorials are innovative grief practices because of the way they take a well-established social practices of constructing durable biographies through loss and give them a particular and effective online form. By being online and accessible from anywhere in real time, the telling of the story of loss and the give and take of support at the heart of solace has become available without either a publishing intermediary or a need to meet each other in the same place at the same time. Online grief practices are more immediate and there is response space – more like conversation, but without the stresses of face-to-face (f-2-f) interactions. A person can log off at any juncture, or can lurk unseen online. Grieving and supportive bloggers can share long dark nights of the soul as they unfold even if they are physically on the other side of the world from each other. The implosion of distance stands counter to the presumption that online grief practices, because of the dispersed and networked nature of the medium, are more isolating.

Virtual networks allow grieving together despite physical separation in ways that rewrite the boundaries between the private and the public. Interapy, grief blogs and web memorials are some of the most popular online strategies for loss management. These online technologies are being used as ways to construct new narratives of self that incorporate their deceased as dead yet still present and influential in their lives. The bereaved use these technologies *and* the communities they enable to incorporate the dead into their ongoing life-stories and retain a place in their biographical narratives. Building the durable narratives of loss through online interapy, blogs and memorials keep the departed present in collective online life-stories. The cyber world has fostered a sea-change in people's everyday grieving practices. It can give *solace* in a form that is appropriate to and constituted through online social interactions.

Christine Valentine's (2008) indication that developing and promoting a

> more relational and inter-subjective understanding of personhood would provide validation and support for bereaved people's attempts to communicate and make sense of their experiences rather than rationalising or pathologising and thereby marginalising these ... calls forth a resourcefulness in other ways of engaging in social life, such as those based on a more intuitive, imaginative and sensory awareness. (p. 176)

The argument presented makes no claims that grief as a complex interpersonal experience and negotiation of loss has been changed by globalization. But that it is not so much that grief has changed but that ways of experiencing or demonstrating grief have changed. As grief can be very difficult to deal with, so people will always reach for solutions that might, in time, prove illusory. Nevertheless, cyber-solace serves to emphasize the disembodied, digitized aspects of contemporary human resourcefulness in the face of such difficult loss.

Conclusion

Death shifts relationships. Mourning has become electronic. Contemporary technologies push us into new and unfamiliar confrontations with ourselves and other people. As we adopt and adapt new technologies and tools, the deeply embedded cultural scripts for grieving are opened up for change. As people use new tools to grieve in different ways, so the solace embodied in the practice of grief also changes. The message conveyed on the screen shot 'Renee has been promoted to glory' hints at the personal emotional crisis that death brings. It also registers broader social practices that include the changed life that the bereaved live. It remembers the dead in personal stories and public tributes. For Goss and Klass (2005), Renee's 'promotion to glory' is a digital object that conveys a perceived presence of the dead as it recalls memories and a sense of identification with the deceased. As such, it is a form of cyber-solace and a means of recognizing and coping with loss. At the same time, this example also demonstrates how grief experiences are shifting. Online blogs and so on reveal the presence of the dead stored and storied in new digital media. These new and easily accessible capacities for storage of information and communication allow new ways of commemorating and new ways of keeping memories and discussion about our dead active. Not least, it also highlights that these novel tools stitch the breach that opens up between those who knew the dead person and those who did not; between living memory and tales of ancestors.

The live video-streaming of Nicholas Uzenski's funeral to family and friends stationed around the world, and their digital tracking of each other – who attended, who blogged, who downloaded – was a collective act of cyber-solace, as those bereaved by his death communicated with each other as they drew on the digital capacities to furnish and ensconce an account of his life in theirs. This capacity to connect the living and the dead unfurls in an epoch that rails against itself as a social form that has ruptured its capacity to take its place in the past.

Questions

This chapter explored the potential effectiveness of online grief support as a form of solace.

1. Name some of the different ways that people reach for solace.
2. Do you think that the pain of loss associated with grief is culture bound? If so, how?
3. In what ways could the notion of a digital divide (where there is inequality of access to the online world) challenge the effectiveness of cyber-solace?
4. Do you think that virtual grieving will completely replace other forms of grieving? What kinds of evidence could you base your answer on?

Chapter 7

Mass Death: Global Imaginaries

'The dead dramatise the polity's relationship to everyday life.'

(Kearl, 1989, p. 310)

Introduction

On 29 August 2005, Hurricane Katrina struck the Mississippi Gulf Coast and broke the levee protecting New Orleans, leaving an unofficial total of 1,383 people dead, some 85 per cent of the affected areas homeless and 6,600 persons still missing as of mid-December 2005 (Takeda and Helms, 2006, p. 398). Katrina struck only four years after 9/11, when a series of four planes were hijacked in co-ordinated suicide attacks on New York and Washington, DC, that levelled the Twin Towers of the World Trade Center in New York, crashed one plane into the Pentagon in Arlington, Virginia, and had another brought down in a field in Shanksville, Pennsylvania.

Beyond the loss of life, a startling feature of Hurricane Katrina is the sharp difference between national responses to 9/11 and to the hurricane tragedy. The debris from 9/11 was removed with unbelievable haste. There was ceremony given to every last steel beam removed from the World Trade Center, with commentary on how billions of tons of rubble, twisted metal and debris were so quickly removed. The New York City memorialization of the event captures a key dimension of advanced modernity: intensified individuality through globalized networks. Each individual killed in the attacks was publicly named and commemorated. The New York fire department gifted twisted shards of metal beams from the Twin Towers to their international counterparts who rushed to search desperately for survivors in the immediate aftermath. Displayed in prominent locations round the world, these graphic mementoes constantly remind passers-by of 9/11 and all that it represents.

The official response to Hurricane Katrina stands in surprising juxtaposition to this rapid, profound and meticulous response to the events of 9/11. The Gulf Coast was unable even to tabulate victims years after the event, and vast tracts of New Orleans remain a disaster area abandoned by populations and civic authorities alike.

The relationship between 9/11 and Katrina is jarring rather than consoling. While the 9/11 response spoke to the core values of white, affluent

America through a narrative of response, recognition, repair and retaliation, Katrina laid bare the less laudable narrative of a people abandoning their own poor, black, Southern American communities to despair and death. Or, more disturbing, an affluent community paralysed by the parameters of their own world, unable even to realize that their class-based inertia was driving the death and destruction.

Compare the response narrative of Katrina again, but this time with the 2005 Boxing Day tsunami. Triggered by an 8.9 magnitude earthquake centred off the West coast of the Indonesian island of Sumatra, tsunami waves slammed into coastal areas across the Indian Ocean and the Andaman Sea, causing billions of dollars worth of destruction, and hundreds of thousands of people to lose their lives in a matter of moments. In terms of the time scale, the Boxing Day tsunami hit without any warning, over a massive area of ocean and coastline that encompassed dozens of the world's underdeveloped nations. Within four days, a massive globally co-ordinated relief effort was under way. Emergency teams from all around the Asia-Pacific region stepped in immediately. Hundreds of rescue ships, helicopters and planes evacuated tourists once the extent of the devastation became clear (AFP-AP Reuters, 2004).

In contrast, the disaster that was Hurricane Katrina unfolded in slow motion. Tracked by global satellites, the hurricane was watched as it formed and traversed the Bahamas on Tuesday, 23 September 2005. Significant breaches of the flood protection systems were predicted, and what emergency evacuation procedures were in place were activated as the water levels around the Gulf of Mexico began to rise with the incoming tide. By Thursday 25 September, the hurricane made its first landfall in Florida. By Saturday, New Orleans mayor, Ray Nagin, announced a state of emergency and called for voluntary evacuation. Louisiana governor Kathleen Blanco requested the then US president, George W. Bush, to declare a state of emergency in order to release federal funding assistance. This state of emergency was extended to Alabama and Mississippi by Sunday 28 September. By the following Wednesday, the hurricane had dissipated and a Canadian search and rescue team had arrived in New Orleans to help the local Urban Search and Rescue (USAR) teams. Meanwhile, up to 20,000 people, as instructed by the authorities, had made their way to the Superdome, a sports arena designated as an emergency support point. As the days wore on, they were beginning to suffer the effects of no food, water, power, medication or sanitation. The sick and the elderly began to die. Round the world, media headlines screamed 'starving survivors die as anarchy reigns' as shoot-to-kill orders guided the thousands of National Guards sent in to restore public order (Reid and Goddard, 2005).

Not known for their democratic political regimes, many of the nations swamped by the Boxing Day tsunami swung into unprecedented immediate and collective action. Narratives were beamed round the world telling of cohesion and effort in the face of such destruction, suggesting nations seasoned by catastrophic hardship and dramatic damage on their lands. Negligence and inertia in the face of the encroaching Hurricane Katrina, despite opportunities to learn from 9/11 and the Boxing Day tsunami, revealed to the world a nation not yet used to numbing disaster on its own turf, and arguably of its own making.

The inability of US infrastructure to cope has left local communities broken and at the mercy of what Naomi Klein calls *disaster capitalism* (Klein, 2007). A brand of corporate capitalism, it executes 'orchestrated raids on the public sphere in the wake of catastrophic events, combined with the treatment of disasters as exciting market opportunities' (ibid., p. 6). The New Orleans of 2005 carries the mark of America subjected to its own brand of neo-liberal economics that came to fruition in the economic crises of 2008–10. The sub-prime mortgages sold to the poor and barely franchised communities of America destabilized many lives in the name of debt society, more familiar to developing nations in the vice-like grip of the International Monetary Fund (IMF).

The contradictions between how the world expected America to respond to another human catastrophe on its own soil and the actual reactions fostered the realization that a new global interdependency between management, prevention and remembrance was unfolding. Broadcast around the world in relays of reports, a new consciousness was cemented about the undeniably global scope of contemporary disaster relief as it came to the rescue of purportedly the richest country in the world. National infrastructures were found to be woefully inadequate against closely woven, yet world encompassing networks of corporations, non-governmental organizations (NGOs) and independent groups. At the same time, the image of the nation, as the institution most able, best-equipped and with the political mandate to act in the face of such devastation, crumbled as incessant images of distraught and dying Americans were repeatedly broadcast across the world's news channels. The images of social turmoil, disorder and despair on American soil stood in powerful contrast to the populist global messages of America as the world's policeman, ready to step into conflict to protect the freedoms of the defenceless. Global commercial and voluntary enterprises played an unprecedented and very public role in the rescues and clean-up. This pushed home the message that even the most powerful and wealthy nation in the world was ill-equipped, unable and unwilling to deal with the consequences of a mass disaster.

As the years go by, the capacity for recuperation tells of two different worlds. South East Asia re-opened its doors to global tourism within a matter of months of the Boxing Day tsunami. In contrast in the USA, desolate New Orleans suburbs remain, now acting as the fodder for dark tourism businesses operating out of the beleaguered city. Comparing international narratives of disasters highlights the interdependencies between polarized groups in the USA *and* between First- and Third-World nations, yet another feature of global society. The new global infrastructure and consciousness made manifest by Hurricane Katrina introduces the topic of this chapter: the sociology of mass death.

It is estimated that every day around the world approximately 155,000 people die. Most of these will die of un-extraordinary causes such as disease, accident or interpersonal violence. Despite the large number, this daily death rate does not constitute mass death or a disaster. Mass death is when many people die at one time, and their deaths are connected to a single overarching issue or event. For example, the single issue that connects recent and ongoing deliberate mass killings in Bosnia, Rwanda, Kosovo and Darfur is that groups of people are deemed to be unwanted and thus legitimate targets for mass extermination by those in positions of power and authority (Campbell, 2001).

Mass deaths are caused by both natural and human-caused incidents. Natural incidents include destructive meteorological and geological events such as storms, heavy rains (flooding), drought, landslides, earthquakes, tsunamis and volcanic eruptions. Naturally occurring events are only seen as disastrous when they disrupt the normal social and economic structure and function of whole communities, causing economic, physical and psychological damage (Benson and Clay, 2004).

Mass death caused by human beings can be a result of responses to natural events (such as not evacuating people from a flood zone), the deliberate destruction of people (war fatalities, deliberate mass killing – for example, genocide, the mass denial of the necessities of life – for example, starvation sieges) and the unintentional consequences of large numbers of people coming together (for example, those crushed to death during religious pilgrimages and football games).

There are also newly emerging forms of mass death that are being created by the very progression of human development, especially science. The Chernobyl and Bhopal disasters are both revealing examples. The Chernobyl accident, regarded as the world's worst environmental disaster, happened on 26 April 1986. A routine safety check of the Chernobyl Nuclear Power Station in North West Ukraine in Eastern Europe went horribly wrong. A steam rupture in Reactor Number Four caused a massive explosion of highly radioactive material. The nuclear cloud spread west over mainland Europe and parts of the UK and into the Atlantic. Chernobyl and surrounding areas were evacuated, yet many millions of people remained in the vicinity to live in and work the contaminated land. Exact details about the numbers of people affected are not known, though there has been a marked increase in cases of leukaemia, breast cancer in women, lung and stomach cancer in men, and thyroid cancer in children (Mara, 2010).

Possibly the most devastating chemical disaster ever occurred in Bhopal, India, in 1984. A US-owned Union Carbide plant released a deadly cloud of methyl isocyanate into the air over the densely populated town of Bhopal overnight, and the official death toll reached 3,787. In addition, many thousands of people suffered blindness and debilitation from the effects of the chemical spill. The Bhopal disaster highlights the potential disasters associated with new technologies. Henrik Harjula, in partnership with the Organisation for Economic Co-operation and Development (OECD), has identified that the potential future liability for any damages caused by wastes disposed into or on to land in the home country is one of the significant stimuli that encourages generators of waste to consider export. Responses to that risk by companies have led to an explosion in the transboundary movement of hazardous waste into underdeveloped countries (Harjula, 2006). The attractiveness of disposing of hazardous waste internationally has increased. From 1993 to 1999, the overall amount of transported waste rose from 2 million to 7 million tonnes per annum (United Nations Environment Programme, 2002). Because moving hazardous waste is so expensive, safety and containment conditions are often overlooked at the final destination. Beck considers disasters such as Bhopal and Chernobyl to be examples of short-term boomerang effects of being involved in an industry that creates manufactured risks – for example, hazardous chemical or nuclear waste – as a by-product of capital gain in the industry. The true long-term costs of disasters always outweigh short-term financial gains.

The destructive power of natural hazards, combined with individual and societal vulnerabilities across a range of exposed elements, can lead to large-scale losses during natural disasters in areas where population and economic investment are concentrated. People are killed as a direct result of the physical trauma of destructive forces as well as the after-effects of the breakdowns in the social systems that ensure the basic necessities of life. People die quickly from physical trauma to the body or, when injured or cut off from the absolute means to support life (clean water, food and shelter), they die from infection, dehydration and exhaustion. Many more also die of indirect consequences associated with diseases of deprivation. In terms of armed combat, the Geneva Declaration Secretariat's report, *The Global Burden of Armed Violence* (2008) estimated that, between 2004 and 2007, an average of around 52,000 people died directly and some 200,000 people died indirectly as a result of armed conflict during that time (Human Security Report Project, 2010). Mass death can be fast, or it can be slow. Fast mass death happens when the forces of destruction are immediate (such as bombing/tsunami), and slow mass death happens when the forces of destruction are enduring (such as famine).

In terms of death and dying, mass deaths are socially problematic because they are *unexpected deaths*. People have died in a manner not fitting the beliefs, values and infrastructure of the society in question. The Superdome deaths in New Orleans were *preventable*, because American society associates death with old age rather than being deprived of the basic necessities of life (water, food and basic medical care).

The sociology of mass death

The sociological study of mass death is concerned, at the most general level, with the effects of radical and unexpected social change on all aspects of social life. Disaster sociology, as a distinctive branch of the discipline, was initiated during the early days of the Cold War, focused on questions relevant to the American government and military leaders, and centred mainly on potential public responses in the event of a nuclear war. Researchers at the time believed that natural and technological disasters provided useful laboratories for studying social behaviour under conditions of large-scale physical destruction and social disruption:

> Classic empirical work in the field challenged widely held myths concerning public panic, post-disaster lawlessness, disaster shock, and negative mental health outcomes. In place of these myths, early research stressed positive behaviours and outcomes that characterise disaster settings, such as enhanced community morale, declines in crime and other antisocial behaviour, reduction in status differences in suspension of pre-disaster conflicts in the interests of community safety, the development of therapeutic communities and organisational adaptation and innovation. (Tierney, 2007, p. 504)

Community studies of disasters carried out in the 1960s and 1970s tended to take a structural functionalist or interactionist approach as they focused on the short- and long-term effects on interpersonal relations as a cipher for wider societal relations. One very well-known study is Kai T. Erikson's examination of the Buffalo Creek disaster, where a dam burst and caused a flash flood that wiped out a small mining community in West Virginia (Erikson, 1976). Erikson explained that the trauma experienced by the survivors was both collective and individual. Collectively, the community lost the key modes of interaction and engagement that held it together. People could no longer meet, work together, share time and food in the small rituals of everyday life, and the places within which they lived out their routines had been swept away:

> By collective trauma I mean a blow to the tissues of social life that damages the bonds linking people together and impairs the prevailing sense of communality. The collective trauma works its way slowly even insidiously into the awareness of those who suffer from it; thus it does not have the quality of suddenness usually associated with the word 'trauma'. It is, however, a form of shock – a gradual realisation that the community no longer exists as a source of nurturance and that a part of the self has disappeared. (Erikson, 1976, p. 407)

Though realist in its overall tone, disaster research has become increasingly open to social constructionist perspectives. The notion that disasters can be socially constructed has gained increasing currency – the idea that a disaster can be understood as both natural or socially caused is an important step in this direction. Sociologists of death and dying have tended to focus on the post-disaster rituals associated with the dead – for example, the different ways that bodies are handled, funerals conducted and the bereaved treated as a collective in their own right. For Anne Eyre,

> Post-disaster rituals and symbols are a valid and important area of study because they have significant implications for disaster management, not only in terms of practical, logistical arrangements such as crowd control, but also in terms of managing sensitively and appropriately the range of psychological, social and political issues associated with these aspects of the immediate post-impact and longer term rehabilitative stages of disaster. (Eyre, 1999)

Social constructivist approaches to disaster studies have also prompted new kinds of connections to be made between broader sociological analyses of the contemporary trend and more specific theorizations of mass death events. Risk approaches to disasters tend to argue that disasters themselves, though triggered by, for example, a dangerous weather event, originate in social conditions far removed from the events. The denudation of the Everglades in Florida is seen by some as a direct precursor to the New Orleans floods. As a natural protection against floods, once drained to make way for progress, large land masses became even more at risk of serious floods in the storm season. These conditions are produced by broader social change at regional, national and global levels (Tierney, 2007).

The sociology of mass death and disaster in its early days stressed social cohesion and altruism – it was a sociology of consensus that can be linked to the structural functionalism of Émile Durkheim, Talcott Parsons and Robert K. Merton. Latterly, the sociology of mass death and disaster broaches social conflict and risk as it explores examples including the Holocaust, genocide and extreme everyday violence.

At the most basic level, social institutions are collectively organized and co-ordinated activities that in some way manage death, where managing means to attempt to influence though organized activity, who dies, of what, when and in what circumstances.[1] Problematic, *preventable* deaths need to be socially managed. The phrase *management of mass death* is used to denote this relationship. It refers to the connections between the social institutions charged with the collective responsibility of carrying out duties in relation to mass death (for example, epidemics, war and natural disasters) and how the social institutions charged with this collective responsibility make sense of such mass death – seeing it, for example, as a punishment from God, a political strategy, or a technical mistake.

Having a sense of the infrastructure and imaginaries for managing mass death can tell much about the society from which they spring. Take the Black Death of the fourteenth century. This was a highly contagious, deadly disease that raged along the world's trade routes from East to West and devastated Europe in the late 1340s. The spread was rapid and devastating. Even with conservative estimates, 'nearly half of the population of England died in something like 18 months' (Horrox, 1994, p. 3). Contemporary chroniclers, though from our current vantage point prone to exaggeration, were so aghast at the extent of death that they thought the plague worse than Noah's flood, because at least then God left some to continue the human race. Its ferocity and spread was a direct outcome of people's lifestyles and beliefs about the world. Trade across the known continents was widespread. The rise in market economies during the preceding centuries had fuelled the rapid increase and shift of populations from relatively isolated rural lives to urban and cosmopolitan towns and cities. The cramped and dirty conditions of city living supported the spread of the species-hopping bacilli across multiple host populations of fleas on rats and humans. It is also suggested that since Europe had been 'weakened' by a mini ice age and consecutive famines in the decades preceding the outbreak, European populations were undernourished and thus highly susceptible to this particularly virulent disease (Canning, 2004, p. 9). The church was the social institution charged by its congregations with managing the plague in its practical causes and consequences; the church and religious belief was also the pivot through which people understood themselves – as sinning plague victims desperate for intercession and mercy.

The causes and consequences of the Black Death in medieval Europe were shaped directly by the infrastructure and imaginaries that underpinned a particular system for managing mass death, even as they instigated profound social transformations and invented new ways of managing mass death. As the scale of the plague deeply challenged the effectiveness of the church and its methods, so other forms of social authority began to emerge. The impact of the plague on people's respect for and belief in authority was profound. As Horrox (1994) explains, the church framed the plague as a punishment from God and called for social order through increased devotion and piety. However, the depth of the devastation, even to the pious and worthy, deeply challenged even the most devout, and the church's authority came under intense pressure and challenge from which, some would argue, it never quite recovered. It is worth noting how the plague helped to seed the Protestant Reformation. The high mortality rate among the clergy caused a shortage of priests as well as a shift in public perceptions of priests' status *and* the devout worshippers' own relationship with God. Clergy had high social status, but because the plague was seen to be caused by sin, people came increasingly to suspect the sanctity of priests, which caused many to lose faith in the institution of the church. Rather than stepping away from the faith altogether, however, the use of private chapels began to spread from the nobility to wealthy commoners, signalling a desire for a more personal relationship with God. This *anti-clericalism* is a contributory factor in 'Luther's later success' (McNeill, 1998, p. 195).

Alongside the challenge to the church's authority, the massive population losses also prompted a revolutionary reworking of economic relations. Medieval society worked on a system of serfdom. Serfs (peasants) worked the land and had to pay a tithe to the lord upon whose land they lived. The lord had many rights over his serfs, including often the right over their lives. Serfs had to ask permission of their lords to move to another place. During the times of plague, there would be insufficient people alive to gather the crops and pay the tithe to landowners. Many wealthy landowners began to give coin to other landowners' serfs to come and harvest their lands, and the practice of moving from area to area and receiving payment for work done began to take hold. Many historians regard this shift as the emergence of capitalist waged labour (McNeill, 1998; Platt, 1996).

In place of church authority, a new culture of secularism and state-building sprang up: 'While chroniclers in 1348 relied on the supernatural and based their explanations on the constellation of planets and bizarre happenings in distant lands, those commenting on the plagues' successive bouts turned to political, social, and hygienic conditions within their own territories to understand the plagues' origins and transmissions' (Cohn, 2004, p. 53). The devastating consequences of the plague served to alter medieval society to such an extent that a whole new system of social life took shape. It was based on the exchange of labour for wages, urban living, the emergence of the nation-state and growing secularism now referred to as modernity. With the benefits of hindsight, the nation-state and science became the new constellations of power, authority and social organization, and the new model for the 'modern' management of mass death.

Any given society will seek to manage mass death. Such management is a multi-dimensional social practice involving the interplay of infrastructures and imaginaries that give form to a society's overarching collective identity. This interplay can be approached by looking at how events-in-time are interpreted: that is, how people make sense of events in the past, present and future. Time and space are key means of locating oneself and others in relation to each other. The term *collective memory* is used, alongside collective agency and collective preparation to help explore the three closely interrelated dimensions in time of events in the past, events as they unfold in the present, and events envisaged in the future. As Zerubavel (2003) explains, the collective narration of the past in collective memory, much like making memories in a person's individual narrative, is a central strategy for societies to define themselves in relation to other groups – that is, their collective identity. This is because having a narrative of how things were done in the past informs what people do when faced with particular events in the present (their collective agency), and how they foresee, and so attempt to bring about, their future actions.

Relations between the past, present and future have a generic character in that those of us in the present are always to some degree remembering the past to allow it to become a resource to cope with the present and at the same time to influence the future. The ways in which traumatic events are recalled and remembered speaks volumes about the infrastructures and imaginaries that manage mass death. The act of remembrance is, as Lennon and Foley (2006, p. 112) put it, 'a vital human activity [that] shapes our links to the past, and the ways we remember define us in the present'. Remembrance is central to personal and collective identity and involves the active construction of the past. One aspect of this active construction involves imbuing what we recall or think about with symbolic significance through visiting the past. For some, this is an act of direct recall – war veterans, for example, summon up events they witnessed or were party to, and are often recounted as being in living memory. For others, remembering the past is an act of imagination and identification where, while not physically present, what happened in the past comes alive in imagination to such an extent that emotional, physical and psychological attachments are generated. Zerubavel (2003) captures this poignantly when recounting the social tradition of remembering that he experienced as a child growing up in Israel and

> in the traditional Jewish belief, repeated every Passover, that '*we* were slaves to Pharaoh in Egypt, and God brought *us* out of there with a mighty hand' and that in every generation a man should see himself as though *he* had gone forth from Egypt. Such a remarkable existential fusion of one's personal history with that of communities to which one belongs also helps explain the tradition of pain and suffering carried by American descendents of African slaves as well as the personal shame felt by Germans about the atrocities of a regime that ended long before they were born. (Zerubavel, 2003, p. 3)

Remembering is a social activity that involves a whole plethora of social products in its task – from mnemonic models of time (including linear, circular and multiple) that shape the sense of shifting events, to the invention of traditions and calendars to mark the passing of time, and the making of relics and memorabilia that imbue objects, places, people and actions with symbolically significant, historically loaded meanings. The ways that the past is maintained (through preserving archives or objects, through folk tales and family stories, for example) are always selective preservations (Coser, 1992) and they reveal much about the beliefs, interests and aspirations of the present. Social practices of remembering span a continuum from the most informal gesture between friends that recalls a shared adventure to the highly formalized, officiated, institutionalized sites of preserving the past in nationally sponsored museums, and every contrivance in between.

Mass death has an enduring place within the generic social practice of visiting the past. For example, the tales of battles, wars, pestilence and persecution through which many thousands, even millions, of people perished fill history books, school curricula and entertainment media, which frame them as significant events for the enduring identity of the society concerned. The First and Second World Wars, for example, were significant historical events for the countries directly involved. This is because remembering the past is seen as a pivotal means to reiterate the official core values of those who won these wars. Remembering the war dead means retelling stories of the wars and is a means of reiterating, for example, the unacceptability of genocide and the need to protect the values of democratic freedom (though the ability to call up these core values to automatically prevent the recurrence of genocide is sadly lacking).

The ways in which past mass deaths are officially remembered and revisited reflects dominant infrastructures and imaginaries. As an example, when nation-states were in the ascendant, memorialization of the war dead took a highly formalized form epitomized in the building of national war memorials and museums (examples are the Australian War memorial dedicated in 1941, the New Zealand war memorial of 1932, and the Canadian National War memorial of 1939). The war memorial and the national museum were the predominant means of officially revisiting the past.

Notwithstanding these general continuities, the ways in which individuals in the present understand the past and look to the future of managing mass death throw into relief the specific characteristics of a given time. Though incidences of mass death are rare relative to the continual juggernaut of people dying (and being born) every second of every day, mass death is an enduring and regular phenomenon: natural disasters directly killed between 205,000 and 220,000 people in 2008 around the world. According to CBC News, 'the UN estimates that nearly 84,000 people died and 54,000 went missing after Cyclone Nargis came crashing into Burma, also known as Myanmar, May 3, 2008. Less than two weeks later, nearly 70,000 people were killed when an earthquake rocked a swath of central and southern China. The numbers of deaths caused indirectly by these natural disasters are difficult to estimate; however, the number of people plunged into absolute poverty can give some indication: about 2.5 million people were left destitute by the cyclone and an estimated 5 million people rendered homeless by the earthquake' (Associated Press, 2009).

The events that lead to mass death cannot always be foreseen or avoided. Despite this randomness, mass deaths are patterned phenomena. The extent to which cataclysmic events cause mass death depends on the social configuration of the society in question. Some, for example, would argue that the high death toll of Hurricane Katrina was not caused by the floods as such – as floods are an enduring feature of that geographic area. Rather, it was because of the consequences of living in a hierarchical society that housed poorer communities in flood-prone areas, failed to maintain flood-protection systems, and had ineffective evacuation plans and an apparent lack of concern for the affected communities among the wider American community. The political, economic and cultural configuration of a society directly shapes the contours of deprivation and destruction experienced as a result of cataclysmic events. Another way to say this is that how people organize themselves formally (the social infrastructures), and how people understand themselves and their world (their collective identity or social imaginaries) has a very close, even symbiotic, relationship with mass death.

The next section brings together examples of how mass death is being managed in a global age. To draw attention to the shift from previous to contemporary approaches to managing mass death, there is a brief synopsis of how mass death has been viewed from a modern nation-state approach to past, present and future. Contemporary approaches focus on how mass deaths caused by natural disasters are managed in the *present* tense (that is, as they are unfolding). *Future* mass deaths are managed in the contemporary period by exploring ways in which perceived threats of mass death are understood and administered. *Past* mass deaths are then considered as being framed in the here and now through a focus on war memorialization. The aim of the next section is to pay attention to the distinctive ways that global infrastructures and imaginaries operate.

Current ways of managing mass death

To begin with the modern management of mass death: the twentieth century is replete with infrastructures and imaginaries that frame the management of mass death as being modern. The modern model, based on rational calculability and technical prowess reached its zenith in the twentieth century's industrial-scale world wars, nation-states and, within them, nationally bounded welfare states. The wars were unique in their scale and form – methods of mass production (industrial technology and rational calculation) were employed for national political ends that saw the persecution and murder of millions of urban dwelling civilians as well as soldiers on the designated battlefields across vast tracts of Europe, the Far East and Africa (Betts *et al.*, 2008). At the same time, medical technologies embedded in newly organized health services in welfare states saw the prevention of millions of deaths from infection and want (Hyman, 1982). Looking back to the past from a modern perspective, mass death was managed through memorializing the dead (especially of war) by way of nationally oriented, rather than religiously oriented, monuments and museums (Williams, 2007).

If mass death is central to social organization, and if it was characterized as industrialized and institutionalized at a national level in nation-state times, how might it be characterized and explained in our global, post-industrial, post-nation-state era? The discussion shifts to consider current ways of managing mass death as a means of exploring this question.

Management: Responding to mass death crises

As already mentioned, devastating natural disasters abound. Hundreds of thousands of people are killed each year by geological and/or meteorological events. Hurricanes and tornadoes literally blow habitations away, floods rinse out towns, tsunamis swamp and smother coastal areas and small, low-lying islands, earthquakes crush communities that straddle tectonic boundaries, while volcanic eruptions and bushfires burn, choke and suffocate. The extent of human devastation depends entirely on where and how people live. People in Tornado Alley in the USA live with a seasonal risk, as do people living on deltas, fault-lines, low-lying islands and drought-prone bush. The trouble is, human beings are boundary-dwellers, and they have made a habit of settling on the edges between water and land, plains and mountains because these areas tend to offer the vital combination of potable water, productive land and passable routes to reach other people. Being killed by natural disasters is an enduring feature of life on this planet, however, but what is new are the globally infused tools, infrastructures and mindsets that people currently bring to these crises.

The tools used for disaster response have always been the cutting-edge technologies of the time: as heavy earthmoving equipment became available, it would be used in disaster situations (for example, tractors and bulldozers to move rubble). We live in an age of globally connected precision instruments and communicative technologies, so it should be no surprise that high-end digital technologies play an increasingly central role in disaster situations. According to the *Guidebook on Technologies for Disaster Preparedness and Mitigation* (Sahu, 2009), a short list of the new kinds of technologies available includes: infrared surveillance systems, DUMB-ONET (a single mobile ad hoc network that allows each node on the internet to communicate with any other node and with remote headquarters), wireless network, MetaSim (a complex disaster simulation platform), and wearable interactive 3D technology (a computer that can be carried in a backpack, virtual reality goggles, and an attached video camera which can convey information to a control room via wireless, LAN and 3G networks. The control centre creates 3D maps and images for field personnel to view through their goggles.) Canine search and rescue technology uses custom camera and audio and communication harnesses that enable wireless transmission of information to a receiver carried by the handler to another responder, or to a receiver located in the site command post. Rescue teams are able to receive real-time video of the disaster site from a dog's eye view, as well as two-way audio. The canine assistance technology also enables search dogs to deliver equipment or supplies to trapped victims long before emergency personnel can reach them.

The use of these new tools represents complex intersections between global technologies and infrastructures, where globally generated and communicated information is one of the key resources that decision-makers use to guide their responses to unfolding events. For example, it was only by combining the satellite mapping of Hurricane Katrina with modelling software and historical data on weather patterns that it became possible for the authorities to realize that a major meteorological event was under way, and that decisions needed to be made. The intersections of different digital mapping, tracking and database technologies allows external organizations to access the information they need to response to crises as they emerge, thus mitigate the worst effects of natural disasters. As an example of this in action, during the South Asian tsunami of 2004, early warning systems that detected the undersea earthquake and subsequent tsunami linked to phone networks that were used to send warnings (both fixed and mobile) that saved many lives. Afterwards, websites were set up and used to help co-ordinate relief efforts and track down missing people.

The infrastructures these tools key into are global in orientation. High-end disaster management tools are used by, and distributed through, sophisticated global infrastructures, where particular kinds of organizations and institutions gather, monitor and respond to disaster information. As the National Research Council put it succinctly: 'in a world now orientated toward map applications popularized by the advent of "Google Earth" and personal global positioning systems for automobile and pedestrian navigation ... [a] seamless link between digital geographic information systems and various types of population data for use in emergency and development programs has arrived' (National Research Council, 2007, p. x).

Similarly, the INSARAG (International Search and Rescue Advisory Group) is a global network of disaster-prone and disaster-responding countries and organizations dedicated to urban search and rescue (USAR) and operational field co-ordination. INSARAG was established in 1991, following an initiative from the international search and rescue teams that operated in the 1988 Armenian earthquake. A country's membership of INSARAG ensures accessibility to international USAR team assistance at a known and agreed-upon standard if required for a domestic disaster *and* if sought and approved by the government in the disaster zone.

The scope, reach and capacity of these organizational infrastructures span the world as communication networks and information hubs interlock with and reach across each other. Transport logistics is a good example of this. One of the major issues in a disaster is that existing transport infrastructures are broken or clogged as those affected attempt to get out while rescuers try to get in. In 2005, DHL, a global transport and logistics company, entered into a partnership with the United Nations Office for the Coordination of Humanitarian Affairs (UNOCHA) in the area of Disaster

Management. Its professional focus and strengths are to eliminate logistical bottlenecks. Teams work on a weekly rota and, according to the DHL website (www.dhl.com), the Disaster Response Team (DRT) can be deployed to a crisis area within 72 hours and for a period of up to three weeks. By that time, the initial wave of international charter aircraft bringing in aid supplies has normally reduced the crisis to a level that is manageable by local authorities. In its own web publicity, DHL explains its work:

> One of the most severe earthquakes of the past hundred years with a magnitude of 8.8 hit the Chilean city Concepción on 27 February, 2010. Around 500 people lost their lives and more than 500,000 homes were destroyed. The DHL Disaster Response Team (DRT) with six team members started an operation to help the Chilean Emergency Agency ONEMI to transport relief goods on 5 March, 2010. At the affected airports of Santiago de Chile and Concepción the DRT organized the packaging of around 10,300 DHL speedballs containing more than 206 tonnes of relief aid such as food, water, and blankets. They were supported by 65 volunteers of the DHL Chile country office. (DHL, 2010)

Not only do the company infrastructures key into all the major transport hubs around the world, they also operate through a global register. That DRTs are drawn from companies at the behest of highly respected international organizations such the United Nations while drawing on local volunteers and employees, shows a remarkable and effective synthesis of global, national and local connections in the name of humanitarian relief.

These infrastructures are present-oriented – that is, they move from one mass death crisis incident to another around the world, from the Boxing Day tsunami, Hurricane Katrina, the Haiti earthquake, hurricanes in Fiji and Samoa, earthquakes in China, winter storms and landslides in Europe, earthquakes in China to bushfires in Australia. To give an example that directly informed this book, on 22 February 2011, a magnitude 6.3 earthquake struck the central city of Christchurch, New Zealand. The central business district sustained widespread damage to its infrastructure and commercial buildings, and there was a significant loss of life. This event was followed just over two weeks later by an earthquake and subsequent tsunami in Japan that resulted in mass death, destruction and nuclear disaster.

Urban search and rescue is the first port of call in a disaster zone, because of the need wherever possible to rescue those who are still alive. USAR teams are able to call on external support and expertise as required in areas such as construction, heavy machinery operation and specialist equipment. In the immediate aftermath of the New Zealand quake in February 2011, the three national USAR taskforces were immediately deployed – quickly joined by their international counterparts. INSARAG mobilized USAR teams from Australia, China, Japan Singapore, Taiwan, the UK and the USA to support the ongoing efforts of the operations already in progress around the city. During the February earthquake, one of the worst-hit buildings was an English school of language on the edge of the central business district. Known as the CTV building, it had pancaked, trapping an unknown number of English language students and teachers, as well as doctors and patients from the medical clinic in the same building. The majority of the students in the school were Japanese nationals.

With the scale of the devastation, many Christchurch residents in the affected suburbs found themselves refugees in their own city after rapid evacuation from their homes. Suddenly, an affluent Western city had become more like one in the Third World, with broken homes, impassable roads, rivers of liquefaction (sticky ancient alluvial mud that squirted up out of the ground), a lack of power, water and sanitation, limited telecommunications and an unstable infrastructure with military personnel restricting movement into the city centre, as well as between and within individual suburbs (Wadmin, 2011).

While the people of New Zealand, and especially those in Christchurch, slowly came to grips with the scale of the devastation, a 9.0 magnitude earthquake, the largest ever recorded in Japanese history, struck the north-east coast of the main island of Honshu on 10 March 2011 at 22.46 hours Pacific Standard Time. Minutes later, a series of devastating tsunamis began to swamp Japan's coastal cities. As a result, the Fukushima nuclear plant was critically affected. Essentially, Japan had to cope with three consecutive disasters: earthquake; tsunami; and the threat of a nuclear meltdown. At the request of the Japanese government, the New Zealand government initiated a New Zealand USAR response. The NZ USAR task force, consisting of 52 technicians, assisted in the search for survivors of the tsunami. The Japanese USAR team that had been helping NZ USAR search in the CTV building were now themselves assisted by the NZ USAR team in their own country – within the space of a few days. The sheer capacity to move to each new disaster confirms that emergency response networks are highly trained with very mobile teams of professionals with extremely specialized and portable equipment.

A particularly global mindset underpins the use of these tools and guides these infrastructures. To offer an example of a disaster management global imaginary: the *Code of Conduct for the International Red Cross and Red Crescent Movement and NGOs in Disaster Relief* (Steering Committee for Humanitarian Response, 1992) is instructive. The *Red Cross Code of Conduct* is voluntary and is self-enforced by each of the signatory organizations. Now ratified by over 400 signatories, the Code has been applied and evaluated in numerous disaster situations and complex humanitarian crises through the 1990s and 2000s. Its ten overarching principles are

the humanitarian imperative comes first; aid is given regardless of the race, creed or nationality of the recipients and without adverse distinction of any kind. Aid priorities are calculated on the basis of need alone; aid will not be used to further a particular political or religious standpoint; we shall endeavour not to be used as an instrument of government foreign policy; we shall respect culture and custom; we shall attempt to build disaster response on local capacities; ways shall be found to involve program beneficiaries in the management of relief aid; relief aid must strive to reduce vulnerabilities to future disaster as well as meeting basic needs; we hold ourselves accountable to both those we seek to assist and those from whom we accept resources; in our information, publicity and advertising activities, we shall recognize disaster victims as dignified human beings, not hopeless objects. (International Federation of Red Cross and Red Crescent Societies, 1992)

The code operates as an ethically explicit conduit between the governments responsible for a disaster area, other governments who seek to offer assistance, and non-governmental humanitarian organizations whose members and infrastructures sit outside of and span these inter-government relations. Though found wanting by some (see, for example, Hilhorst, 2005), it has become an active set of guiding principles for humanitarian relief in disasters around the world. As the Red Cross Code is actively interpreted as a globally applicable prescription for the ethical practice of humanitarian relief, it operates as both a set of organizational rules that frame the relationships between the various infrastructures *and* an overarching statement of values that guides these complex state practices. Since the humanitarian principle that underpins the code of conduct is based on the principle of human rights where *every* human being has rights, the Code puts into practice what Shaw (2000) calls the global state, and what Levy and Sznaider (2006) call global cosmopolitanism.

Another striking feature of the global imaginary that underpins disaster response is that not only do emergency response teams know and respond instantaneously, the world also knows about them instantaneously too. It is possible to watch as natural disasters unfold – and now a common feature of global media organizations is to be early, if not first, on the scene. At the same time, the proliferation of digital communicative technology enables people who are actually experiencing the disaster to transmit images and footage via their mobile phones and laptops. Once transmitted, these images can circulate widely and rapidly (Boxing Day Tsunami, 2009).

An abiding feature of cosmopolitan codes of conduct and the immediacy of global communication is in their effect. A call on human rights demands that all people are recognized, a flash of footage that relays the devastation of an earthquake unleashing prompt emotive, networked responses in the viewer. The American Red Cross *Text to Help* is a mobile fund-raising initiative that allows people to send a text to their crisis of choice – for example, the Tahiti or Chile earthquake appeal. The sent text automatically donates US$10 to the appeal (American Red Cross, 2011). At least US$10 million had been raised this way for Tahiti relief.

What do these examples of disaster response technology, organizations and value statements reveal about the character of the global management of mass death in the *present*? Disaster management infrastructure and imaginaries are brought together in specific global technologies, organizations, systems, rules and legislation. Part of this global scope and intention is not just the physical reach of information and transport systems but also in the values and economic systems that underpin these activities. The immediate response to devastating natural disasters reveals the emergence of global practice – infrastructures and imaginaries in the form of pragmatic and task-based interactions dispensing humanitarian relief across the globe as and where it is needed, and prompting highly visceral responses from people who are not there but are watching.

At the same time, these interactions are given definite form through neo-liberal economic relations. Returning to the Christchurch situation, the rebuilding of the city is funded from a long-standing insurance arrangement with the Earthquake Commission (EQC). The EQC was established in 1945 to provide coverage for earthquake and war damage for New Zealand, extended to cover other natural disasters. Every homeowner in New Zealand has to pay an annual levy to EQC. In the event of a natural disaster, the EQC operates like a commercial insurer to cover damage to buildings up to a certain value. At the September 2010, 7.2 magnitude earthquake, the NZ fund managed assets of NZ$5.93 billion, but the scale of damage in Christchurch overwhelmed the well-planned and long-established EQC. The New Zealand government established a project management office to oversee the rebuild, and appointed Fletcher Construction (one of the biggest construction companies in New Zealand) to run it. Fletcher Construction sub-hires construction workers to carry out the repairs on behalf of the EQC.

On the face of it, this is a needs must recovery strategy. However, on closer inspection, calling in private firms to undertake civic responsibilities *also* bears the hallmarks of disaster capitalism, because it brings 'for profit companies into the functioning of the state' (Klein, 2007, p. 15). Naomi Klein coined the term *disaster capitalism* to characterize how the widespread social disorientation following massive collective shocks (wars, major natural disasters or radical political change) is exploited by corporate leaders and their political and military allies to shift wealth in massive ways from the public sector to select powers in the private sector – with resultant widespread social dislocation and misery. Fletcher Construction was named by the EQC to run EQC's Canterbury earthquake project management office after the September 2010 earthquake. Fletcher Construction is also one of five companies working with the Christchurch City Council and the NZ Transport Agency on between NZ$2.2 billion- and NZ$2.7 billion-worth of infrastructure repairs.

While the present-oriented management of mass death focuses on the infrastructure and housing stock rebuild to enable material and economic recuperation, the long human saga of mass trauma begins to emerge. In Christchurch, between February and September 2011, there were over 4,000 aftershocks. During this destabilizing time, the rates of unexpected preventable deaths rose: more elderly people, especially the displaced, were unable to withstand everyday illnesses over the Southern hemisphere winter; incidences of broken-heart syndrome (or stress cardiomyopathy) increased. Christchurch Hospital has an average of six cases a year, but around that number were admitted in the first week after the September 2010 earthquake. The condition is brought on by sudden emotional strain, but unlike an anxiety attack, part of the heart stops working. The condition mainly affects women, and generally they are middle-aged or elderly. It is usually caused by an emotional trigger, such as a relationship ending or being the victim of a crime (Wright, 2011). The number of suicides also increased.

Prevention: Preventing mass death

The previous section discussed disaster response to focus on in-the-moment ways of managing mass death. In this section, the challenge is to focus on the ways that future mass deaths are approached, operationally and conceptually. A way to do this is to articulate how future mass deaths are imagined and embodied in social practice.

Collectively legitimated global institutions that concern themselves explicitly with the management of mass death encompass a variety of institutions and actors that include academics, politicians and professional practitioners. Focused predominantly on preventive medicine/healthcare and peacekeeping, the emphasis that informs their practice is that mass deaths (caused by illness and warfare, especially genocide) ought to be prevented. The most well-known global institutions are the World Health Organization and the United Nations. Both of these organizations focus their attention on different aspects of global relations that have a direct impact on the management of mass death into the future. As organizations, WHO and UN are embedded in dense, cross-cutting networks of smaller and more specific subnational and transnational organizations that feed into and monitor the activities of the UN and WHO. For health, these include Global Health Watch and the Centers for Diseases Control. For warfare, and in particular genocide, these include International Alert Against Genocide and Mass Killing, Amnesty International, the International League for Human Rights, the International Commission of Jurists, Cultural Survival, Survival International, and the Minority Rights Group (Gellert, 1995). These all focus on the prevention side of managing mass death in the future. There are also many unofficial organizations that seek to prevent mass death.

Similarly, there are many official and unofficial organizations and networks with a global span that seek to manage mass death in the future by using the threat of it. Ironically, governments, including the USA and the UK used the potential threat of weapons of mass destruction (WMD) to launch Operation Iraqi Freedom on 19 March 2003 – a military campaign that has in the interim period seen thousands of international military and Iraqi civilians killed (Operation Iraqi Freedom, 2009). Organizations such as Al Qaeda regularly use the threat of mass death (through, for example, suicide bombers) as a strategic tactic for global political attention (Moghadam, 2008).

Whether health reformers, global peace activists or combatants, those who seek to manage mass death in the future do so by drawing on the power of threats to elicit the desired behaviour change. For example, the WHO actively imagines global health threats as a strategy to prepare real action plans that will be implemented if and when the envisioned scenario unfolds (as was the case with the swine flu epidemic of 2009). Though the statistical and managerial techniques to do this have been available for some time, it is only recently that ICT technologies of surveillance have opened up the world for observation. The new technologies that gather, store and compute vast amounts of information make it possible to track the movements of individuals, goods and groups across the day. They also make it possible to calculate and map out future scenarios based on currently identified threats to global food, oil and water security.[2]

The United Nations charted a debilitating global food crisis which came perilously close to fruition during 2008. The crisis was caused by soaring global food prices in early 2008, which were in turn the result of

> the cumulative effects of long-term trends, like the increasing demand of food due to the growing world population and a decline in agricultural investment, more immediate supply and demand dynamics, including those related to the rapidly increasing oil prices and diversions of maize to ethanol production, and responses like hoarding which exacerbated price volatility. (United Nations, 2009)

The UN saw the global food crisis threat as real and present, and responded by setting up a global task force that included 'the Heads of the UN specialized agencies, funds and programmes, as well as relevant parts of the UN Secretariat, the World Bank, the International Monetary Fund, the Organisation for Economic Co-operation and Development and the World Trade Organization'. The task force developed a Comprehensive Framework for Action, a set of policy directives that 'aims to be a catalyst for action by providing governments, international and regional organisations, and civil society groups with a menu of policies and actions from which to draw appropriate responses' (United Nations, 2009). These directives were explicitly inclusive and participatory – key elements of a cosmopolitan politics of global relations.

More recent tensions between relatively wealthy nations continue as they seek to future-proof their food security. For example, in March 2010, Chinese investors in Hong Kong looked to buy New Zealand dairy farms for NZ$1.1 billion (Associated Press, 2010). This action was seen to be as a result of the tainted infant milk scandal in China (melamine was added to infant formula to boost apparent protein readings; however, many infants were poisoned and some died). While China saw its role as protecting the future quality of food production, many New Zealand commentators regarded the buy-up as a means for China to secure its own future food supplies by having ownership of and controlling the food produced in other nations, regardless of local New Zealanders' own food needs (Bennett, 2010).

To discuss the model of the future that underpins these future-oriented activities, the implicit assumption for those who actively eschew mass death *and* those who use it as a political strategy is that future mass deaths ought to be prevented. This implies that it is possible to change the contexts and circumstances that are understood to bring about the conditions for mass death to occur (through preventive planning or manipulative threats). Such an approach to the future is optimistic in that it is believed that organized human intervention can alter the course of events in the world, rather than its obverse, a pessimistic approach which presumes a fate-driven model of the unfolding of events.

This optimism is progressive in that it is believed by those who practise it that human intervention will bring improvements rather than merely changes to people's lives. This is the case for all concerned, even though the improvements envisioned by a WHO health worker will be quite different from those imagined by an Al Qaeda cell leader. And it is backed up by some evidence. Regarding worldwide health, people are living longer, and fewer people exist in conditions of abject poverty even as the world's population is increasing by the billion. Regarding the political use of religion, more people are aware of Al Qaeda's political aims to install Islamist states throughout the world at the same time that many nations are engaged in managing the revival of religiosity across the globe (Turner, 2007, p. 126).

This progressive optimism is technology-driven, as it is believed that on one level the technologies that are now available can be used to predict and control the future more than ever before. It is also process-driven in that relations are conducted that will dictate whether desired outcomes are achieved (that is, forestalling the precipitative circumstances of mass death). To focus on by far the largest component of mass death prevention – namely, global health and peacekeeping initiatives – the weight of discussion falls squarely on a focus on human rights and cosmopolitanism as the most appropriate, effective and efficacious means to conduct global health care, peacekeeping and reconciliation initiatives. Collaboration, negotiation and intercultural dialogue are the favoured interactive approaches in UN and WHO global initiatives to forestall mass death (see, for example, Campbell, 2001; Brizio-Skov, 2004; Kiernan, 2007; Misztal, 2010). The future-oriented management of mass death embeds an idealized future, where technologies and social relations are in harmony at a global level to forestall global mass death scenarios. The terms of this future orientation are built on acknowledging a conscious and explicit connection between global technology networks and groups of people across the entire planet that are brought together in supposed safety under the banner of cosmopolitanism and human rights.

Global infrastructures and imaginaries rely on a particular way of looking to the future, to manage mass death that combines calculated projections of calamity (the calculation of risk) with an integrated approach to bring about social change that should forestall the precipitating conditions of mass death. This approach to the future regards it as a territory that can and should be mapped out and manipulated for the benefit of those living in the present, even if the means to do so are to invoke the fear of future calamity to engage people's attention and encourage behaviour modification. This reliance on a fabricated (or to use Beck (2006a) and Giddens' (1999, 2004) phrase, *manufactured)* fear of the future serves to connect people through an emotional experiential register.

It is also worth noting that even as global infrastructures and imaginaries are reworking the territories of the future to shape current behaviour, good old-fashioned international politics are still involved when mass deaths occur on home territory. Unfriendly nations have for decades played an international game of partial information exchange. China, for example, even through the darkest days of the Cold War, would still share its meteorological measurements with the world, as a means of helping to model, and so identify, potential weather disasters. Yet information about disasters in China has been hard to come by. And, for years, the USSR censored all information about its aircraft crashes and casualties resulting from natural disasters, and the USA turned down post-Katrina offers from Cuba.

The next section focuses on the ways that the past is constituted for the global management of mass death.

Remembrance: Remembering mass death

Ways of visiting the past are closely linked to how a society is organized. For example, the oral transmission of history dominates in non-literate cultures, while writing cultures use literary tools to engage with the past. Even bureaucratically inclined cultures transmit history through the tools of their organization – in the form of minutes, agendas and reports (Ong, 1982; Zerubavel, 2003). In the contemporary era, there are many possible means of visiting the past that incorporate old and new, and tangible and intangible technologies for inscribing the past. Recent shifts to global economies and globally oriented flows of products and people, and the expansion of communication have had a significant, observable impact on ways of revisiting mass death in particular. Part of a more general rise in the public's interest in the past,[3] there are distinctive trends in contemporary ways of remembering mass deaths that involve new tools, new infrastructures and new mindsets for visiting the past.

The means of visiting the past have taken on the technological innovation of digital recording. The capacity to create, store and transfer overwhelming amounts of digital data is coupled with the ever-increasing accessibility of the equipment that captures the digital information. In not much more than a decade, digital photography and sound recording have advanced to such an extent that what were in the mid-1990s very expensive and unwieldy digital cameras and digital storage facilities are now available on mobile phones *as a standard accessory*. People can record, send and store events as they unfold. The shift in capacity and accessibility has moved the practice of archiving from the professional realms of the library, museum and institutional records departments into many hands, including children and teenagers whose parents can afford these relatively cheap and easy-to-use technologies. The de-institutionalization of the archive has allowed many millions of people to develop their own accounts of their everyday lives and the lives of past events relevant to them. Much of this activity takes the form of heritage and genealogy, and a significant branch of this involves researching family histories that were lost to war, and in particular the Holocaust. Using the technology to demonstrate its capacities, a Google search in May 2012 generated 10,700,000 hits for Holocaust heritage sites in 0.34 seconds. A way to think about this is that everyday people are now able to contribute and explore the historical record of mass death events in ways that were not possible before. Moreover, this can be done from the comfort and safety of their own homes using everyday objects and ephemera.

The expansion of everyday memory-making into public domains has prompted the proclamation that

> We are in the midst of a worldwide obsession with memorializing ... [f]rom the crosses and flowers left by the roadside as transient memorials to the accidentally dead, to the transformation of 'the world's largest building project' – the rebuilt World Trade Centre [*sic*] – into a huge functioning memorial, everywhere are found new spaces dedicated to the commemoration of the past, and usually a past involving violent death. (Tonkin and Laurence, 2003)

There is a shift away from the 'official record' to many accounts of the past that are a mix of official and lay perspectives. One way to generalize is that a consequence of technological advances in recording leads to the multiplicity of histories of mass death rather than a single history of mass death. Another consequence of the mainstreaming of history-making is that it is much more likely for mass death events to be recorded and broadcast outside official channels. This has consequences for future retribution and reconciliation work.

The capacity to store massive amounts of information in a non-tangible digital form has, some believe, lead to an obsession with memorializing built on a generalized fear that, as we rely more on digital archives, we may eventually become 'the era without memory' (Huyssen, 2003, p. 29). To reflect on the infrastructures for remembering mass deaths, while digital technologies allow accounts of mass deaths to multiply into unofficial domains, there has also been a shift in both how official remembering is organized and how official remembering is communicated to those who are involved in it. Two closely connected shifts have occurred. One is the rise in what are called *memorial museums*, and the other is the emergence of dark tourism as a social practice. Together they represent a distinctive and very contemporary way of visiting past mass deaths.

To mark out what a memorial museum is, Paul Williams sets out the interrelated, though distinctive, attributes of memorials, museums, memorial museums and memorial sites. His definition is worth repeating in full:

> a *monument* is a sculpture, structure or physical marker designed to memorialize. A *museum*, as we know, is an institution devoted to the acquisition, conservation, study, exhibition, and educational interpretation of objects with scientific, historical or artistic value. I use the term *memorial museum* to identify a specific kind of museum dedicated to a historic event commemorating mass suffering of some kind. A final term, the memorial *site*, is used to describe physical locations that serve a commemorative function, but are not necessarily dominated by a built structure. (Williams, 2007, p. 8)

So many memorial museums have been erected in recent decades that Williams argues there is a global rush to commemorate atrocities that bears a signature template.

At the same time as we are seen to be obsessed with the (violent) past, our obsessions are deeply contested as they are characterized by unresolved struggles over *which* past examples of mass death, and *how* they should be memorialized. Dilemmas of commemoration prevail no more so than for the question of commemorating the multiple mass deaths of fallen soldiers and civilians in the Second World War, and the *Shoah* (the deliberate extermination of Jews by Nazis). The Holocaust and remembering Nazi Germany has grown in significance as that time and place recede from contemporary reality. One prevalent dilemma is over how Germany should at the same time memorialize its soldiers killed during the Holocaust. After the war, the Allies forbade the Germans to build war memorials, and this order was not relaxed until 1952. From then on, monuments to the fallen soldiers concentrated on generalizing the experience of war and playing down references to heroism. 'The Germans themselves in the western zones of occupation suggested that new war memorials should no longer contain inscriptions honoring national martyrs, but a simple dedication to "our dead"' (Remmler, 1997, p. 44). At the same time, how to memorialize those obliterated in the *Shoah* remains problematic. As Remmler notes

> The desire to save a demolished culture from oblivion speaks to the impossibility of an authentic reconstruction. Even if it were possible to recreate Jewish life as it existed in the 1920s, is it even desirable to claim authenticity? Does not the very idea of reconstruction become unconscionable, since a fabricated past, like the one familiar to us at Disney World, would reduce past Jewish life to folklore and rob its methodically planned destruction a second time of its tragic dimension through Klezmer music and nostalgic *Shtetl* anecdotes? (Remmler, 1997, p.45)

The dozens of Holocaust museums and lesser-known examples including the Tuol Sleng Museum of Genocidal Crimes, Phnom Penh, Cambodia (1980); Nanjing Massacre Memorial Hall, Nanjing, China (1985); Le Mémorial de Caen, un musée pour la paix, Caen, France (1988); Ukrainian National Chernobyl Museum, Kiev, Ukraine (1992); Museum of Genocide Victims, Vilnus, Lithuania (1992); Memorial to the disappeared, General Cemetery, Santiago, Chile (1992); Simon Wiesenthal Center's Beit Hashoah-Museum of Tolerance, Los Angeles, USA (1993); District Six Museum, Cape Town, South Africa (1994); Tsitsernakaberd Armenian Genocide Memorial and Museum, Yerevan, Armenia (1969/1995); the Atocha train station memorial, Madrid, Spain (2004); the World Trade Center Memorial, New York, USA (2009); and plans for a Khmer Rouge theme park in Cambodia are striking in their shared concern with telling the history of mainly civilian victims killed in circumstances that 'range from the morally problematic to the utterly inhumane' (Williams, 2007, p. 20). In each event, 'the motives of the killers and the mode of killing loom large in the public consciousness, hence the histories have a dramatic quality that lends itself to evocative reconstruction and that issues of identity, culpability and punishment of perpetrators are often contentious or unresolved' (ibid.).

Memorial museums depart markedly from the conventional historical exhibitions, in that usually the site of the museum is significant, often located in the place where the atrocities occurred; and their clientele also often have a special relationship to the museum (as former inmates, or family members of the victims, for example); they hold politically significant events; they function as research centres for serious scholars who are geared towards identifying victims and aid the prosecution of perpetrators;

they are often aligned to truth and reconciliation commissions and human rights organizations, and have a strong pedagogic mission to work with survivors and link education to contemporary issues in society (Williams, 2007, p. 20–1). The capacity and wherewithal to memorialize the past is an explicitly politicized activity. As many scholars of political reparation argue, it 'is within this complexity of remembering and forgetting by actively constructing and attempting to "represent" the multiple stories of victims and survivors of conflict that memorialization has the promise of promoting human rights, pursuing issues of transitional justice and nation building' (Naidu, 2004).

Within the sites, Williams (2007) notes that the enduring tension between authentically preserving significant historical objects and sites, and constructing emotive and dramatic visitor experience often comes out on the side of emotion and drama – achieving a visceral, intense experience in visitors is considered more important for the impact on peoples' attitudes and understanding of the events. This is because an overriding aim for these memorials and installations is that they need 'to be able to speak to generations who were not there ... it must speak in a public way for the next generation who will not have been there, who will not have those memories' (Goldberg, 2006). This is done by encouraging people to take a particular message away; visiting a memorial museum is a heavily scripted encounter (Strange, 2000). One example is drawn from my own experience of visiting a site of multiple mass death events – Port Arthur in Tasmania. A former colonial prison colony for men who had been imprisoned for extreme offences on multiple occasions – a prison for violent recidivists located in a secluded, shark-infested bay, this model prison sought to retrain men into the habits of civilized society by imposing harsh behaviour modification programmes which were the early seeds of prison reform. Many men experienced extreme conditions of isolation and illness. The threat of capital punishment always loomed, and in the two decades that the site worked as a penal colony (1833–1850s), men were hanged, died of infectious diseases or were burnt alive as fire swept through the prison blocks on at least two occasions. Notwithstanding the fascination of the colony's grind of death for passing tourists, in 1996, Port Arthur became the site for the worst mass murder event in post-colonial Australian history.

On the 28 April 1996, Martin Bryant shot and murdered 35 people and wounded 21 in various locations around local area and in the colony site, including a café and car park, before being captured. Since the mass killing, the site still remains a significant and popular tourist destination. However, for any tourist visiting the site, there is an explicit script to be followed. At various locations there are signs telling visitors to refrain from asking local guides and workers on site about the killings, as many were there on the day and lost co-workers, friends and relatives. Tourists interested in the shootings (one must ask, who wouldn't be?) are requested through signage to make their way to the site of the café where many were killed. Though the café burnt down soon after the tragedy, a water memorial of a calm pond has been erected, where visitors are prompted to reflect on the murders in a way that encourages silent, yet thoughtful tranquillity. The dedication stone to the massacre reads:

> Death has
> Taken its toll
> Some pain knows
> No release
> But the knowledge
> Of brave compassion
> Shines like
> A pool of peace

(Dedication to the Port Arthur massacre, 1996)

An integral aspect of this rush to commemorate atrocities that Lennon and Foley (2006), among others, have drawn attention to, is the related phenomenon of 'dark tourism'. This is the business of visiting such sites of mass death precisely because they are the places where atrocities have unfolded. While sites of massacre and carnage have long held a fascination for visitors, what Lennon and Foley are concerned to note is the new mobility and hybridity they embody. The mobility of those with expendable incomes to make sometimes arduous journeys to the real sites of mass death is historically unparalleled. More people travel to more sites of mass death than have ever done so before.

The key practice at the memorial sites is indication and interpretation (showing visitors where the sites are and how to interpret their experience of visiting them). Attention is to the experience of the visitor over the preservation and presentation of authentic artefacts (ibid.). There are some very revealing points made by Lennon and Foley as they examine a series of dark tourism sites around the globe. They note that these sites now promote multiple histories. Not only that, but commercialization, education and historical documentation are all intertwined in a shift towards the experiential aspects of the tourist visit:

Global communication technologies play a major part in creating the initial interest [in specific dark tourism sites] and that the objects of dark tourism themselves appear to produce anxiety and doubt about the project of modernity; the educative elements of sites are accompanied by elements of commodification and commercial ethic which accepts that visitation is an opportunity to develop a tourism product. (Lennon and Foley, 2006, p. 11)

Dark tourism has become a global industry that maintains the past by invoking empathetic experiences in the growing number of people interested in histories of mass death:

> Globalization is not just about processes of economic exchange, it involves cultural processes. Ideas, attitudes, people, technologies, media, and cultural commodities and symbols now flow across the globe in what were once unbridgeable temporal and spatial distances. If globalization is about the compression of time and space, then it has profound consequences for identity and in particular people's cultural affiliations, and ... the politics of remembrance (Rizvi, 2003, p. 209)

People no longer define themselves exclusively through their nation or their ethnicity. Now, as Levy and Sznaider (2006) argue, it is possible to discern the emergence of a global collective memory. What makes it global is that collective memories are achieved in ways that reach across the globe as a physical space – they are not keyed into or locked in reference to a particular location, and are not bounded by legal territorial borders (aka the nation-state). A shared sense of ethics – a shared set of values of what is understood to be right and good – is discernible in the global human rights movement; seen as an example of supra-national ethics that forms the basis of a global collective memory. These memories are enacted in and through cultural institutional practices associated with a new way of memorializing – managing past mass deaths that are themselves disengaged from particular national territories, but are seen to move back and forth between nations. The series of markers across the world that denote the Middle Passage Monument is a case in point. As a monument, it spans the historical trade routes of slavery in a way that emphasizes the interdependence of wealth and human exploitation, and of ongoing inequalities long embedded in race relations (Ater, 2010). The purpose of the Monument is to serve as a gravestone on the world's largest graveyard, the Atlantic Ocean's infamous Middle Passage, where millions of African people are estimated to have died en route to the slave trade in the Americas between the fifteenth and nineteenth centuries, their bones forming a trail across the ocean.

How does this reading of memorial museums and dark tourism contribute to this discussion of the contemporary management of mass death? They are examples of contemporary commemorative practices that are vehicles to elaborate the particularities of the management of mass death in a global age; they manage the past in new ways that synthesize a multiplicity of meanings, global travel routes and digital media for experiential effect. These infrastructural and ideational approaches achieve the management of mass death in ways that conform to the contours of a global age. Connectivity and experientiality are the vehicles for collective remembrance, and so the means through which collective belonging may be being achieved in a global age. Dark tourism and memorial museums are two examples of how the past is being institutionally and ideationally reorganized and re-understood. The shift is from nation-focused museums that attend to the solidities of national identity, to event-focused museums. These new ways build on visitors' emotional experience of being in the place, or surrounded by the objects. They reconstruct a version of the past that makes sense in a world where national boundaries are superseded by transnational institutions, corporations and personal identities as people migrate and communicate across borders as never before.

Conclusion

This chapter began with the terrible events of Hurricane Katrina in August 2005 as a way to highlight the contrast between old and failing and new and successful strategies to manage the mass death instigated by a natural disaster. It then laid out a conceptual framework for approaching mass death in a global age – mass death is central to social organization and this relationship is usefully explained in the concept of the management of mass death. This way to understand mass death (as a keystone for social organization) can be explained by looking at institutional ways of managing mass death. Using three examples to demonstrate how institutional organization is involved in managing mass death in the past tense, unfolding mass death scenarios and the prevention of future possible mass deaths, it has been feasible to build an account of how the contemporary management of mass death is unfolding as a global rather than a national phenomenon.

The management of mass death is a fundamental social practice. A global management of mass death is already in place and Janus-faced as it encompasses both cosmopolitanism and disaster capitalism. To return to the question of how it might be characterized and explained in our global, post-industrial, post-nation-state era, this global management of mass death can be identified in the distinctively globalized infrastructures and imaginaries that prevail. The institutional frameworks for managing mass death are spread across the globe, and are intensified in particular kinds of ways (experiential participation though seeing, hearing, being involved in the playing out of disasters, epidemics and wars in ways that were not possible before). This is made possible because of contemporary economic, technological and communicative capabilities that stretch over pre-existing national boundaries and international relations.

The character of the infrastructures for managing mass death are achieved through global networks of surveillance and social policy. This is seen in the examples of interconnected and interdependent rapid response teams and long-term reparation and reconciliation tribunals. It is also seen in thinly veiled complicity in pogroms. For example, the limited international response to Serbian attacks on Bosnian Muslims in Sarajevo in 1992, and the world's indifference in the face of media reports of secret camps, mass killings and the destruction of Muslim mosques and historical architecture in Eastern European ethnic cleansings in the mid-1990s indirectly implicates United Nations member states in the ethnic cleansing of approximately 200,000 Bosnian Muslims. The Janus-face of these global infrastructures raises questions about the character of globalization. On the one hand, the benign and empathetic response to people in distress suggests a move to what Beck and Grande (2010) would call institutionalized cosmopolitanism, where there is a certain recognition of global threats, discussions and responses that are co-ordinated through global networks discussing how best to prevent such events happening again in the future. At the same time, a quite different reading can be made of the same set of responses, courtesy of Naomi Klein's theory of disaster capitalism (Klein, 2007). Based on the premise that the growing global bureaucratization carried out in the name of risk management fosters a particular style of rapacious capitalism, it turns disasters into commercial opportunities through 'orchestrated raids on the public sphere in the wake of catastrophic events, combined with the treatment of disaster as exciting market opportunities' to use moments of collective trauma to engage in radical social and economic engineering (ibid., pp. 6–9).

Imaginaries incorporate technical means with bureaucratic, computational, algorithmic approaches to the shaping of human activity in the name of forestalling mass death. Mass death is imagined through a conscious recognition and acceptance of connection at a global socio-political economic level, where causes and effects can be mitigated (if not fully thwarted) through globally co-ordinated agency. The networked infrastructures are pragmatic and task-focused in character, while the imaginaries draw both explicitly and implicitly on enduring emotions such as empathy and fear to make experiential connections between vastly different groups of people around the world.

We in the present are engaged in archiving the past as a resource for our present as well as for our plans for the future. We are doing this in distinctive and identifiable ways grounded in pragmatic and task-focused connections between the infrastructures and imaginaries that manage mass death.

In 2011, the Arab Spring, combined with shattering earthquakes and tsunamis in New Zealand and Japan, are fertile ground for institutionalized cosmopolitanism *and* disaster capitalism as countries come together to alleviate distress and to support those in relatively wealthy countries who find themselves in dire need, while millions starve in the not-so-lucrative markets of Darfur in the Sudan, for example. The question of why abuses of power and authority can and do still occur, even as the world likes to understand itself as one global community, can be explained by pointing out a belief in the capacities of technological innovation. To map, plan, detect and respond to mass death situations does nothing to alleviate power structures and struggles for ascendancy. In fact, perhaps the lack of reflexivity on behalf of those who develop and market these new ways of managing our past and future is the means through which existing inequalities and exploitations become re-articulated in a global age.

Questions

This chapter was about the management, prevention and remembrance of mass death.

1. If you have ever been to a site of mass death (for example, a battlefield, historic site of executions, famine area and so on) describe what the experience was like. If you have never been to one, write a few words on how you imagine it would be to visit such a place.
2. Imagine that you are a schoolteacher and you are to take a class of 10-year-old children to a site of mass death (for example, a trip to Ground Zero in New York). How would you prepare them for the trip? What expectations would you have for their and your own behaviour there? What would you think of other people being frivolous at the mass death site? Why?
3. Compare and contrast two recent incidences of mass death through natural disasters (for example, the 2004 Boxing Day tsunami with Hurricane Katrina or other, more recent, mass deaths such as the 2010 Pakistan/2011 Australia floods). Search online for news articles that were released at the time the disasters were unfolding. Concentrate on the main headlines and think about the kinds of messages they are putting across. Work in a group or with a study buddy and consider what kinds of effects each disaster has had on the communities concerned. How might media responses shape individual, organizational and governmental responses to these disasters?

Chapter 8

Religion: The De-secularization of Life and Death?

Introduction

> Hale Bopp's approach is the *marker* we've been waiting for – the time for the arrival of the spacecraft from the Level Above Human to take us home to *Their World* – in the literal Heavens. Our 22 years of classroom here on planet Earth is finally coming to conclusion – *graduation* from the Human Evolutionary Level. We are happily prepared to leave this world and go with Ti's crew. If you study the material on this website you will hopefully understand our joy and what our purpose here on Earth has been. You may even find your own *boarding pass* to leave with us during this brief *window*. We are so very thankful that we have been recipients of this opportunity to prepare for membership in Their Kingdom, and experience Their Boundless Caring and Nurturing. (Heaven's Gate home page, 1997)

On 27 March 1997, the *Higher Source* group, led by Marshall Applewhite committed the largest mass suicide in US history. CNN reported that the 39 members were found dead in a Californian hilltop mansion. The carefully orchestrated mass suicide probably took place over three days and involved three groups, proceeding in a calm and ritualistic fashion. Some members apparently assisted others and then cleaned up, then went on to take their own dose of the fatal mixture, mixed with apple sauce. The last two victims to die were found with plastic bags over their heads. Lying on cots or mattresses with their arms at their sides, the victims each carried identification. All the victims wore black pants and Nike athletic shoes, their faces and chests covered with purple shrouds. Their bags had been packed neatly in the dormitory-type rooms. The officials were tipped off to the suicide after videotapes and a letter were sent by the group to an ex-member. In those communications, every member of the organization gave a brief statement prior to their death; the essence of those statements was that they were going to a better place. Members were 'quite jovial and excited about moving on to the next stage' and an ex-associate of the group said he was told that *Higher Source* believed that a UFO was hiding behind the Hale Bopp comet (CNN, 1997). *Higher Source* believed that aliens were planning to take over the planet.

174

On investigation, it became known that, in 1975, the leader, Marshall Applewhite, with his partner Bonnie Nettles, had set up a movement called Human Individual Metamorphosis, which later became Higher Source, and preached that death could be overcome through physical ascension into another realm beyond the confines of planet Earth (Robinson, 1997). At their talks, they predicted various mass landings of UFOs. The group became disillusioned when none of them ever ascended, and the mass landings never happened. The initial group disbanded, though a core group continued and recruited with pamphlets and other print publications for two decades before moving to California and actively using the internet to transmit messages in the mid-1990s. Members of the cult opened a Web consulting business, called *Higher Source* as a means of financing themselves as they waited for their marker (Robinson, 1997). Members left no instructions for the disposal of their earthly remains, which were cremated and returned to family members at the end of the official investigation (CNN, 1997).

Allāhu Akbar

On 11 September 2001, 19 young Muslims commandeered passenger jets and killed themselves, taking with them 2,937 people. Subsequently, the FBI released a letter reportedly handwritten by the hijackers and found in the form of three separate copies on 9/11 – at Dulles International Airport, at the Pennsylvania crash site, and in Mohamed Atta's suitcase. It included a checklist of final reminders for the 9/11 hijackers. An excerpt reads: 'When the confrontation begins, strike like champions who do not want to go back to this world. Shout, '*Allāhu Akbar*', because this strikes fear in the hearts of the non-believers' (FBI, 2001). Instructions for their last night included a series of rituals to purify body and soul in preparation for their passage to Paradise the following day. The hijackers were, among other things, to make an oath to die and renew their intentions, shave excess body hair, shower and wear cologne; read Al-Tawba and Al-Anfal (traditional war chapters from the Qur'an) and reflect on their meanings, and remember all of the things God has promised for the martyrs. Remind their soul to listen and obey [all divine orders]; purify their soul from all unclean things. Completely forget something called this world [or this life]. The final instruction was always to remember God. They should either end their lives while praying, seconds before the target, or make their last words: 'There is no God but God, Muhammad is His messenger' (Loeterman, 2002). In the cockpit voice recorders found at the crash site of Flight 93, the hijackers are heard reciting the Takbir[1] as the plane plummeted towards the ground (FBI, 2001). In subsequent months, remains of two of the World Trade Center hijackers were identified and removed to an undisclosed location from Memorial Park in New York, the mass memorial cum storage facility for unidentified remains from the World Trade Center (Kelley, 2003).

Like Christianity, Islam teaches the continued existence of the soul and a transformed physical existence after death. A Muslim theodicy[2] believes that there will be a day of judgement when all humans will be divided between the eternal destinations of Paradise and Hell. If granted admission to Paradise, those souls will enjoy physical and spiritual pleasures for ever – or if condemned to Hell, to suffer physical and spiritual torment for eternity. Two exceptions are: warriors who die fighting in the cause of God are ushered immediately into God's presence; and enemies of Islam are sentenced immediately to Hell upon death.

Elsewhere in this book indirect reference is made to the place of religion in death practices. It discusses the increasing secularization of funeral rites in relation to the professionalization of medicine and funeral directors in Chapter 4 and the significance of the distinction between the sacred and profane, with specific reference to the representation of death, in Chapter 9. This chapter sets out to examine the ways in which sociology has approached the question of religion in society more generally, and how the sociological insights gleaned can be brought to bear to help explain events such as Heaven's Gate and 9/11 in terms of the place of religion in contemporary globally-oriented societies.

What becomes clear from reading the official accounts from the Del Mar, California Police Department (CNN, 1997), and the 9/11 Commission Report (Zelikow, 2004), given the difficult task of reverse-engineering the deaths, is that both of these murder-suicides shared much common ground. They signalled to the world at large that they were religiously derived, ritualized deaths that were understood by those who carried them out to be legitimate. Moreover, both Heaven's Gate and 9/11 were contemporary exemplars of complex relations between religion, death and society. The ways in which these deaths were religiously derived took a form that drew on partial yet extreme interpretations of existing world religions (Christianity and Islam) and the easy accessibility of current technological capabilities to enable both groups (Higher Source and Al Qaeda) and their respective leaders to achieve their figurative and literal ends.

These tragic incidents embody a well-accepted trend that has been witnessed over recent decades, which is a growing religiosity that takes two main forms. One strand is a rise in organized fundamentalist religion and is seen in the growth of Christian fundamentalism, especially in the USA, and Muslim fundamentalism, especially in the Middle and Far East. This strand is noted for its political activity and extreme views on, for example, abortion, the death penalty and euthanasia (Kearl, 1989; McLennan, 2007). The other strand is the increased religiosity seen in the mushrooming of alternative religious practices and beliefs, often referred to as the 'New Age' movement. Though not often formally organized (unlike world religions), nevertheless many millions of people today are interested in spiritual dimensions (Lee, 2008).

Also, both events can be interpreted as contradictory rejections of contemporary global social relations, in that both can be regarded as a backlash against global times and what they represented: Al Qaeda of perceived Western dominance of and through global capitalism; and Heaven's Gate, a rejection of this sullied world for an interplanetary future. At the same time, and in tension with their rejection of life today, these acts were enabled through global technologies and relations: Al Qaeda's ability to infiltrate American aviation, and Heaven's Gate capacity to finance itself and to access satellite images of the Hale Bopp comet.

The contradictions that Heaven's Gate and 9/11 symbolically carry are a contemporary form of two long-standing tensions: between faith and reason; and between religion and science. As carriers of contradiction, they are a helpful device to introduce a chapter about the nexus of death, religion and society. What they demonstrate is a set of concerns about the growing place of religious belief in global social relations, and the place of death within this post-secular context.

This shift in people's engagement with religion(s) has been described as a 'post-secular' move within advanced modernity (McLennan, 2007). This shift has generated much debate in general sociology and is also present in the sociology of death and dying. Post-secularism represents a change in the way in which death and religion come together in advanced modernity. During the twentieth century and onwards, a significant drop in church attendance and religious observance has been interpreted as a secularization of, in particular, modern Western societies. Within sociology, the secularization of industrial society was also cast as the disenchantment of modernity; this will be discussed later in the chapter. It has now become evident that while well-established world religions may not have the same level of social influence they once had, this does not mean that people's religiosity has reduced. It may in fact mean that it is taking new forms that draw on the capacities of the societies within which they emerge: a re-enchantment associated with post-secular society.

The next section outlines the different ways in which sociology has theorized and studied the question of religion, and ongoing debates that inform scholars' engagement with religion and contemporary society.

Sociology, religion and death

Sociology has been cast by some as the science of the problem of religion in society (Lemert, 1999), the science of examining what is this thing called religion. Though there are a variety of ways in which the roles of religion and death in society are explained, each shares a common feature, which is that there is a deep conceptual acceptance that religion has a central place in any attempt to describe and understand society. Also, regardless of the theoretical perspective taken, 'to study the institution of religion is to study the basic tensions within the relationships between individuals and their society' (Kearl, 1989, p. 198).

To gain an understanding of how sociology has conceptualized the nexus of death, religion and society, it is, according to Kearl, important to understand the concept of a thought system and how it links to systems of institutionalized actions and people's beliefs about what they do. An institutional thought system is the way that the reality that people take for granted is socially generated and personally internalized (ibid., p. 172): 'The social worlds of everyday life are groupings of individuals bound together by networks of communication and universes of discourse, each producing a distinctive constellation of consciousness. Institutions are carriers of this consciousness, acting as both cognitive blinkers (perception, for instance, is highly selective) and stabilizers of experience (Berger 1972)' (ibid., p. 174).

Sociological interest dovetails into anthropological concerns with symbolism at this point in the links between social structure, symbolism and people's actions, and how this shapes cultures/cultural belonging more broadly. Institutions offer habituation of thought and action, which minimizes doubt and frames action. Social institutions are templates for the social world. This way of approaching religion (as a social institution that shapes people's behaviours and beliefs in various ways) allows patterns to develop between structures of consciousness (ways of thinking) and particular institutional processes (ways of doing). For example, the thought systems of the 9/11 bombers and Heaven's Gate participants was a particular version of reality embodied in the charismatic views of Osama Bin Laden and Marshall Applewhite, respectively. Members of both groups shared a sense of belonging based on the belief that they were already the chosen ones. Both groups had prepared over a long period for their final reckoning. Both groups were in a holding pattern, prepared but waiting for a signal from their leader that the time had come to trigger the final rituals of departure. And as their own ends approached, both groups signalled their faith as they transitioned from the present world to their hereafter.

Social institutions provide the legitimation and sanctions for those thought systems: Al Qaeda and Higher Source were the social institutions that provided the support networks and sanctions for their members. These institutions can be read as religious because they both had a developed theodicy: their worldviews addressed the three core human difficulties: the meaning of life, suffering and death.

Death is highly ritualized and entwined with religion as an institution because, as

> Berger and Luckmann [1967] have pointed out, one of the most important tasks in any society is legitimating death. According to those authors, death obtains legitimacy through the existence of symbolic universes, which serve to explain and justify social reality. There is a

strong need in every society to cope with death and the legitimise its place in society, since the awareness of death, a knowledge specific to humankind, and the fact of death, can underpin the meaning of society as a whole [Malinowski 1948]. Therefore, in most societies, death is a highly ritualised event, accompanied by certain rites that take place while a person is dying, and often more elaborate ones taking place after death. Last rites rank among the so-called rites of passage (together with birth, initiation and marriage [Gennep 1960]), which give structure to human life, and during which the new social stage that the key actors are in acquires social acceptance, secure from the collective character of the rites or their parts. (Nesporova, 2007, p.1177)

However strange and disturbing to those not within their interpretation of reality, the legitimation or validation of these deaths was achieved by them reading certain symbolic meanings into what they were doing as individuals in a group. With ceremonious repetition, they ritualized their preparations, and these last rites[3] served to both explain and justify their subsequent actions. In a connected way, as death is ritualized because it is a way of legitimating *specific* deaths in terms of the broader social symbolic worlds (of Higher Source and Al Qaeda) within which the deaths took place, the overall effect also explains and justifies that broader social reality. Another way to say this is that these deaths are legitimated for those societies to make sense.

Religious practices are set apart from ordinary everyday living and doing. By approaching time in this way (as beyond the everyday) it makes death a transition instead of an ending, and allows religions to conceptualize and integrate the net sum of human activities: 'Our separate endeavours, as well as those of our ancestors and successors, are but unrelated, discrete events – unless there is some overarching frame of reference – and part of religion's role is to establish this broader perspective on everyday life' (Kearl, 1989, p. 180). Coherency in the continuity of generations is achieved by *transcending* the individual. Continuity gives order to biographical experiences, There is a need to transcend, as it achieves experience of community through continuity of generations where (Kearl quoting Michaels, 1949, p. 160), 'a tradition carried from generation to generation [wherein] the living acknowledge the work of the dead as living on in themselves forever' (Kearl, 1989, p. 180). Religions are therefore a major institutional source of that continuity and community.

At the individual level, how Heaven's Gate and 9/11 protagonists were ritualized connected their deaths to the group's *last rites* universe in a meaningful way and so made these deaths (both the suicides and the murders) legitimate. In Heaven's Gate, the participants were all dressed in androgynous clothes and the men had been castrated some time before their demise. They all lay in the same position, left the same message to the world and died together at approximately the same time, when the comet was closest to the earth, in the shared belief they would be transported to the spaceship hiding in the tail of the Hale Bopp comet to take them to Heaven where they would meet and become one with androgynous angels there (Robinson, 1997). The 9/11 protagonists saw themselves as warriors for Islam who were cleansed, body and soul, to go immediately to God's side at their death, in the expectation of eternity in Paradise. And their victims, by definition infidels and enemies of Islam (because they were in America, the symbolic belly of the beast of Western capitalism), would go straight to Hell for ever when they died.

The opening examples are acts of killing (of selves and/or others) construed through a form of religious belief. Heaven's Gate and 9/11 were specific types of suicide-murders where a cult organization and millennialism came together in the form that the promise of a different world *relied* on death in this world – that is, death is deliberately brought about through the actions of the cult leaders to achieve their ends. Other famous events include the so-called Jonestown Massacre, in 1978 in Guyana, where cult members poisoned themselves.

One other general point to be made is that in such murder-suicide situations, there is a stark disjuncture between the meaning of the world from within these groups and the meaning of the world that is held by the broader society within which these groups exist(ed). What is significant about that disjuncture is that it helps to reveal the moral dimensions of relationships between different groups in society – from a majority point of view it is quite likely that Heaven's Gate and 9/11 groups can be seen as 'deviant' from the dominant moral order, though seen from within these groups, their actions were legitimate and logical. This is an interesting tension, especially in death studies when it comes to problematic social issues that also include other deaths that can be seen as potentially bad, such as suicide, abortion, murder, execution, euthanasia, genocide etcetera. For death studies, it is important to be able to approach these bad deaths from an understanding that judging a death as bad is only possible if there is a model of what a good death should be. And understanding what is an appropriate, socially sanctioned death for a particular time and place must recognize the religious/symbolic dimensions of how they play out across institutions and actions.

The idea that societies and groups work with a concept of a good death/bad death to guide people's social actions underpins much public debate about euthanasia and the death penalty, for example, and also informs hospice practices, medical end-of-life care and other issues that have been introduced in this book. One other aspect that informs discussion of good deaths/bad deaths is the potential social contradictions that these moral precepts can take. For example, in the USA, high-profile anti-abortion and anti-euthanasia lobbies have emerged in federals states that are willing to take the lives of their people (in the form of executions) to ensure the rules are upheld (Kearl, 1989).

Formal religions are seen as the repository of moral guidelines: the institutions through which moral rules are defined and enforced. It is interesting to think about the place of good and bad deaths in relation to good and bad lives. A core aspect of this area of death studies is getting to grips with the concept of good deaths and bad deaths. This links to the different moral statuses of deaths as legitimated because they are good, but also legitimated in the sense that they are given credibility and explanation in terms of broader cultural beliefs when they are labelled bad deaths. They are categorized, which means that they are given a place in systems of justification – that is, systems of legitimation. What is understood to be acceptable socially has been mandated through organized social practices and social institutions.

Currently in Taliban-ruled societies – for example, in Iran – a person who is seen to break the moral code can be put to death. The public stoning to death of adulterers is seen as a means of rectifying the shame of a badly lived life. The death through stoning atones for the mistakes and sins of the living; it is a good death in that it repairs the moral standing of those shamed through the actions of the adulterers. The USA death penalty can also be seen in a similar light. Institutionally imposed death for perceived wrongdoing is more of a symbolic act about punishment for breaking moral and legal codes than it is about rectifying what was done. The good deaths rectify the damage wreaked by the bad lives of those who are punished.

Of course, given the power differential between different groups in society, it should come as no surprise that the actual operation of the death penalty, whether in the Middle Eastern Taliban-ruled areas or in American states, embodies wider power relations. It is those in weaker positions within the society that are more often punished, and more brutally, than those in positions of power and authority. Again, this also introduces the point that moral rules are not outside the realms of economic and political power. Some would argue that one of the significant trends in religious practice in recent decades has been the resurgence of religion in politics and, conversely, politics in religion. This phenomenon is closely connected to discussion and debate about growing fundamentalist movements which do not recognize the separation between politics and church that is seen, for example, in secular societies.

It is no surprise that classical sociological scholars all had something to say about religion in society. Some spoke out more than others, and what they had to say is deeply embedded in their understanding of society. Classical sociology approached religion in ways that befitted their overall ways of understanding the social world. For example, Karl Marx understood religion as *the opiate of the people*, because it instilled a focus on the afterlife, and on religious belief as false consciousness that aided and abetted the continuation of systems of oppression such as feudalism and, to a degree, capitalism. It was an enemy of the people.

Durkheim is justifiably famous for his work on religion on society. He placed religion at the centre of his sociology as he sought to close the circle between social institutions, beliefs and symbolic practices in his quest to decipher the laws of society. For him, religion is a social phenomenon that can at the same time be a formal social institution and a personal disposition that is not necessarily shared by all or entered into by all in the same way within a given social system. The role of religion is to help to bind society together. It does this by being one of the main ways that ideas, institutions and actions come together.

Many of Durkheim's concepts and ideas associated with society and religion inform sociology to this day. A significant concept is that the function of religion is to ensure the continuity of society – a significant piece of social machinery that does the job of linking beliefs about the world, institutions and people's actions. Through studying religions from non-modern Western societies, specifically from Australian Aboriginal peoples, he and others who developed and refined his ideas laid out a schema for making sense of any religion as well as the place of death within religion (Durkheim, [1912]1995).

While his work gave conceptual architecture to an understanding of how religion in general worked, he also brought to the table an attuned sense of the effects of modernity on religion and death. He understood that the growing influence of science (of which he was a part) forced a significant confrontation with the terms of religious belief. If the role of religion was to ensure the continuation of society, then God came into significant question because whatever deity was in place would either be demoted (to be in service to society) or diffused. This crisis in religion, in both its institutional form and in the form of religiosity as the moral compass for people in society, caused Durkheim considerable concern and, as already noted in the Introduction to this book, he developed a potential solution to the reduced role of religion in modern society. The role of morality would be translated into professional ethics, and that would be the core sets of beliefs and practices that could, and possibly should, guide people through the new times of industrial modernization at the start of the twentieth century (Durkheim, [1890]1957). Even if modern society became fully civic, death rituals would remain central to group solidarity.

Weber developed an alternative account of religion, society and death. Though not as clearly worked out as Durkheim, Weber argued that religious attitudes and beliefs did have a profound impact on what people did in the world. He had a deep fascination with religion and undertook to try to decipher the role of religion in modernity and the emergence of capitalism and a way to organize society. This came to fruition in the argument put forward in *The Protestant Ethic and the Spirit of Capitalism* (Weber, [1904]1958), that the way in which capitalist entrepreneurs approached the world was in large part an outcome of the Protestant Reformation. And a consequence of the growth of capitalism was the increasing influence of instrumental rationality – so much so that Weber believed it would super-sede the magical, mystical and spiritual aspects of modern society and trap people in a miserable *iron cage* of instrumental rationality. Life would have no symbolic meaning, and within this scenario, death would be treated merely as a material demise. Death rites would wither away, people would no longer care about who had gone before, and dealing with the remains of the dead would be organized along the lines of the most rational form of disposal. This line of thought is embedded in many arguments that explain the turn to utilitarian, uniform cemeteries, the rise of cremation and the decrease in funeral rites over the twentieth century and into the twenty-first as a sure sign of the over-extension of instrumental rationality. It has to be remembered that Weber was diagnosed as having depressive episodes throughout his life that might have prevented him from recognizing and acknowledging that while religions might have altered alongside the exten-sion of bureaucratic rationalities and systems of social organization, running parallel, people still went to church, and developed different ways of engaging their spirituality, in some cases through mediums or psychics (Lee, 2008).

The ways in which classical theorists grappled with conceptualizing and interpreting religiousness continues to influence profoundly both the soci-ology of religion *and* the sociology of death and dying. More recent perspectives have rejected, accepted or adapted the classical approaches to death, religion and society. For example, coming from a structural func-tionalist perspective, Kearl (1989) saw that religion provided the basis of moral solidarity for society. It also acted as a cultural check and balance against (technologically driven) forces of change. The *legitimation thesis,* used to explain the place of death in society, relies on a structural function-alist perspective with its emphasis on the effects of what people under-stand, behave and do in the workings of society. A critical realist approach allows for an emphasis on the inherent tensions and contradictions that drive society forward, while conflict theorists, on the other hand, typically approach religion as 'a tool by which the social elite maintains their social power, such as by diverting the motivations of the subjugated from the here and now to the hereafter' (Kearl, 1989, p. 197). One key area of contemporary theoretical interest is the differences between the ways that concepts of time and space, and divisions between the sacred and profane, religious and secular, and between good and bad deaths, are thought through and experienced as boundaries that are always in a state of flux, and how the transitions between these categories are achieved (Hockey *et al.*, 2010, pp. 6–7).

Contemporary sociologists of death and dying suggest that their concern with religion focuses predominantly on the relationship between the living and the dead (Howarth, 2007). For example, it can be approached as a form of social practice; that is, how the relationship between the living and the dead is conceptualized is linked to cosmologies about the afterlife and how people deal with death. In terms of dying, how it is understood as, for example, an end in itself, or a passage to another world and so on, and regarding disposal, how disposal of the dead is symbolized. This in turn helps to explain the form and content of funeral rites. Also, how grieving for those who are dead is understood, and how long-term memories of the dead are incorporated into the lives of the living: formally, for example, in the form of ancestor worship, or less formally in personal recall and a range of other ways.

Howarth suggests there have been two dominant ways to conceptualize the relationship between the living and the dead, and each way seems to have an elective affinity with a particular form of society. The first one is to understand relations between the living and the dead as continuous, where life merges into death, and death is omnipresent in life. This frames the relations between the living and dead as a continuum. Howarth draws heavily upon anthropological work on non-Western societies, particularly the work of Maurice Bloch, to draw out how a continuum between the living and the dead takes shape. For example 'As Bloch argues of the Merina culture of Madagascar, such a continuity relies upon the notion that death and birth, or fertility, are interrelated, 'that it is the dead who have been and will be the suppliers of life' (Bloch, 1971, p. 222, cited in Howarth, 2007, p. 216). Ancestor worship, which is particularly prevalent in Polynesian and Mexican societies, is a form of this continuum, where the dead are venerated and called forth and consulted to offer guidance in the lives of the living. There is a continuing dialogue between the lives of the dead and the lives of the living.

The second is a dualism, where there is a profound break between the lives of the living and the dead. There is a binary opposition between the living and the dead. This dualism can take different forms. For example, Tibetan Buddhists who practise sky burial (as mentioned in an earlier chapter) see that the body is a mere empty shell after death. The soul of the departed, though needing help from the living state through the transition to other realms, is on a one-way track and there is no enduring engagement with the lives of the living. Similarly, post-reformation Protestant Christian sects are marked by the rejection of the notion of Purgatory. What this means is that, once people die, they have gone to meet their Maker and there is nothing the living can do to intercede regarding the future fortunes of the souls of the departed. The relationship between the living and the dead terminates at death. This stands in sharp contrast to the continuum at the heart of Catholic theology, where it is possible for the living to intercede in the fate of the souls of the dead (through prayer) and this could have an impact on the duration and quality of the soul's stay in Purgatory before ascending to Heaven.

Moving away from Christian theology, there are some strands of New Age belief that conceptualize death and the decomposition of the body as a transformation of the human form back into its component parts, which are, ultimately, space matter or stardust. The matter that makes up human beings continues past and present for ever, but there is a decisive break between the here and now and this other particulate state. Another form of this dualism is in humanistic approaches to death, where the death of the body is believed to be the real ultimate final end and that nothing survives. The differences *within* this dualistic relationship between the living and the dead are a good way to introduce the idea of immortality. This rather complicates explanations because it shows how different kinds of cosmological beliefs meld with each other as a source of quite complex and variable human understandings of death and how they relate to human practices in death. Thinking in terms of bodily disposal, sky burial makes sense as a dualism between the material and the spiritual. Having ones ashes shot into space (as did the American science fiction writer, Timothy Leary) makes sense in the context of beliefs about humans reverting on death to become stardust. Burying relatives in one's garden, a common practice in Pacific Island communities to this day, speaks of continuity between life and death. The dead literally remain in the domestic living space, from where they are continually called upon to advise and adjudicate in the trials and tribulations of the living.

Through the ages there have been decisive epochs of religious history linked to particular types of society, and these influence the relations between the living and the dead. In Western societies heavily influenced by institutionalized Christian theology over centuries, Howarth (2007) argues that post-Reformation societies (from which sociology emerged in the nineteenth century) constituted the relationship between the living and the dead in a binary way:

> In the sixteenth century, Protestants rejected the doctrine of purgatory and the belief that the living could mediate for the dead. This was undoubtedly an important factor in the development of a philosophy (prevalent in modern Western societies) that perceived life and death as binary opposites rather than a continuum. (Howarth, 2007, p. 219)

This move to binary opposition, when coupled with the radical doubt of the Enlightenment bubbled through as a growing humanistic attitude to death and a growing secularization of the state as the social institution charged with enforcing the moral–legal codes of that society. It was more socially permissible for people to take a humanist position without incurring public wrath and possible retribution. With the growing humanistic attitude to death there was a parallel material transformation in the sacred spaces of the dead to become garden cemeteries (Hockey *et al.*, 2010, p. 16). Church graveyards became municipal cemeteries and were set out as parkland on the semi-rural edges of newly urbanized populations (Rugg, 2006).

Modernity and the disenchantment of death

Though it continued through the centuries, this binary situation transformed in post-Enlightenment times from one between the body and the
soul to one between the body and the mind. This point is reiterated and
usefully theorized by Finucane (1996), who has charted a shift in the status
of the dead (ghosts) through the changing contours of Anglo-Saxon society
as the social relations of religion transformed from classical to Reformation
and to Enlightenment and modernity.

Finucane discusses this binary state through the impact of secularization on Christianity and how it intersected with popular beliefs about
ghosts. In the 1850s, there was freer thought on religion, and the people
of the time understood public debate about the status of ghosts as
evidence of a battle between reason and faith were often regarded in this
light (for example, the works of Jeremy Bentham, John Stuart Mill,
Herbert Spencer or Karl Marx). Reactions to such public debate were
varied:

> some Christians left their faith behind, others ... entrenched themselves
> amidst the tenets of evangelical fundamentalism. Yet others, like some of
> the founders of the Oxford movement, looked to Mediaeval Catholicism
> for inspiration, while probably the majority simply went on going to
> church out of habit. Many Christians hungered for assurance and grew
> anxious in an atmosphere of scepticism, doubt, and confusion far more
> pervasive in an age of mass media and rising literacy, than that experi-
> enced in the past. (Finucane, 1996, p. 175)

There were many other manifestations of the effect of radical doubt that
included the emergence of the Romantic Movement as a deliberate
counter to the overbearing rationalism of the sciences. Culminating in the
re-enchantment of the Victorian era with its peculiar attention to funeral
rites, taphephobia (a fear of being buried alive), grief, the afterlife and all
things strange and ghoulish: 'All of the curiosity, dread, anxiety and sentimentality in Victorian attitudes toward death are to a degree products of
the Romantic Movement ... this movement was itself a reaction to the
scientific and agnostic tendencies of the period, especially during the
second half of the century' (Finucane, 1996, p. 169). Finucane theorizes
his account of the vicissitudes of the afterlife in relation to the ebbing and
flowing currents of reason and Romanticism.

It is understood that modernity brought a profound challenge to religious beliefs and practices, because the impact of the scientific method as
an empirically based means to understand the world rejected faith in God
as the appropriate vehicle for understanding the universe and all that
occurred within it. This is sometimes referred to as *disenchantment*:

In Weberian terms, the edifice of modernity rests on the inseparable processes of disenchantment and rationalization. The modern world is considered only monumental and not intimate ... In so far as these values are concerned, modernity comes to stand for a sort of anti-transcendentalism that earmarks the mystical and hidden realms to the waste bins of the here and now. Death seems to have no relevance within the monumentality of modernity. (Lee, 2008, p. 749)

Sociology has been particularly influenced by this view of modernity as disenchantment thesis, which has taken shape as the death taboo. A good example of this is Becker (1973) who brings together psychoanalytical and religious existential writings of Sigmund Freud and Søren Kierkegaard to explore what he sees as the pivotal feature of modern, dis-enchanted society, namely the 'denial of death' (ibid., p. 68).[4]

Taking Weber on his own terms, the way that people understand their own actions is absolutely central to understanding how they act and organize their lives. It took those who came after Weber to apply the same logic to his, as perhaps one might label it, monotheistic account of modernity as disenchantment. According to Lee (2008), while Weber did not discuss the death taboo or the denial of death directly, nevertheless 'his critique of modern culture implicitly addresses the nihilism of death as a reflection of the increasing relativism of values' (ibid., p. 747). Hence it would not be too far-fetched to argue that this relativism underlay an outlook on suppressing death as the mirror of the senselessness of life. Under this canopy of relativism, the death taboo can indeed flourish as a boundary marker of the modern world by repressing any hint of pointlessness. People can go about their daily lives without having to confront death as reflecting the pointlessness of their routines. In short, modern relativism constitutes an unacknowledged source of the death taboo.

A paradox lies hidden in Weber's account of modernity as disenchanting. Modern society could not resolve the suffering; in fact, Weber saw that it aided and abetted it in his metaphor of the Iron Cage of Rationality, yet this sits in a contradictory relationship to his account of the consequences of the Protestant Spirit for the successes of cumulative capitalism. It is through people's belief in the afterlife and their attempts to resolve the eternal conundrum of seeking signs of being chosen within a doctrine that stated all had already been chosen and nothing done on Earth could change the path of salvation. Lee notes that other theorists picked up and reworked Weber's seemingly contradictory explanations of modernity. Among them, Edward Tiryakian reframed the relationship between modernity and enchantment by explaining that modernity does not remove or exorcize re-enchantment, but that those enchanting elements of modernity are subsumed by what he calls 'mundane' ends, referred to as the 'secularization of magical consciousness' (Lee, 2008, p. 749). This more complex account of the relationship between modernity and enchantment gives space to recognize and acknowledge that enchanting activities still take place within modernity, even in areas previously seen as avowedly rational and anti-transcendent, such as scientific and technological advances.

Lee's contribution to contemporary debates on religion, death and society is to identify the deeper, broader concerns of modernity as *both* dis- and re-enchanting. His discussion of enchantment helps to introduce a productive, paradoxical approach to modernity, which is that it is not an all-or-nothing contest between two diametrically opposed positions (the rational *or* the romantic) but a steering through the confluence of the tension between rationalism and romanticism. Rational and romantic impulses *are constantly pulling through each other* (a dynamic tension).

Ronald Finucane offers a similar kind of theorization. His claim is that the way the afterlife is present in modern societies is just a continuation of a long-standing cultural contradiction. Societies with an Enlightenment heritage and other societies that come into contact with Enlightenment beliefs, practices and processes experience a gradual secularization, not only of their social institutions but also of their beliefs about the dead. This secularization is experienced as an enduring contradiction between reason and faith, and made manifest in the personalization of the dead even while there is a continuing belief in the afterlife. For Finucane, as this contradiction is a deep driver of post-Enlightenment society, his perspective is a form of critical realism.

What Lee's and Finucane's arguments boil down to is the growing presence or growing realization that there has been a co-presence of dis-/re-enchantment. Lee points out the long-standing recognition of the tension between rationalism and romanticism as a feature of modernity. Lee sees this struggle between dis- and re-enchantment as a central tension/paradox of modernity that informs much of the ongoing permutations and transformations in religion and death.

Post-secularism: negotiating the non-negotiable

> Society is dynamic and continually changing, and this is also true of the rituals it adopts to generate meaning as it relates to death. As societies become more culturally diverse, death rituals become more differentiated and numerous. Cultural groups may discard, retain or revise traditional rituals as well as develop new ones. This is particularly the case in advanced modern, increasingly multi-cultural societies where rituals may be adapted to take account of the practices of dominant or minority ethnic groups. (Howarth, 2007, p. 234)

If death is ritualized because it legitimates the specific death in terms of the broader social-symbolic world within which the death took place, then the way it is ritualized is a means of understanding what that social-symbolic world looks like as it transforms in a highly technologized post-secular environment, as it is clearly the case that 'contemporary technological developments can have a significant impact upon social and cultural forms, and upon the ways in which people encounter and experience religious phenomena' (Mellor, 2004, p. 358).

One effect is that belief and non-belief are forced to confront each other. Jupp (2008) explains this challenge in terms of contemporary Christianity's double-imperative of elaborating on and offering ways to contend with the tensions faced by being practising Christian (ministers) in a secular society. Even within multi-cultural contexts where secularism is a significant mode of belief and personal practice,

> the responsibility of those who conduct Christian funerals abides: to set each death within the death and resurrection of Jesus Christ; to choose vocabularies and rituals from the Christian armoury and beyond with which to give personal support to individuals and communities in their specific needs; and to address the challenges that mortality poses for all societies. (Jupp, 2008, p. xv)

The double-binding task of finding ways in which Christian funeral ministry can be made more meaningful in secular surroundings is a case of negotiating the non-negotiability of faith, whatever form that particular faith may take.

When considering the consequences of globalization on the configuration of religion in society and how it links to death ritual, given the rise of fundamentalisms in East and West, it is acceptable to expect an increase in the religious ritualization of funerals in post-communist countries as they emerge from a strictly secular communist to a more pluralist socio-political environment. Also, a move towards the increasing personalization of funeral rites could legitimately be expected in a post-secular environment, and as a consequence of globalization.

A very interesting example is the symbolism associated with funerals during the communist era in Czechoslovakia. According to Czech sociologist, Olga Nesporova (2007) communist regimes were marked by their radical humanism. Part of their political standpoint was to reject religious doctrine of any sort as being antithetical to the aims and objectives of the communist project to release workers from the chains of capitalism. People living under communist regimes often experienced a radical and violent displacement of religious institutions. This had significant impact on the legal and legitimate form of funeral rites.

Communist regimes, with their attachment to state apparatuses, embodied a high degree of humanism when their death views were considered. No otherworldly or spiritual domains were legitimate under these regimes, and simple cremation was seen as the most appropriate from of body disposal (though the mummification of key communist leaders for ongoing public display is a moot point within this logic). Yet the symbolic need to legitimate deaths remained. For Czechoslovakia, Nesporova notes, 'the system attempted to comfort people (the dying as well as the bereaved) by referring to lifetime achievement, particularly in terms of work' and communist party involvement (Nesporova, 2007, 1177).

The strong need for the ritualization of the liminal stages of life held sway in that the communist regime introduced the concept of the *secular funeral* ceremony. Nesporova's study examined the consequences of this change in death ritual doctrine for trends in funeral rites in succeeding decades of communist rule. There was a widespread acceptance of secular funerals during the 40 years of communist rule. However this cannot be taken to signify the capacity of communism to easily sweep aside religiosity. While Czechoslovakia seemed to embrace the secularization of death, other areas under communism were much less acquiescent. For example, in rural areas and in particular Moravia, Nesporova (2007) highlights that 'the replacement of the religious funeral ceremony with a state civil ceremony was less successful than in towns'. Similarly, the situation in the Slovak Socialist Republic was also very different, as there was more a widespread and stronger affiliation of Slovaks to the mainly Roman Catholic Christian churches. The secular funeral has never been particularly popular in Russia, probably because of the Russian Orthodox Church's opposition to cremation.

The impact of the fall of the communist regime in the late 1980s and through the following decades has thrown up interesting, and one could argue quite unexpected, trends in Czech funeral rites. As this aspect deals directly with social change that can be linked directly to forces of globalization, the Czech case will be discussed again in a later section of this chapter. For now, the task is to make the general point that Czechoslovakia seemed to embrace secular funerals while their counterpart communist comrades in the wider Soviet bloc were much more reticent. According to Nesporova,

The widespread acceptance of this kind of funeral ceremony could be explained by the already existing atheistic social climate and the fact that Czechs were quite open to the idea of cremation. Unlike Orthodox Russians, many Czechs favoured cremation even before the communists came to power [and] although Catholics did not recognise cremation as an alternative to burial until the 1960s, Protestant churches had no objection to this method of disposal. (Nesporova, 2007, p. 1177)

As the communist regime began to crumble in the late 1980s and through the 1990s, there was a significant decrease in the number of religious (Catholic) funerals, and a significant decrease in the number of funeral ceremonies, religious *or* secular, recorded during the communist era. For those that did take place, there was an overall simplification of the funeral rites in Czechoslovakia within the secular majority and in religious minorities. Nesporova's explanation for this trend is useful because it draws attention to ways in which existing cultural contexts come together with changes to symbolic doctrine for the dead.

However, this has not been the case in the secular or religious sections of post-communist Czechoslovakia. In approximately one-third of all Czech cremations, no ceremony is organized through an undertaker, which in most cases means that no funeral ceremony is held (Howarth, 2007, p. 216). Omitting the funeral altogether has been on the increase among unbelieving Czechs, and those who hold to religious beliefs are seen to have simplified their rites over this period too. Reasons for this are multi-layered. Respondents interviewed by Nesporova stated their reasons being that funeral rites were too expensive, and that people wanted to avoid the emotional stress that funerals were bound to elicit in those who attended them. This explanation cannot on its own fully explain the reduction, because it is hard to believe that people could forget the deceased just by avoiding a funeral ceremony:

> Czech society [like Britain; see Walter, 1999] favours more reserved expressions of grief, and this choice enables them to avoid an emotionally stressful situation in the presence of others. It is a short step from holding a private ceremony for just a narrow circle of relatives (which Czechs often do nowadays) and omitting it altogether. When a ceremony is not seen as being somehow useful for the future existence of the deceased, for honouring the dead, or useful for the bereaved, then some bereaved decide to omit the funeral ceremony especially in urban communities with their associated anonymity and decline in mutual dependency. (Nesporova, 2007, p. 1189)

Nesporova's explanation for why secular funeral rites were the favoured form serves to demonstrate the importance of long-standing cultural attitudes in shaping death rites, even when the formal worldview and the overarching justification of the organization of a given society is switched, in this case, from monarchy to communism. It raises the point that the ways in which church funerals are organized and the process of their organization makes sense only in terms of the broader context of society. It also raises interesting questions about how to explain the growing secularization of capitalist Western nations throughout the twentieth century and into the twenty-first. Often touted as a response to an increasingly material society fuelled by capitalist enterprises, there may be other reasons for this secularization of society and death rites right across Western and Eastern Europe. What aspects of a society dispose it towards a more secular worldview? One striking similarity between Eastern and Western bloc nations of the twentieth/twenty-first centuries is the rise of the nation-state bureaucratic infrastructure. Could this be, as intimated by

Weber at the start of the twentieth century, what really transforms symbolic life away from formalized religion and towards secularism? If this is indeed the case, what are we to make of the transformation of institutional life that is brought about by forces of globalization. The argument for the dismantling of nation-states and of their bureaucratic infrastructures may, it could be conjectured, be a transformation in social institutions that wreaks significant change upon symbolic worldviews and a transformation in social institutions that in turn transforms how people organize death rites.

Religion in post-secular death studies

Sociology is engaged in the debate, employing various positions and strategies to approach post-secularism in a way that will foster and further the tenets of democracy without debasing or hollowing out the capacity to appreciate religiosity, or reducing it to a mere institutional form. On the one hand, the turn to religious revival is dangerous in its potential to submit human freedom to religious doctrine, while on the other, a truly democratic position must be able to engage genuinely with others who hold deeply to a completely different worldview – who regard democracy itself as a brand of monotheistic dogma. The conundrum at the heart of post-secular debates is whether, and how, faith and reason can be brought together in an emancipatory project, and whether the definitive features of sociology can survive such a move. Sociology is caught in a difficulty because it has a heavy-duty historical, conceptual and political attachment to secularism, strongly rooted in the application of reason to substantive questions about the world. At the same time, sociologists have sought to contend with the otherworldly both in the form of religious institutions and religiosity as a central feature of society and sociality. Currently, a move to post-secularity calls into question many of the objectifying tendencies in sociology's approach to religion (as, for example, merely a function of society, or as just another cultural resource) and so also its capacity to describe and explain the whys and wherefores of the resurgence of religion as a political force and an aspect of identity. And the related question of what is the source of cultural and moral legitimacy in a global society.

In an engagement with the conceptual dilemmas posed to sociology by the post-secular turn, McLennan (2007) lays out constructively some of the terrain in sociology of the 'post-secular' debates, drawing on key contemporary social theorists and a selection of four perspectives that feed the current debates – poststructuralist vitalism, transcendental realism, multiculturalism and epistemic dialogism – to pose sociological questions about how secularism and religiosity are being defined and set up in relation to each other, and the possible place for sociology in debates on post-secularity.

For McLennan, sociology has not reached, and may never reach, a convincing resolution of this inherent tension beyond the recognition that there are aspects of the social world and social reality that lie beyond the empirical, and that sociology may have to content itself with playing its part as an approach to the world that is forever grounded in the substantive. There may be aspects, such as the non-empirical, that, like it or not, sociology cannot ever become part of while remaining true to itself. The tension within religion and science, then, helps to define the boundaries of sociology (as a substantive discipline). It also then demarcates what can be countenanced in the name of a sociology of death and dying – it can engage with the substantive and seek to describe, explain and critique on those terms; however, it cannot hope to find a place at the table of explanation defined through religious belief. This has implications for giving an account of how the sociology of death and dying broaches the nexus of society, religion and death.

How do these broader debates about the ways that sociology and religion can engage with each other in a post-secular world link with the sociology of death and dying? It is important to note that some of the leading scholars in the sociology of death and dying are *in faith* or have spent much of their careers engaging with religions organizations. Their professional practice is premised on *standing in* the tension between faith and reason. For example, Peter Jupp, as a committed Christian, has been fully engaged in elaborating key social issues in death and dying. Especially as it concerns the elaboration of ways to contend with the tensions faced by practising Christian ministries in secular surroundings. For example, Jupp's edited collection *Death Our Future* (2008) draws together the challenges that those who minister in the multi-cultural and person-oriented culture of contemporary Britain, and to offer suggestions of how to negotiate ways in which Christian funeral ministry can be made more meaningful in secular surroundings from a perspective where

> The responsibility of those who conduct Christian funerals abides: to set each death within the death and resurrection of Jesus Christ; to choose vocabularies and rituals from the Christian armoury and beyond with which to give personal support to individuals and communities in their specific needs; and to address the challenges that mortality poses for all societies. (Jupp, 2008, p. xv)

Douglas Davies, trained in anthropology *and* religious studies, engages theoretically with the interface between theology and sociology by pushing back from a Christian theology into a social history of theologies of death as a means of revealing the different ways in which Christian theology has engaged with death 'by thinking of theology as the actual process of quest and reflection in the ongoing life of believers rather than a single set of answers' (Davies, 2008, p. 2).

Howarth remarks that 'the way in which more innovative contemporary rituals might suggest that some elements in Western societies are moving, whether consciously or not, towards a view of life and death as a continuum' (Howarth, 2007, p. 230). She sees relations with the dead as being more mobile and more visible. As living people move physically more frequently, ways of connecting to the past also shift. Her insight into the multiplicity of practices and the inherent pluralization of what may have hitherto been monotheist beliefs and practices to do with the dead is a vital point to make. Howarth argues that a useful way of conceptualizing and explaining the kinds of changes in societal relationships between the living and the dead that are linked to the increasing mobility and ease of communication across great distances, is a more general move to a continuum of relations based on fragmentary lines of descent that 'may be more appropriate as societies and communities within them are ever more socially and geographically disjointed. Such fragmented patterns enable mobility and visibility to both the living and the dead who may now accompany them' (Howarth, 2007, p. 232). In this formulation, while formal religious institutions still do play a part in people's engagement with the dead, religious beliefs and practices are secondary, (an effect of) changing social conditions and relations rather than the pivotal and primary explanation for people's behaviour towards their dead.

Other theories have also sought to explain contemporary social phenomena associated with religion and death. One such is Finucane's argument that the way afterlife is presented in contemporary societies is just a continuation of the long-standing personalization of the afterlife:

> As in the 1880s, the banality of 'real' spectres stands in sharp contrast to the horrendous and frightening powers they wield in literature, or in the 1980s, in television and cinema. (Finucane, 1996, p. 178)

> But on the whole, there is no essential difference between twentieth century apparitions and their nineteenth century prototypes. This is the most striking impression left from a random sampling of modern reports … contemporary perceptions, most of them 'pointless', unknown spirits, represent a continuation of Victorian attitudes toward the other world. (Finucane, 1996, p. 189)

These different theories are attempts to explain and account for an increasing multiplicity of complex views about the dead in a post-secular era. The dead are certainly present in the lives of the living, but the forms they take is influenced by the current context of tension between faith and reason, religion and science. Bringing Finucane's and Howarth's theorizations together, it is possible to suggest a synthesized approach where it is perhaps not quite a continuum between the living and the dead that is emerging in the multiplicity of contemporary practices. A continuum suggests many discrete practices that exist alongside each other as a part of a potentially infinite set of variations between two extremes. Instead, drawing on Finucane's and Lee's insights about the deep-driving contradiction of reason and faith, alongside Howarth's recognition of the complexity and variation in what people actually do, the notion of a *new articulation* of a long-standing cultural contradiction may be more useful. An articulation where the culture-defining tensions of reason and faith in the post-secular phase, where societies, and the secular and sacred, are integrated differently, neither through binary separations nor a washing-line continuum of variations, but by way of dis-enchantment *and* re-enchantment are constantly pulling through each other. This may offer a more fruitful way to explain the contemporary sets of religiously infused social practices that encompass suicide bombers, New Agers and post-soviet funeral rites.

Nesporova's study suggests that the situation is much more complex and multi-layered, harder to predict than globalization equals multi-culturalism, which begets a fundamentalist backlash and a parallel transition to a post-secular society and a general increase in religiosity, especially in relation to bad deaths, the afterlife and death rites. This may be one strand (for example, in the case of Holy Wars, the war against terror, and Jihads) and suicide bombers and so on, but it is certainly too early to extrapolate from this in any coherent and substantiated way. And though there may be intimations of innovative couplings between spirituality and funeral rites, there is as yet not enough evidence to generalize about or predict with any degree of accuracy the character of the abiding relationship between globalization, religion and death. The suggestion is that there are multiple sites and trends that may seem contradictory but are not when considered with the insight that social context (historical and existing cultural practices) continues to exert powerful influence even as the everyday social institutions for death, and society more generally, have radically transformed.

This points to a significant need to examine this aspect of contemporary death and dying. It is not appropriate to presume that living in a post-secular, globally connected world means either a slewing towards an uptake of religiosity (as some would see in the increasing political influence of fundamentalist religions in secular institutions such as government) that is a backlash against the expansion of secularism across many aspects of social organization and belief. Or a complete disengagement from funeral rites in general (dualism taking form as groups polarized against each other either opposing fundamentalism or between fundamentalists and secularists). This either/or approach to understanding what is happening in the world in relation to religion, death and globalization is, it is argued, better to be approached as a both/and situation, where multiple viewpoints and means of engagement are both present. But this is explainable not through the notion of a continuum, as this merely describes rather than explains the relative relationships between the various positions. It is better to consider it by using the notion of embeddedness in the sense that it means paying attention to the influence of social context as being able to explain the different ways in which people are carrying out their funeral rites, if they do so at all. To return to post-communist Czechoslovakia's trends in death rites: with the opening up of the communist bloc from the late 1980s onwards, a return to religious rites in death practices could be expected as the censure and prohibition associated with the eschewal of religion eased. A return to religiosity would be in line with arguments about one effect of globalization being the increased presence and power of fundamentalist religious movements in relation to world politics. However, this does not seem to be the case in Czechoslovakia for either the religious *or* the secular minded.

It is acceptable to expect two linked trends – the increased personalization of funerals and the increased spiritualization/religiosity of funeral rites in a post-secular era. Furthermore, it is legitimate to interpret these trends as an outcome of increasing cultural diversity that is a consequence of migration and communication across cultures and a pluralist political environment (see Howarth, 2007, ch. 11). What is interesting about post-communist Czechoslovakia is that a return to religiosity, or a re-enchantment embedded in a post-secular era is not immediately apparent. This expectation does not seem to be borne out empirically. On the one hand, for those who are of a secular disposition, people are moving away increasingly from funeral rites altogether (instead of there being an increase in the personalization of secular humanist funerals). Those with a religious disposition find that religious codes have not fully reasserted themselves in the content of religious funerals. Because, institutionally, 'in the Czech Republic, control of the funeral industry has been granted to private businesses in the form of funeral directors who pursue activities that were formerly (till 1990) regulated by the state'; that is, funeral directors provide a secular funeral template within which religious figures can only partially influence proceedings (Nosporova, 2007, p. 1189). Added to this, the Czech Republic has remained, through all these profound cultural transformations, a relatively ethnically homogenous country with a very small proportion of immigrants.

What consequences does the Czech case have for a discussion about the influence of globalization on the nexus of death, religion and society? It highlights that there are limitations as to how globalization can be used as *a sufficient explanation* for changes in death rites. One effect of globalization on death rites (for example, the rise in fundamentalism and the use of good deaths within those political objectives) cannot be generalized unproblematically across all contexts within which globalization is having an impact. How globalization impacts on death and religion cannot be generalized without taking stock of the existing contexts within which these broader social changes have taken place.

Conclusion

Globalization is recognized as a contemporary set of processes that bring about cultural mixing. In terms of death rites, it has been argued that this effect appears as the individualization of funeral rites in response to the pluralization of beliefs and the greater ease with which people can pick and mix the symbolic resources they would draw upon in their death rites – the personalization of funeral rites is a recognized feature of funerals, especially in Western Europe, the USA and the Antipodes. Theoretically, this move towards increased personalization is often cast as a re-enchantment because many personalized funerals tend to combine a focus on the individual with more spiritually symbolic rites (balloons, candles, spreading ashes at a sacred place for the deceased, for example). A general re-enchantment is argued to be a means of understanding the rise in religiosity (fundamentalisms as well as New Age and Green movements) in advanced modernity. There are strong conceptual connections made between the evident surge in religiosity, the increase in the public presence, and the everyday acceptability of spirituality connected to the well-documented personalization of funerals. However, this line of argument and explanation – advanced modernity, post-secularity, religious revival and personalization – is not necessarily borne out when it comes to substantiating these claims and expectations for the nexus of religion, death and society under these conditions.

Both Heaven's Gate and 9/11 protagonists bear the hallmarks of a technologically sophisticated post-secular social contradiction. They were simultaneously in contempt of yet drew upon the advanced modern world to achieve their aims. The Czech case also highlights the enduring influence of cultural traditions and history as profoundly influencing shifts in social practice from expected/sanctioned secular funeral rites to a more open acceptance of both secular and religious rites. The unexpected trend for *not* personalizing funerary rites and actually stepping away from them completely in an increasing number of cases calls into question the direct connections presumed to exist between globalization and its concomitant cultural mixing, which sees fundamentalism or democratic pluralism as a widespread response. The expectation for both increased numbers of religious of funeral rites and the increased personalization of funerals, is not borne out.

Debates about secularism and enchantment, while not ever likely to be resolved conclusively, shed useful light on explaining the current social contexts within which religiosity and death are played out. There are multiple ways in which globalization, religion and death are connected in contemporary debates and in people's everyday actions. The existing literature on death and dying offers various ways of conceptualizing the multiplicity and complexities of contemporary death rites in relation to religion. Ways in which death and religion are approached within the sociology of death and dying suggest that globalization is necessary but insufficient to explain adequately the different ways in which death and religion are playing out on the global stage today.

Questions

This chapter was concerned with religion, death and society. A central argument in this area of death studies is that religion's influence over death rites and beliefs has waned in contemporary society.

1. How would you explain the rise in the use of religious beliefs for political ends?
2. Would you agree that there has been a re-enchantment of advanced modern society (for example, seen in the popular resurgence of interest in communicating with the dead). Why/Why not?
3. Do you think it is it possible to be a sociologist and adhere to a religious faith? Whether you answer yes or no, explain how your answer influences your understanding of death.

Chapter 9

Representations of Mortality: Watching Real Death Is Good?

Introduction

> Just hours before the Olympic Opening Ceremonies in Vancouver for the start of the 2010 Winter Olympics, a Georgian luger, Nodar Kumaritashvili, was killed in a horrific accident on a training run ... Witnesses to the accident say the 21-year-old was near the end of a practice run when something went wrong and he suddenly went airborne, hitting a steel pole. Rescue workers performed chest compressions for less than a minute before airlifting the young luger to a nearby medical facility in Whistler. Ruben Gonzalez, a member of the Argentinean luge team who had once trained with Kumaritashvili, told ABC News Sports Radio, 'Everybody gasped, a collective gasp, and I've been in the sport since '84, and I've never seen anybody fly out of a track before. (Yahoo Voices, 2010)

A video of the crash went viral on the internet within minutes of the incident.

The moment of Kumaritashvili's death unfolded in full view of a global audience. Some part of the Winter Olympics held in Vancouver, Canada, in 2010 was watched by 190,000,000 people. At least 2 million people replayed the video of the fatal impact on YouTube before Google, who control access to YouTube, pulled the footage on a copyright technicality lodged by the International Olympic Committee. Briefly the focus of intense media scrutiny, the footage of this man's death changed status. The clip was banned from repetition on the internet and went underground for approximately six months before beginning to reappear in a repackaged format. The footage was exactly the same, but the viewing architecture had transformed. This time, the clip was a eulogy. Sombre music played quietly in the background as the associated text talked of Kumaritashvili's death as sacred – he died doing what he loved for the benefit of his country and for that, viewers are guided to feel pride and awe as well as shock and curiosity. The footage remained the same, yet the meanings associated with consuming it altered drastically from newsworthy information, to illicit and perverse entertainment, then finally to sacred homage.

Kumaritashvili's demise epitomizes the terms and conditions for representing death in a global age: the immediacy and communicative reach of the graphic, real-time footage of his demise *and* the unstable moral status of these few fleeting seconds of footage reveal the interplay of new global communicative technologies with moral codes for representing death.

Death has always been a vector for cultural communication. Death can only ever be thought about in the abstract world of representations, and perhaps because of this, it has an enduring presence in the realm of cultural production. Death has been the muse of cultural producers from time immemorial, be they painters, playwrights, philosophers, novelists, comics, politicians or priests. From the dawn of human time, the earliest cave paintings depict hunts that are life-threatening escapades for both hunters and hunted alike. Even though we may never know what life was really like back then, their use of media to communicate about life and death leaves a message for us to ponder.

With its focus on social formations, change, institutions and identity, sociology cannot but concern itself with the methods and processes of sense-making. These methods and processes are closely aligned with culture. In this discussion, culture is taken to mean all the different objects, meanings and practices that people devise to give meaning to (and take it from) their formal and informal social actions. While the cultural domain is expansive, it always involves a connection between the collective media (the methods) and communication (the processes) of sense-making in society. How and what people communicate with each other shapes society, and vice versa.

The enduring presence of death images in cultural communication suggests that there is a close relationship between the depiction of death and forms of social life. Theoretically, the enduring challenge for sociologists is to explain how communication about death links to broader social beliefs, behaviours and organization. This chapter introduces ways in which sociologists have examined and explained the media's relationship to death and society. It details how death images are used to give form and meaning to society in general, and how they alter over time as social formations change. It also considers sociological theories about the significance of these changes for the nature of contemporary death ways.

When sociologists interested in death and dying focus on the media they have a large set of more general intellectual resources from which to draw. Sociologically oriented studies of the media are concerned to recognize and study the impact of communication media on every aspect of social living. Scholars of death and dying tend to pay most attention to the presence, form, impact and influence of death messages on the living. Chapter 1 discussed how the anthropology of death and dying draws strong connections between the cultural and moral dimensions of death to reveal how death rites give shape and meaning to people's worlds and help to re-establish social order.

The sociology of media and communication is also concerned with aspects of culture, but instead of rituals and rites, it focuses on shifting institutions, form and content to focus on the effects that the media have on people's behaviour and wider society. For example, does watching violent deaths on television, even highly stylized, fictional ones, increase the chances of cultural consumers killing innocent others in their everyday lives? Or is there a threat to democracy posed by the question of whether governments have the right to censor images of war casualties as part of the need to manage troop and enemy morale?

From a sociological point of view, the media can be analysed on three interconnected levels: production, text and audience. Production concerns the material organization of its production and reception (for example, the organization of the film industry). Text analysis is about understanding how the stories are told – that is, the genre. It examines how symbols and messages frame the readers' interpretation of a text, and what their symbolic intent may signify about the society that consumes the images. For example, the rise in popularity of the 'un-dead' genre in recent popular culture is striking, with its dozens of vampire and zombie television series and Hollywood films both in circulation and in production. Howarth suggests that, symbolically, this explosion of interest in the un-dead conveys the long-held connection between death and sexual lust, and that their rise in popularity coincides with a growing awareness of the moral dangers of unprotected sex in an age of HIV/AIDS: 'the vampire's association with blood and sexual lust could thus be viewed as symbolic of the moral panic of the period when both blood and sex were associated with death' (Howarth, 2007, p. 107). Pushing her analysis further, Howarth suggests that their popularity is a cultural recognition and articulation of the fragility of the boundary between the living and the dead, a boundary effectively dismantled by medical practices, as discussed in Chapter 2 of this book.

The third analytical approach focuses on media influence on the audience, and includes debates about the processes and consequences of ideological effects, and audience reception and consumption on human behaviour. In terms of death and dying, there is a pervasive belief in the power of the media to affect people's behaviour in problematic ways. For example, such a belief underpins any attempts at censorship and explains why in many countries the media are legally restricted in, if not outright banned from, reporting details about suicide in the press and the broadcast news.

Nervousness about the power of the media in relation to death has a long history. More than 200 years ago, the belief in the power of narratives to influence people's thoughts prompted German authorities of the time to ban the novel *The Sufferings of Young Werther* by Johann Wolfgang von Goethe (Goethe, [1800]1957) because it had been found in the possession of some young men who had killed themselves. Much more recently, at the end of the twentieth century, concerts by musician and artist Marilyn Manson were banned by certain states in the USA because it was claimed that those responsible for the Columbine massacre – a school shooting in which 12 students and a teacher were killed – had been listening to Marilyn Manson's music just prior to their onslaught in April 1999.[1] Despite these strongly held beliefs, and even though indirect associations between reporting and rates of suicide are evident, it has been impossible for researchers to find a *direct* link between consuming death representations and bringing about death in others (violence and murder) or oneself (suicide) (Stack, 2003). The ambiguity in the scientific literature centres on the problem of how to understand the way that people interpret what they see, and how those interpretations link to their behaviour. The great majority of people have read about or seen thousands of deaths in fiction, and been informed of just as many real deaths through the news media, yet the proportion of people who have become killers or suicides is infinitesimally small in comparison.

To gain as accurate a sense as possible of the connections between death representations and society, it is best to understand that these three dimensions, of material, textual and audience reception, are linked, albeit indirectly, to each other. Changes in the material organization of the media, such as a technological shift from mass to networked media, or a shift from national, state-run media to global corporate media, will be implicated in shifts of the kinds of genres (texts) that are distributed and may become popular. Also, the ways in which people take up and interpret the images and narratives they consume will depend on the kinds of interactions that the media technology supports – whether that is shouting at the TV or blogging with thousands of others about a YouTube upload. Pulling these three strands together and tracing the kinds and effects of death images can be a complicated business. The strategy employed here is to categorize all the potential ways that death can be portrayed, along two axes. One axis is that death representations can be about ordinary or extraordinary deaths, and the other axis is that representations are about either real or fictional deaths. This generates four categories of death representation: fictional accounts of ordinary deaths, actual accounts of ordinary deaths, fictional accounts of extraordinary deaths, or actual accounts of extraordinary deaths. Every news item, story, painting or communiqué about death can be organized into these four categories. Their relative presence (for example, the predominance of extraordinary fantasy death representations) within a particular society helps to reveal the broad social messages about death that prevail there.

A fascinating feature of the ways that these material, textual and influence dimensions come together in death representations is that they are *always* concerned with the moral order. Media representations of death are more than the sum of their parts. The way they come together helps us shift and shape our moral worlds. The sociology of death and dying is wise to pay attention to how death images play a part in the making of people's moral worlds, because the collective sense of what is moral and just under-pins individual and collective action in any society. Understanding how death is portrayed through the media is part and parcel of understanding a society and its potentially contradictory concerns, be that supporting the production of nuclear warheads or protesting against their production.

Sacred and profane representations of death

When we see images and video footage of death, those images are *always* morally loaded. Chapter 1 introduced the idea that death is central to social relations, and one way this happens is through taboo. In *Purity and Danger*, Mary Douglas tells us that taboo 'confronts the ambiguous and shunts it into the category of the sacred' (Douglas, [1966]2002, p. viii–xi). The purpose of a taboo is to preserve the boundary between the sacred and the profane, and to prevent the sacred from being defiled by the profane. The mixing of sacred and profane has the effect of polluting what was once sacred; it becomes morally dubious and open to censure. Consider the following example of a Holocaust float in the 2008 Rio de Janeiro carnival: a float made up of a pile of models of naked and emaciated dead bodies atop a collection of shoes and personal objects recalled the horrific sights with which Second World War allies were faced with when they gained access to Treblinka, Belsen, Buchenwald and other death camps run by the Nazis (see Figure 9.1). These death camps were set up by the Nazis in their quest to exterminate people from across Europe of whom they morally disapproved, including Jewish people, gypsies, mentally and physically infirm people, and political dissidents such as communists.

The float, a fictitious rendition of extraordinary deaths, caused great consternation and debate among the carnival organizers because, on the one hand, the float was seen as a respectful reminder of those who had been persecuted and tortuously killed, a lest we forget *memento mori*, but on the other hand, it was also interpreted as disrespectful because it mixed up symbols that were not supposed to be combined. A carnival float is under-stood as a symbol of joyful, playful celebration of the everyday fun of living, and this stood in sharp contrast, illustrating the pervasive fear and sense of evil that is symbolically associated with the Holocaust. The sacred status of Holocaust victims was sullied, profaned, made bad and preten-tious because it was intended to be used in a profane or everyday context of celebration and community participation. The float was later banned from appearing in the carnival.

The status of real images of death is even more contentious. If such images are sacred, part of that status means that they carry a symbolic load. They are taken to represent or embody significant meanings and values. This can be seen in public controversies about broadcasting executions. In 2002, Daniel Pearl, an American journalist was kidnapped while in

Figure 9.1   Worker prepares a float for Rio de Janeiro Carnival, 2008

Source: Tranz International (representing Reuters Image in New Zealand). Photographer Sergio Moraes, Brazil, 2008.

Pakistan investigating Al Qaeda, who captured and beheaded him. His capture, internment and subsequent execution were recorded and a video was released to the media. The video was edited with voice-over and images to convey the point that Muslims were subjected to the same kinds of terror, capture and murder, and that, as a consequence, all Americans could be subject to Pearl's fate if stated demands were not met. Another example, a video of Taliban members stoning a Pakistani couple to death for alleged adultery shows how footage of violent deaths is used deliberately to instil fear and in this way attempt to control the actions of other members of the same society. These executions and their public dissemination were used deliberately as part of a political strategy of fear and intimidation. This is morally problematic because such actions are evidence of breaking a globally held value (the basic human right to be protected from mob rule and violence). At the same time, watching the footage is also deeply problematic, because the viewer becomes party to the victims' disempowerment and defilement. The pollution associated with breaking the taboo of murder and watching murder was captured ably by the US media, who branded them political snuff films.

Sociologists, then, are concerned with categories of death representation that prevail, the moral significance attached to them, and the social forces (material, textual and influential) that underpin them. To be able to see what is specific about codes of death representation in advanced modernity, it is important to have as clear as possible a sense of what the existing codes of death representation are in contemporary Western societies and how they are explained (theorized). The focus is on Western societies because it is from within their modern midst that global technologies and relations emerged and took full shape on the world stage.

Moral codes representing death

The codes and conventions for representing death in cultural artefacts in Western society have long been the subject of study. Philippe Ari s' discussion of *Ars moriendi,* in *Western Attitudes toward Death* (Ariès, 1974) is taken as a classic account of the changing moral codes for approaching death associated with the emergence of individualism and linked to the Late Middle Ages. Thornton and Phillips (2010) comment on the cultural status of the text:

> At a time when dying could be viewed as a performed battle against damnation, the *Ars moriendi* codified a set of moral precepts that governed the expression of autonomy, relations between the dying and the living and orientation towards God. In these images, dying well is a moral activity that results from active decisions by the dying person to turn from earthly preoccupations to contemplation of, and submission to, the divine. (Thornton and Phillips, 2010, p. 94)

Thornton and Phillips and Ariès' discussion of *Ars moriendi* describes the special circumstances under which these representations of death were to be used. *Ars moriendi* books and woodcuts were representations of death that were set apart in that they had a specific and solemn moral purpose of guiding people towards appropriate behaviour during their death by highlighting the rewards of choosing the good and the terrors of choosing the bad. As cultural artefacts, the *Ars moriendi* were themselves taboo in that they were specialized texts for the specific task of communicating the socially sanctioned way of dying. They depicted everyman's death, from pauper to king. The dominance of ordinary realistic death representations has been linked to the prevalence and visibility of death in everyday pre-modern European and American life (Stannard, 1977; Llewellyn, 1997; Hallam and Hockey, 2001).

Through the centuries, as popular culture has transformed from woodcuts and ballads to novels and newspapers, popular texts that exercise reflections on death continue to be popular. For example, the novel *Little Women* by Louisa May Alcott (1832–1888) follows four girls – Meg, Jo, Beth and Amy – as they face the trials and tribulations of growing up in New England during the American Civil War. Almost autobiographical, the declining family fortunes and the death of Beth are key plot devices for Alcott to explore American attitudes to the role of women and the effects of grief on family relations. Of interest here, Alcott uses Beth's death as a catalyst for her sister Jo to pursue the goal of financially supporting her family through a writing career. Here, the death caused by marauding infectious disease prompts significant distress and disruption of the close-knit family and a highly individualized personal re-evaluation. The emerging American values of industriousness and personal fulfilment are in direct response to death. Alcott's story offered a way for readers to interpret Beth's death as sacred because it embodied the new values of a transforming society. Again, a fictitious account of an ordinary, everyday death is a pivotal point in the narrative.

While Alcott and other writers used the novel genre and the death plot device to explore emergent new social values, other cultural analysts have paid attention to the ways that representations of death alter as communication technologies advance. The impact of photographic and visual mass media (especially film) technologies on the representation of death has garnered special attention from sociologists. In *Ways of Seeing*, John Berger (1972) grapples with the generic limitations of representing death while at the same time explaining the new social possibilities associated with the advent of visual accuracy and the capacity for exact and limitless reproduction embodied in photographs.

The link with the once-living that photographic and filmic technologies capture, draws a powerful distinction between fictional representations of death and a record of a real death. This is profound, because documentary images 'ask us to consider it as a representation of the historical world rather than a likeness to or imitation of it. The image of the death of an individual purports to record the *actual, physical* death of that person rather than a mimetic representation of death' (Nichols, 1991, p. 110; emphasis added). The symbolic challenge of physically accurate representations of real death was not possible until the invention of photography and film.

Joy Ruby's *Secure the Shadow* (1995) examines in detail how this new technology engaged with existing cultural rules, regulations and stylistic conventions associated with death. She fleshes out many of the specific codes that set out the limits and signs of appropriate behaviour around death relations in the USA from the 1840s to the late 1980s. For Ruby, photographs of the dead have been socially sanctioned cultural artefacts associated with legitimate and healthy mourning practices: 'In the nineteenth century, the personal desire for a corpse or funeral photograph was socially appropriate and the behaviour was supported by the culture. One could publicly display the photographs without fear of being regarded as pathological' (Ruby, 1995, p. 188). Corpse photography involves using the mediating technologies of the stills camera to emphasize the significance of direct personal relations between the deceased and those who grieve for them. Ruby charted the growing restriction of death representations, where the use of corpse photographs became 'more guarded, absent from family albums and shown only to selected people' (Ruby, 1995, p. 161).

Berger's and Ruby's work points out how new technologies can have multiple effects: they offer new ways to represent death; but these technologies also give rise to new moral ambiguities that need to be re-incorporated into the prevailing moral order. Sometimes they are absorbed into the status quo, while at other times they herald a shift in the position of death in society.

Ruby talked of a re-calibration of death images, with ordinary deaths receding into the private realm of family memorabilia alongside the increasing individualization and privatization of the modern American family of the twentieth century. This re-calibration involves the resolution of moral dilemmas that show the connections between social values and social practice. Viewing the images of real dead people provokes contradictions that seek moral resolution in the communities of concern. Quoting writers from the *Atlantic Monthly* and the *New York Times*, Meinwald (1990) explored how new technologies (photography) quickly become subject to rules for appropriate engagement. The first war photographs showing dead soldiers were from the Battle of Antietam, in the American Civil War. When the photographs were put on public display, prominent commentators in highly influential papers (the *Atlantic Monthly* and the *New York Times*) modelled the way for viewers to approach and interpret these exhibitions as horrific yet honorific images, because they attested to the gruesome, but necessary, war:

> Many people would not look through this series. Many, having seen it and dreamed of its horrors, would lock it up in some secret drawer, that it might not thrill or revolt those whose soul sickens at such sights. It was so nearly like visiting the battlefield to look over these views, that all the emotions excited by the actual sight of the stained and sordid scene, strewed with rags and wrecks, came back to us [yet] the end to be attained justifies the means, we are willing to believe … yet through such martyrdom must come our redemption. War is the surgery of crime. Bad as it is in itself, it always implies that something worse has gone before. Where is the American, worthy of his privileges, who does not now recognize the fact, if never until now, that the disease of our nation was organic, not functional, calling for the knife, and not for washes and anodynes? (Meinwald, 1990)

Meinwald shows the special terms for when the representation of death is permissible.

Debate over whether or not to hide the casualties of war from the American populace has a long history. During the Second World War, it was not until 1944 that President Franklin D. Roosevelt lifted the ban on publishing photographs of dead American troops as it is said that he was worried that Americans at home were becoming complacent about the war. The iconic *Three dead Americans lie on the beach at Buna* photograph taken in Papua New Guinea helped to galvanize the war effort at the same time that it told readers they did not need to know the identity of the soldiers to appreciate what they had done. The publication of images of war dead continues to cause public consternation. In January 1991, the Pentagon made the decision not to allow the public dissemination of photographs of caskets being returned from the wars in Iraq and Afghanistan. Though contested in the US Court of Appeals in 1996, and subject to ongoing criticism from media organizations and the bereaved relatives of the soldiers killed in combat, the ban has been upheld. The public display of the war dead confronts the ambiguity of death and shunts it into the category of the sacred. Viewing war dead is appropriate *only* when it helps to explain this war as for the greater good. Otherwise, it is illicit and to be condemned.

Geoffrey Gorer theorized this transformation in death representation as the *Pornography of Death* (1955; 1965). The increasingly restrictive rules associated with emotionally repressive culture has rendered death images illicit and relegated them to the realms of titillating fantasy similar to the burgeoning sexual pornography of the sexually repressive Victorian era. As sex becomes pornographic when divorced from the emotion of love, so death becomes pornographic when divorced from the emotion of grief. Gorer's theory of the *pornographic turn* in death representation hinges on a particular understanding of how modern Western societies work. The rise in the belief in science and the pressure to individualize has led to the profound dismissal of existing Western death culture. Alongside other social theorists, such as Philippe Ariès (1974) and Norbert Elias (1985), Gorer proclaimed that death was badly handled by modern society. Ritual elements had been cast aside and death was no longer an appropriate topic of conversation, leaving people unsupported and so unable to cope with the painful losses of death. Their form of understanding the taboo of death is to regard it as fully banned, and since needs must come out, it has reappeared in illicit fantasy, forming 'a society that refuses to talk of death personally becomes obsessed with horror comics, war movies and disasters' (Walter, 1991, p. 295).

One effect of taboos is that as they load special significance and meaning on to particular objects and values, and these things become fetishized. Gorer's pornography of death is about death becoming a focus of unusual attention and used as an avenue for gratification that leads to the likes of the website SeeMeRot.com. This is a site linked to a webcam purportedly placed inside a coffin that allows viewers to watch a corpse slowly decompose in real time. Whether real or fake, SeeMeRot.com is associated with the adult entertainment business, and highlights the close links between sexual and other fetishes and the taboo of representing death.

The unique contours of this modern Western death taboo on representing death is deftly outlined by Sobchack (1984): in modern Westernized societies, representations of actual deaths are rendered nearly invisible, and fantasy deaths are almost always unusual (violent) deaths. The vast majority of death representations are *fictitious*, and these deaths are also dominated by unusual, often violent, deaths (Sobchack, 1984, pp. 285–6). The dominance of fictitious, extraordinary deaths and the near invisibility of ordinary factual deaths in films and photography of the twentieth century is because the capacity to capture death in image and film was used in service of prevailing pornographic death taboos of the mid-twentieth century. The status quo prevailed. The representation of *real* death has become severely restricted. Not only has the event of natural death been removed from everyday sight, but when real deaths are represented, they are almost always extraordinary – for example, as the result of murder or war.

It is worth noting that the theory of the pornography of death considers the media to be merely a conduit for existing moral orders. Attitudes to the media have changed: it is now widely accepted that it has significant influence over the meanings and values it disseminates in its own right. Brought to public attention by cultural studies,[2] contemporary sociologists of death and dying are now mindful of the multi-faceted ways in which the construction of news media items influences their reception and interpretation. One consequence of this raised awareness is that sociologists of death and dying have paid increasing attention to the influence of material production on the form, content and reception of death portrayals. This has become particularly significant in recent decades, because of the ways that the material organization of the media has been transformed and the media's presence in everyday life has grown.

Current debates around the sociology of death and dying recognize the increasing presence of the media in everyday life. This has drawn the pornography of death thesis into question and caused researchers to revisit the issue of whether death itself is still taboo in advanced modern society. For example, Walter (1991) points to how multiple social trends – such as the move to an expressive society heralded by the counter-culture of the 1960s, the hospice, green and feminist movements – suggest the ongoing reworking and transformation of the rules of engagement embedded in the death taboo. Walter's work, amongt other contributions,[3] clearly points out that taboos – that is, the rules for appropriate behaviour around an ambiguity – are dynamic social relations, constantly under negotiation and review as broader social contexts change – and those contexts have changed markedly in recent decades.

The world of representation has undergone significant technological transformation. Humankind now lives in an era of global instantaneous communication by many for many, where the technology for capturing and transmitting high-quality images and sound is within the reach of a large proportion of the world's population. There has been a general increase in all forms of the representation of death, in line with the proliferation of media images in general. This shift is increasingly acknowledged and documented in death studies and media research (Gibson, 2007). The relative weight of different kinds of death images is also shifting. In 1989, Michael Kearl shared startling statistics that 'by the age of 16, according to the National Institute of Mental Health, the typical American had witnessed some 18,000 homicides on television' (Kearl, 1989, p. 383). In comparison, today's 16-year-old will not only have witnessed many thousands of homicides on TV, is likely to have also participated in the virtual killing of many more thousands in video games; viewed increasingly realistically graphic content on prime-time crime shows; come across dramas that make death their focal point week after week; replayed YouTube uploads of war footage, torture, violent political agitation and retaliation; contributed to Facebook pages of friends, or friends of friends, killed through their own or others' risk-taking behaviour, and if they live in the Netherlands, have watched a game show where competitors vied for the organs of a terminally ill judge.

In recent years, the sociology of death and dying has sought to explain how the ways that death is represented in the media have altered, and link this to the ways in which the role and presence of the media has shifted in general society. After examining how disasters are currently being portrayed in the mass media, Walter (2006) interprets the changes at the level of social institutions. For him, the increasing influence of the media in everyday life and portrayals of death is because they are coming to replace the church as the social institution responsible for guiding communities through the morass of ethical dilemmas elicited by the ever-increasing media presence of real deaths. Focused more on the subjective experiences and understandings of death (which link to identity formation; see Chapter 1), Margaret Gibson (2007) theorizes that the shift in death from private experiences and places to more public spheres highlights a paradox peculiar to globally mediated societies. Though new technologies increasingly blur the distinction between real and simulated deaths, paradoxically new media forms lay bare the brute fact that 'all the narratives and images which have shaped and informed an individual consciousness do not necessarily prepare for witnessing death and experiencing grief' (Gibson, 2007, p. 423).

Recent technological transformations have had a profound influence, not only on the number but also on the kinds of images of the death that are publicly available. There have been changes to the terms of the taboos associated with representing death that, to extend Walter, reveal the different ways in which the media are now using death to embody shared values. There has been a revelatory turn, seen in the corpsification of prime-time television, the increasing number of detailed depictions of ordinary deaths in documentaries, the emergence of reality death television, and the increasing presence of actual footage of real deaths in news media. Though not able to resolve the enduring gulf between death representations and life experience, the shift in media practice highlights the increasingly public negotiation of ambiguity and ambivalence that informs ethical practice in the everyday world.

Representing death in advanced modernity

The distinctive feature of the portrayal of death during a global age is that 'death is more real in the mediatized world of global communication'. To explain what this means, and also give examples of this incongruous phenomenon, this section shows how the component relationships of death representation (fictionalized and actual accounts of ordinary and extraordinary deaths) have become reconfigured. Before explaining this reconfiguration more fully, we first outline the new technological advance in representation that has made the shift possible: media convergence.

Media convergence means the bringing together of computing, communications and content. This has happened at two interlocking levels. One is technologies where 'creative content has been converted into industry-standard digital forms for delivery through broadband or wireless networks for display on various computer or computer-like devices, from cellular telephones to personal digital assistants (PDAs) to digital video recorders (DVRs) hooked up to televisions' (Flew, 2010). The other is at industry level, where 'companies across the business spectrum from media to telecommunications to technology have merged or formed strategic alliances in order to develop new business models that can profit from the growing consumer expectation for "on-demand" content' (ibid.). One consequence of media convergence with implications for death representation

> is the growth of a 'flatter' publishing structure that allows one-to-one and many-to-many distributions of content. This development contrasts sharply with the one-to-many distribution that was characteristic of twentieth-century mass communications. Digital publishing also has empowered many ordinary individuals to become involved directly or through collaborative efforts in creating new content because of the dramatically reduced barriers to producing and distributing digital content over the Internet. (Ibid.)

The culture of electronic media is characterized by full aural and oral sensory experiences, and global real-time coverage gives events immediacy and salience despite geographic dislocation. Some would argue that a result of technological innovation and worldwide expansion is that multiple forms of the media have become powerful agents of international affairs. The process is known as mediatization (Briggs and Burke, 2009).

One consequence of media convergence is the increasing mediatization of death. This is where communication about death is almost without exception relayed via communication and IT technologies. The influence of media convergence on the representation of death is yet to be fully understood, but it is possible to discern some changes in the types of representations of death that are now possible. The task of the next section is to give some examples of how representations of death may be being done differently as a consequence of media convergence, mediatization and the media effect. It discusses the relative shift between the four types of death representation and the new kinds of moral dilemmas they instigate.

Fictional accounts of ordinary deaths

Until the mid-1990s, ordinary deaths had little presence, either in fiction or documentary form, thus upholding Vivian Sobchack's claim about the ways in which the taboo of the pornography of death made itself felt in mid-twentieth-century representations of death. A tongue-in-cheek analysis of types and rates of death suffered by characters in the genre most associated with representations of everyday issues and struggles concluded that

> staying alive in a television soap opera is not easy. Standardised mortality rations for characters were among the highest for any occupation yet described, and this was not just because all causes of death were overrepresented. Deaths in soap operas were almost three times more likely to be from violent causes than would be expected from a character's age and sex. A character in *Eastenders* was twice as likely as a similar character in *Coronation Street* to die during an episode. (Crayford, 1997, p. 16)

Since the late 1980s, the depiction of believable narratives of ordinary deaths has been catapulted into the limelight of the global broadcast mass media. The worldwide explosion of fictionalized narratives of ordinary deaths is embodied in the focus and unprecedented success of the first television series to take the subject of death and dying as it explicit theme, HBO's *Six Feet Under*, a

> critically acclaimed television series that averaged 5.7 million viewers for its first two seasons and earned six Emmy awards, two Golden Globes and was syndicated around the world. Each episode begins with a portrayal of a common, everyday situation in which one of the people involved meets his or her death, typically portrays the impact of death in those closest to the deceased, as well as providing an ongoing account of the personal lives and careers of each member of the Fisher family [who were running a business as undertakers]. (Schiappa *et al.*, 2010, p. 462)

Since *Six Feet Under* broke the ground for the accurate portrayal of ordinary deaths, more series that have death as its narrative driver have followed. For example, Showtime's *The Big C,* released in 2010, promotes itself as a series where a suburban mother, diagnosed with terminal melanoma, tries to find the humour in the disease, and there is a unifying theme of 'how one woman deals with being told she has Stage 4 Malignant Melanoma but who decides to not inform anyone of her diagnosis, instead going after the outrageous way of living that has always been foreign to her obsessive/compulsive teacher personality' (IMDb, 2010). Within two months of its first USA airing (August 2010), *The Big C* was being broadcast in Canada, Israel, Australia, Turkey and New Zealand.

Apart from covering everyday deaths as an integral part of the narrative of each episode, series such as *Six Feet Under* also contain realistic depictions of events, contexts and consequences of death:

> A number of episodes provide information about what happens to the body after death, including portrayals of bodies in various states of preparation in the funeral home, identifying the body at the morgue, post-mortem erections, bodily noises and smells, preparation of the body for open casket viewings, and the speed at which the human body decomposes. (Schiappa *et al.*, 2010, p. 463)

Everyday deaths are now present in fictionalized accounts of death and dying in ways that they have never been before, and they rapidly gain international recognition.

Ordinary deaths now hold a significant and growing profile in fictional representations of death in globally syndicated multi-media programming. What is pertinent for this chapter is that the growing presence of ordinary believable death scenarios suggests an emerging headspace for realistic deaths in the realms of global entertainment.

Actual accounts of ordinary deaths

In step with the rising star of realistic narratives of fictionalized deaths, the presence of actual ordinary deaths has also emerged from the shadows. There has been a long literary tradition of writing about sickness, death and loss. This tradition transposed as new multi-media cultural forms emerged. As television and films became popular and accessible, the real life *death dramas* of the stars became the topics of public consumption and integrated into celebrity life. There are numerous examples of Hollywood death watches that include John Wayne's and Freddie Mercury's terminal declines in1978 and 1991, respectively. In the latter few months of 2010, the trajectory of Michael Douglas's throat cancer was charted unremittingly in numerous globally syndicated weekly magazine stories, even though at the time of writing (March 2012) he is still alive.

Ordinary deaths have also become the focus for artistic exhibitions: photographers and multi-media artists set to gather and document accounts of their own and other's everyday dying. One early example, *One Woman's Story*, documents the last two years of Joan Robinson's life with ovarian cancer (Markusen *et al.*, 1980). This was followed by *One Dark Mile: A Widower's Story* by her husband, Eric Robinson (1990). Between them they reveal a shift towards self-reflexive narratives made by the dying people themselves, and their immediately bereaved. Another example is by British photographer, Jo Spence, who shook the art world with her thought-provoking and poignant self-portraits about her struggle with breast cancer, which ended with her death in 1992. Joan and Eric Robinson's and Jo Spence's publicly acknowledged personal reflexivity over their mortality paved the way for many more such explorations. One could almost say that their work, became the advanced guard for a trend towards the public support and consumption of representations of actual ordinary deaths. For example, Ellen Innis developed the project of 'photographic self-portraits made in the presence of mortality' that was published as *Reveries: Photography and Mortality* (Ennis, 2007). This series of texts and photography explored many deaths from many places. The distinctiveness of the project is emphasized by the way it brings together personal images that encompass surgery scars, mortuary portraits and body preparation in funeral homes 'to raise public awareness about aspects of death that would otherwise be hidden' (Ennis, 2007, p. 37). November 2010 saw the opening of *Stardust: Some Thoughts on Death* – the result of a year's work by Glasgow-based artist, Gillian Steel, who had been exploring the theme of mortality through a series of interviews with people whose work touches on the subject of death (Steel, 2010). Ordinary Glasgow people are both subject *and* audience in this installation. They reflect upon their own and others' mortality in a public space for others' consumption.

Moving from high to popular culture, the depiction of ordinary deaths has become an acceptable topic for documentaries that explore the ways in which contemporary societies institutionally organize for death in a context of ageing populations, mobile individuals and digitally connected communities. Some examples include the UK's Channel 4 documentary series *Death*, first transmitted in July 2002 and now globally syndicated through Sky TV. This series explores the end-of-life trajectories of a handful of British people with terminal cancer, of different genders, sexualities, life stages and ethnicities. Another, a one-off documentary for the British series *Dispatches*, by sociologist Laurie Taylor, called *On Pain of Death* (2005) examines the limitations of the British National Health Service's palliative care delivery.

Everyday difficulties with ordinary deaths are similarly explored in the context of those who die with no next of kin (a growing scenario in an ageing and mobile global population). Set in Los Angeles, award-winning directors Blue Hadaegh and Grover Babcock (2005) reveal the complex and at times very moving bureaucratic procedures that are set in train when public employees handle unclaimed and sometimes unidentifiable bodies found in the jurisdiction of Los Angeles County. What is striking about this documentary is that it shows the audience the ways that contemporary

American society deals with people who die alone. Through impersonal bureaucratic procedures, people who die alone and unclaimed are assured a certain social acknowledgement. The authorities embalm and hold the deceased and their belongings for a long period in case somebody who knew them might appear. Any possessions are liquidated, and estates are duly calculated and held in trust, bar associated costs, for a considerable length of time. Even when no one appears, the person's remains are disposed of in the same way as millions of other Americans: they are cremated. Again, the cremated remains are held for a number of years, should someone wish to claim them. After such time has passed, the remains are deposited, with a short but respectful service, in marked plots for the benefit of potential future grievers or descendants. The audience is guided to understand that North America is a highly bureaucratized and technologically advanced society, and that also, as a society, it places human remains at the centre of its death practices. Authorities have taken it upon themselves to make sure that, even in the most socially-isolated of circumstances, dead people are treated in ways that fit with the contemporary way of disposing of the dead. This documentary highlights that even if a person dies alone and his or her remains are unclaimed in Los Angeles, there are hundreds of state employees involved in a highly elaborate set of procedures that focus on disposing of the deceased in appropriate and accountable ways that befit the society within which they died.

The award-winning documentary *Mademoiselle and the Doctor* follows the relationship between a 79-year-old French woman, Lisette Nigot, who lives in Australia and Dr Phillip Nitschke, a doctor who has gained worldwide attention for his active support of physician-assisted euthanasia. Mlle Nigot, though fit and healthy, has decided that she does not want to live beyond the age of 80 and the film documents the conversations between Mlle and the Doctor, wider public debate on physician assisted euthanasia (briefly legal in the Northern Territories of Australia for nine months before it being repealed in 1997), her eventual decision and the ensuing publicity. The director Janine Hosking deftly documents the contradictions inherent in societies that have ageing populations and that simultaneously laud individual autonomy while refusing citizens the legal right to be assisted in their own deaths (Hosking, 2004).

Documentaries about dying and death examine the dilemmas that face contemporary society and offer ways of informing the audience about the underlying issues of ordinary death, be they the tough decisions that worry people who are ageing in a country beset by limited health care funding, or the magnanimous role of faceless bureaucrats in the decent disposal of the unclaimed dead. These kinds of documentaries reveal the ambiguities of contemporary death practices while also encoding what is morally acceptable and unacceptable to the wider societies of which they are a part.

Reality television is a new and very popular genre of competition-based entertainment. Relatively cheap to make, reality television is premised on the belief that people enjoy watching groups of other ordinary people in competition with each other. A British talent search television series, *Pop Idol*, captured the interest of producers and consumers alike as it set everyday people with unusual talents against each other while performing for a celebrity panel of judges. The series is now syndicated globally, with over 150 countries around the world either producing their own annual *Idol* series or involved in competitions with other countries. The generic format was taken up in a most interesting way by the Dutch reality show, *De Grote Donorshow* (The Big Donor Show), broadcast in the Netherlands on 1 June 2007. Contestants were people who needed a kidney transplant, which would come from the judge, a terminally ill, 37-year-old woman. Audience members and viewers could text in who they thought most deserved her kidney, and profits made from the show were to go to the Dutch Kidney Foundation.

Revealed as a hoax during the course of the show, it courted great controversy because of the way it combined the sacred with the profane and blurred the boundaries between what was real and what was not. The reality show was a hoax; in real life the judge was an actress who did not have a terminal illness, but the contestants really did need kidney transplants. It also mixed the sacred with the profane because the show crossed existing boundaries between appropriate and inappropriate ways to raise awareness of, and raise money for, the beleaguered organ donor system in the Netherlands. Making those who are at the mercy of failed organs compete with each other for a chance of life was going too far. This was, with hindsight, not an appropriate form of entertainment. Despite, or perhaps because of, the hackles it raised, the people who devised the show reached their goal, which was to raise awareness and money for kidney donors. It brought together people facing their own mortality as a form of public entertainment and broke existing taboos, but in doing so, raised awareness of a serious social issue *and* won an International Emmy Award in 2008 for the best non-scripted entertainment.[4]

A distinctive feature of multi-media in a global age is when different media link with each other. This can be seen on the Video Nation webpage www.bbc.co.uk/videonation/network/. Since the early 2000s, Video Nation has hosted a series of amateur videos of people talking about death, sometimes their own, as a means for everyday people to both document their own take on death and dying, but also to share these musings with the world. This web presence facilitates the meshing of different though related media products and a host of individuals and communities around the world. For example, in November 2010, Video Nation linked its community documentary website with a one-off documentary on the BBC2 TV channel about changing the way the UK cares for the dying, called *How to Have a Good Death*. Containing footage of people who are terminally ill, linking across an archive platform that contains many ordinary accounts of death, and connected to a professionally produced documentary, it seeks to change contemporary social behaviour associated with the care of the dying. This cultural production sets out deliberately to change the institutional organization of the care for the dying to be more in line with the expectations and dilemmas of mobile and interconnected societies.

Terry Pratchett, the acclaimed fantasy author, having himself been diagnosed with early onset Alzheimer's disease, translated the attention drawn to his own terminal prognosis into a documentary about assisted dying, where he travels to Switzerland to film the final moments of 'Peter', a British man suffering from motor neurone disease who had chosen to end his life at the Dignitas clinic. In an advance publicity interview with *Radio Times*, Pratchett captures the moral dilemma of assisted death as he recalls his feeling just after Peter died:

> I was spinning, not because anything bad had happened but something was saying, 'A man is dead ... that's a bad thing', but somehow the second part of the clause chimes in with, 'but he had an incurable disease that was dragging him down, so he's decided of his own free will to leave before he was dragged'. So it's not a bad thing. So, then, is it a good thing? And you are trying to resolve these things. Because it is a good thing, I think, that in those circumstances Peter got what he wanted – a good death. (Dougary, 2011)

Chasing celebrities with terminal illnesses sells magazines and makes money, as do death memoirs, artistic exhibitions and fake reality television shows. Kate Berridge's *Vigor Mortis* (2001) charts the growth in this international market for terminal documentaries, personal reflections and artistic endeavours since the 1980s. What has changed in the public demand for these death-dealing cultural forms? One suggestion by Margaret Gibson is that

> the opening up of private experiences of death and grief shared with strangers is the result not just of the growth in communication and media technologies, but also the will and desire to record one's own or another significant other's existence in the face of death and its annihilations ... the rise of the individual in Western societies has enhanced the symbolic and emotional value of selves and identities to the extent that gaining celebrity, or some form of media attention or public record is a common desire. (Gibson, 2007, p. 422)

Cue Jade Goody.

Jade Goody was a dental assistant turned reality TV star who died of cervical cancer at the age of 27. Goody gained fame at 21 in 2002 when she joined the reality television show *Big Brother*, in which contestants live together for a number of weeks and are filmed constantly. Loud and brash, she became a highly divisive star – initially mocked, but later celebrated as a forthright everywoman by a hungry tabloid press. She became a national touchstone who sparked debate about race, class and celebrity. During filming of a celebrity version of *Big Brother*, in the summer of 2008, Goody was given a diagnosis of cervical cancer by telephone from a doctor in Britain. The camera captured the deeply personal moment, which was shown repeatedly on TV. The progress of her illness was chronicled in detail in the tabloid press and weekly magazines, to the unease of many. She underwent surgery and chemotherapy in the public eye, filming part of the experience for a different television series. Bald and frail, Goody married fiancé Jack Tweed in an elaborate event staged at an elegant country hotel outside London. Goody, who reportedly sold the wedding photographs for more than US$1 million, defended being paid for interviews and photo shoots: 'People will say I'm doing this for money,' she said. 'And they're right, I am. But not to buy flash cars or big houses – it's for my sons' future if I'm not here. I don't want my kids to have the same miserable, drug-blighted, poverty-stricken childhood I did' (Associated Press, 2009). This brief, apocryphal account of Jade Goody's life and death illustrates how ordinary deaths now, more than ever before, are articulated through the global mass media-fuelled cult of celebrity.

Fictional accounts of extraordinary deaths

Fictional accounts of extraordinary deaths, according to Gorer, Sobchack and others, have been the epicentre of pornographic representations of death, and taken as the central pivot of the confusing contradiction between lack of real representations alongside an abundance of extraordinary, unrealistic representations of dying and death. While recognizing the symbolic weight placed on these kinds of representations of death, given that there has been a significant shift in the place and status of ordinary deaths, this shifting configuration has an impact on the high status of fantasy extraordinary deaths (Lee, 2008, p. 746).

A curious and potentially significant trend in the representation of fictionalized extraordinary death has been the meteoric rise in popularity of a new rendition of a long-established fiction genre – the detective story. On 6 October 2000, a new genre of crime drama television series aired with the first episode of *CSI: Las Vegas*. Like *Six Feet Under*, *CSI: Las Vegas* broke ground in the popular culture representation of the dead as it placed the dead body and the lab in the centre of the dramatic arc of each episode and the series more generally. The role for the dead body is to act as the indisputable source of the truth, and the role of laboratory science is the analysis of the body that in combination will bring the killer(s) to justice. *CSI* (Crime Scene Investigation) focuses on crime scenes and this means that the deaths, because they are under criminal investigation, are by definition extraordinary. They are unusual and unexplained. They are also fictional in the sense that the crime and death scenarios are not attempting to depict everyday death scenarios. The crimes are fictional, the characters are fictional, and the CSI lab is also fictional in the sense that there is no attempt made to portray accurately the real Las Vegas crime lab.

An immediate rating smash for CBS, the network quickly capitalized on its hit with spin-offs *CSI: Miami* and *CSI: NY. CSI* has been called the most popular television series in the world with its worldwide audience being estimated at over 73.8 million viewers in 2009 (see http://en.wikipedia.org/wiki/CSI:_Crime_Scene_Investigation). *CSI's* popularity relies on the global multi-media capacities that facilitated its rapid syndicalization, but also in the spin-off series *and* its transmutation into a video game. Ordinary people can themselves play *CSI* in their own home at their leisure. People's engagement with programmes such as *CSI* can be seen in what is called *the CSI effect,* a term coined by legal authorities and the mass media to describe a supposed influence that watching the television show *CSI* has on juror behaviour. Though the *CSI* effect cannot be established empirically as true (Tyler, 2006), that the concept has been heard of in the US court system testifies to the effect that fictitious representations of extraordinary deaths can have.

What *CSI* brings to the representation of death is in the way that death and the effects of death on the human body are depicted, explained and analysed at levels of detail never before seen outside of the crime scene investigation profession. Programmes such as *CSI* offer graphic and realistic depictions of the effects of trauma and decomposition on dead bodies:

> Shot in HD, and framed in extreme close up with enhanced visual and auditory, it could be said that CSI trades on its hyper-real representations of death and discussion forums add emotional weight and substance to the enigmatic framework offered by the show itself; a circuit of debate that often feeds back into the series, as the programme's creative personnel add themselves to the mix. (Allen, 2007, p. 8)

It is significant that the narrative structure and format of CSI is mediated through internet forums in ways that elicit and sustain emotional engagement with the material. It raises the more general point that the ways in which multi-media technologies enable the participation, not just of the protagonists in the stories, but also the audiences, creative personnel and production managers in the scenarios. This constitution of communities, where the lines between those who produce and consume is blurred, is called *remediation* and it promotes engagement with and discussion of the ambiguities and ambivalences in the programme. This is a necessary moment in the enactment of taboos, where subtle nuances are examined and decided on by the constituent communities.

Sue Tait (2006) theorizes the social effect of the corpsification of prime time TV as the means through which social values and attitudes about science are promulgated. *CSI* valorizes the rational over the emotional in professional contexts associated with explaining death. Clinicians, pathologists, police and health care professionals would corroborate such a need for a professional face. Remediation and strategies that encourage professionalism in death show how realistic depictions of death can mimic and guide everyday activity.

As already noted, *CSI* is also available as a video game. In her analyses of the representation of death in the increasingly popular Second World War video games such as *Medal of Honor: Frontline,* films like *Saving Private Ryan,* and TV series such as *Band of Brothers,* Eva Kingsepp (2003) draws attention to the different ways in which death is represented across the different media. Customers demand realism and authentic experiences to such an extent that 'the images, their sequence and camera angles are the same to such an extension that if after recently having played the game *Medal of Honor* you watch a documentary on D-day, the latter may seem almost as a replay of your own experience' (Kingsepp, 2003, p. 4). Yet, for Kingsepp, a key difference between the two mediums is the different ways in which authenticity of death plays out:

> the films create not only authenticity by nostalgic representations of the way it was, but, actual authenticity in an emotional sense by focusing on issues that include ethical decisions, inviting the audience to partake in this reflexive project. Authenticity would then partly lie in the audience being led to experience the same range of feelings as the characters on screen – kicks of adrenaline in combat and danger as well as other of more philosophical character. In the games on the other hand, I would say that authenticity lies only in the material representation, since the emotional experience is reduced to thrills offered basically by your own performative skills. (Ibid., p. 11)

The symbolic representation of death is through ethically ambivalent scenarios. Main characters have to make difficult and emotionally fraught decisions, and ultimately the goal of these decisions is to serve the nation in war. The player is assumed to be a good guy. The aim of the game is to kill as many of the bad guys (the enemy) as possible. Extrapolating, Kingsepp suggests that

> there is a very clear-cut division in the game between Good Guys and Bad Guys, us and them, which are of course Americans and their friends … and Germans and their evil allies. All of us are *a priori* Good and all of them are *a priori* Evil … [and the enemy within] is the threat of you yourself not proving to hold against the required standards. In the mission instructions it is often stressed that you are alone on this secret and dangerous mission, there is no one to help you but the High Command have trust in you, and if you fail you are finished on your own

account. Thus the enemy within is not a trait of decadence (or even evil) within yourself that may lead you astray from righteousness; it is individual incompetence and failure in the service of the Nation. (Ibid., p. 8)

The realism and authenticity suggests a transformation in the representation of death that offers important knowledge about cultural processes and self-understanding in contemporary society. Changes to the fictional representation of extraordinary deaths are that fictional accounts are more real in that they engage the emotions of the viewer/gamer more effectively. At the same time as they are more real, they are also more prevalent in the sense that millions of people are emotionally entwined with the same narrative scenarios of *CSI*, *Saving Private Ryan* and *Medal of Honor*. The ways in which the taboos on representing death play out serve to reiterate existing moral codes of what is right and wrong, good and bad. These new digital media use death representations to simultaneously reveal and resolve deep-seated moral ambiguities.

Factual accounts of extraordinary deaths

A composite shift in the representation of death has been charted, where ordinary deaths now have an acknowledged place in the real and fictional representation of death. It can also be seen that the representation of fictional extraordinary deaths are more present and more real in the ways in which they heighten emotional engagement with, and graphic renditions of, fictional death. Attention now turns to the most morally sensitive domain of death representation, and that is the presentation of real extraordinary deaths. The actual depiction of the death of a real person opened this chapter, and it is to that form of death representation that the discussion returns.

Online, anybody can upload anything. The amount of actual extraordinary death that can be viewed online is symptomatic of the fact that citizen journalists and amateur cameramen are not effectively beholden to any laws regarding the publishing of death-related content. This points to a significant dimension of the increasing accessibility of global communications technology, which is the growing popularity of footage of real deaths. As Giroux (2006) notes, according to journalist Hamza Hendawi, in Baghdad

real-life horror has become the view fare of choice, supplanting the explosion of pornography that filled the post-Saddam Hussein vacuum. In outdoor food markets in Baghdad, crowds gather to watch video footage of a truck bomber seated behind the steering wheel smiling and murmuring his last words before crashing into U.S. military vehicles on an overpass. As the public executions, assassinations, and beheadings continue in Iraq, they are followed by an endless stream of videos that can be purchased as DVDs ... and also viewed online across the globe. (Giroux, 2006, p. 54)

This raised a significant point about the use made of these online death representations. It is argued that 'terrorists have been quick to understand that the camera has the power to frame a single atrocity and turn it into an image that sends shivers down the spine of an entire planet. This gives them a vital new weapon' (Giroux, 2006, p. 57, quoting Ignatieff (2004)).

The beheading of Nick Berg by a jihad extremist group that was accessible via You Tube as TruthTube TV 2009, is another chilling example of the internet as a means of viewing real death online. The global syndicated media reported the killing but not one mainstream media outlet has ever shown the actual beheading. Even so, this was a popular item, with almost three-quarters of a million online visitors in a single day (Giroux, 2006, p. 54).

A more complex example arrived on the world stage in spring 2004, when the online bulletin board, NowThat'sFuckedUp.com, was created as a website for amateur pornography. According to Anden-Papadopoulos (2009), it became popular with overseas US military personnel, but hit a problem because credit card companies blocked charging from high-risk countries such as Iraq and Afghanistan. The website administrator decided to grant US troops free access if they posted an authentic picture proving they were stationed overseas in these areas. Initially, the majority of images posted were benign, but graphic battlefield pictures began to appear, such as 'close-up shots of dead Iraqi insurgents and civilians, many of them horribly mutilated or blown to pieces. Accompanying the photographs was a running commentary celebrating the killings, cracking jokes and arguing over what kind of weaponry was used' (Anden-Papadopoulos, 2009, p. 926). In September 2005, the site made the international news and a Pentagon investigation was launched. By the end of the same month the inquiry was suspended, the web administrator's home was raided and he was charged with obscenity. He pleaded guilty to five misdemeanours, but the charges were dropped when he agreed to shut down the site and hand control of the domain over to the local county sheriff.

The display of horribly mutilated war dead by those who were involved in the killings on the internet was morally problematic to the US military, because the power to gloat over one's victories has long been recognized as a sure-fire means to boost troops' morale and play a part in the psychological battle with the morale of the enemy. At the same time, the fact that the images were easily accessible to any person around the world who was over 18 years old and with access to a credible credit-card severely compromised the US military's war propaganda that it was engaging in a clean war:

The ability of global audiences to access the soldiers' own images and stories directly through war blogs, mass emails and popular video-sharing sites such as YouTube and MySpace is opening up a new window on modern warfare ... that brings to a head the ongoing debates on the forms of witnessing called forth by the representations of distant suffering in the media (e.g. Boltanski, 1999, Chouliaraki, 2006; Hesford, 2004; Tait, 2008). If the moral justification for publicizing the death and agony of others lies in the potential for fostering an active public response, then the soldiers' explicit exposures challenge such assumptions about an educational link between representations of violence and the production of public forms of engagement and action. (Anden-Papadopoulos, 2009, p. 921)

The posting of war images by soldiers, and the ensuing public debate and legal (in)action reveals significant dimensions of contemporary representational technologies as well as the negotiation of rules of appropriate behaviour which signal the reworking of taboos associated with death representation.

Another example is the visual global spectacle of 9/11. Collating many images taken by ordinary people who happened to have a camera at hand when the commercial aircraft slammed into the Twin Towers, David Friend notes that

what had mesmerized every one of these men and women with cameras, surely, was the gravity of sudden death, in numbers of such magnitude. But they were also gripped by the pure visual spectacle – by the sense that this irreconcilably infernal scene was somehow *meant* to be seen. Skyscrapers, along with hundreds and hundreds of lives within them, were being ravaged, with passenger planes, *in order that* the violence be witnessed. Terrorism, by definition, demanded frightened eyes ... This was terror enacted as sadistic, global reality show. (Friend, 2006, p. xvii)

Friend interprets the visual global reality show as sadistic, cruel and debased; however, we also have to face the fact that many people around the world would also regard US military action in the same light. 'US administrations have also used spectacles of terror to promote US military power and geopolitical ends, as is evident in the Gulf war of 1990–1991, the Afghanistan war of fall 2001, and the Iraq war of 2003' (Kellner, 2004, p. 41). It is not unlikely that a sizeable proportion of the global audience of 9/11 may perhaps have interpreted the footage as a successful strike back against an invading imperial force.

Global viewing of actual footage of extraordinary deaths is only possible in advanced modernity. New, globally connected tele-technologies create access to geographically remote events as well as the ability to

exploit this interconnectedness of the world through mass media [and] the interplay between the global and the local; how people have access to events in different parts of the world; and finally how this access can also be used for political purposes by creating spectacles their purpose, ultimately, is to be a representation of itself for the consumption of global mass media. (Project: Carousel!, 2010)

The documenting of actual extraordinary deaths on the internet generated unsettling discrepancies that prompted some kind of official or institutional response. Each one has ambiguous footage that allows for multiple readings, so prompting ambivalence and attempts at formal or informal censure. It is significant that it is only through the technology of global mass media that such things are able to have these effects. But at the same time, one of the consequences of the spectacle is that the *ambiguity* of what the spectacle means *also* becomes undeniable.

How can these examples of the production and consumption of online death further our understanding of the taboos of representing death? Surely the prevalence and accessibility of the footage suggests that the taboo, the distinction between appropriate and inappropriate use, is dissolved? But no, the distinction between acceptable and unacceptable representations of real death pivot on what is deemed to be newsworthy versus entertainment. These brutal images tend to be located on video broadcasting sites next to hardcore pornography. Though not directly under surveillance, they are restricted indirectly, either through legal manoeuvring or through other forms of institutional control of access to information.

The more-real-than-real effects of the media reveal that the construction of newsworthiness has the related effect of shaping expectations about what everyone should know and feel. Global news television coverage, YouTube footage and reality television, for example, all rely on the power of being there as a way of building expectations about what everyone should know and feel. Drawing on recent personal experience of living through devastating earthquakes in Christchurch, New Zealand: shortly after the 22 February quake, standing in the garden at home, which is in the flight path of the airport. No planes are flying. The majority of the electricity is out. There is barely any water coming through. Roads are gridlocked with people fleeing from their workplaces to get to their children, partners, parents, friends and pets. Cell-phone coverage is becoming intermittent as the lines jam with people desperate for the 'I'm OK; are you OK?' text to get through across the city and around the world. The abiding sensory memory is the silence of the airport broken by the sound of two helicopters. One, an Air Force chopper, probably with the prime minster at the time, John Key, making his way to the crushed and still shaking city centre. The other, the prime-time media programme helicopter, so that its lead presenter could be here with microphone in hand for viewers round New Zealand and the world to watch him tell us of how he felt as the aftershocks brought his adrenalin rushing, as he told of his sense of anguish and fear, of his sense of hope and determination.

The descriptions and the emotional tones of the commentators telling viewers, in case we hadn't noticed, that this really was a traumatic and horrendous thing, the cameras dwell – relentlessly – on the grief or the situation of those affected or present. The media-production of the reality effect is again another way that expectations and understandings about death, good and bad, sacred and profane are established in this global, mediatized age.

Conflicts produce martyrs, and with present-day mass transmission capabilities and global interconnectivity, international populations can watch martyrdom in creation. Long-entrenched authoritarian regimes have fallen like dominoes as the images inspired mass protests in non-contiguous states, from Tunisia to Egypt, from Egypt to Libya, Yemen, Bahrain and Iran. It was a YouTube video that changed things for ever in Iran. Following the disputed presidential elections of June 2009, the streets of Tehran were filled with hundreds of thousands of protesters. Neda Agha-Soltan, a young woman of 26, while watching the protests with her father, was shot through the heart and died. Her death was captured on video by bystanders and broadcast over the internet. The footage became a rallying point for the political opposition and her death 'a symbol for the thousands of people who suffered under the government's heavy-handed crackdown' (Mahr, 2009). *Time* magazine rated it as probably the most widely witnessed death in human history.

There has been a distinctive change in the codes of representing death. The change involves a double shift in the existing configuration of ordinary, extraordinary, real and fictitious representations of death. To paraphrase Vivian Sobchack (1984), as a result of the influence of new technologies and new modes of communication, the representation of death has shifted so that, on the one hand, fantasy deaths are marked by the new presence of ordinary credible death narratives *and* the ever-more biologically accurate graphic depictions of fantasy deaths. And actual deaths, both ordinary and extraordinary, feature more readily in documentary representations. Figure 9.2 helps to describe the double shift to increasingly 'real' deaths in actual and fantasy representations.

Death is mediated to a greater degree than ever before, and the proliferation in the variety of communication allows for more heterogeneous and ambiguous representations. Representations of real death are more available, more graphic, more varied and more emotionalized. A significant consequence of these multivalent, emotionalized and mediatized representations of death on the symbolic landscape is that they are a means through which particular social practices are marked out as acceptable or not, good or bad, allowable or punishable. This suggests that taboos have remained in place in contemporary death practices, but that their terms, content and application have transformed in step with revolutions in the technologies of representation.

Figure 9.2   The double shift to increasingly 'real' deaths in actual and fantasy representations

The way death taboo manages ambiguity has shifted

'Pornographic' death:
Representations of actual death
are rendered nearly invisible,
fantasy deaths are nearly always
unusual (violent) deaths stripped
of emotion

'Reality' death:
Representations of actual death
are more available, more graphic,
more varied, more mediated, more
emotionalized – meanings are
publicly negotiated

Type of death/type of representation	Ordinary death	Extraordinary death
Fantasy (fictitious accounts of death)	Increasing presence of credible 'ordinary' death narratives	Increasing presence of more realistic and emotionally engaged narratives and audiences
Real (accounts of actual deaths of people)	Increasing presence of real 'ordinary' death trajectories	Increasing presence of morally ambiguous real extraordinary deaths that demand explicit negotiation of meaning

Conclusion

There is an increasing presence of realistic and actual deaths on our screens, and these images convey powerful messages about how death is to be approached. This is what the phrase *death is more real in the mediatized world of global communication* seeks to convey. Contemporary taboos about the representation of death can be summed up by saying that representations of real death are permissible when they are used for the sacred purposes of defining the good death. In terms of the increasing presence of ordinary deaths, they designate that what is normal equates to what is good, acceptable and expected, however wrenching and testing it is. In terms of extraordinary deaths, in both fiction and documentary modes of representation, these kinds of death delineate the parameters of bad death; death that is unacceptable, unconscionable. It is not that violent deaths are in themselves bad, but it is the purpose and the motives that precipitated the extraordinary deaths and their viewing that becomes the focus of moral opprobrium. Turning back to the opening example, Kumaritashvili's death on-screen was not in itself a bad death; it was when the underlying purpose of watching him slam into the concrete pillar was repeatedly viewed outside of the mass-media news context that, in the act of watching the clip and viewing his death as a voyeuristic or entertaining experience, his death became profaned.

New technologies enable the previously impossible broadcast of events that prompt unheralded ethical dilemmas, such as the global broadcast of an Olympian death, a global broadcast of war atrocities, or mediatized terrorist activities (9/11). By watching these truly globally imbued events, we are involved in the struggles to find ways to manage the ambiguities that they shake to the surface. We designate some interpretations of death as sacred and others as profane, and in doing so, we tend to emphasize and reaffirm what is perceived to be threatened – loss of democracy, loss of decency, and loss of respect for the dead in a social context of instantaneity, hyper-reality and multiplicity. These threats reveal the ways that death is morally regulated in a global age.

Questions

This chapter drew together a wide range of examples to focus on the way that the representation of death has shifted in contemporary times. A central debate in death representation is about death as a taboo subject.

1. The opening vignette was about the wholesale broadcast, then censorship, of an athlete's death. Do you think that his death should have been broadcast on the new global networks? Explain how you came to that answer.
2. With combat imagery there are tensions between political message, battle morale and public sentiment. Note down the last time you witnessed dead bodies on broadcast news media. What were the main messages being conveyed by broadcasting these images of the dead?
3. When is it legitimate and appropriate to censor images of the dead available on the internet? Explain the reasoning behind your answer.

Chapter 10

Conclusion: Death in a Global Age

This book has set out to examine death in advanced modernity as a means of introducing key concerns and debates regarding the sociology of death and dying. For example, how will we die (and *will* we die?) in 100 years' time? How are we to think about this? What is going on in global society that might suggest that, in spite of death being always with us, its social forms and significance may change.

Death in advanced modernity is qualitatively different from modern death. Now the task is to evaluate this claim and speculate on the future under this scenario. It is clear that globally oriented social relations and practices do have an impact on death ways. These social changes have prompted a significant rethink of how sociology can best approach the study of death. There is a growing interest in and concern for the interplay of different societies today, and how ideas of death shape and are in turn shaped by those interchanges. The introduction highlighted the place of the individual in modern death, and across the chapters it is clear that individualization continues to inform death ways in many ways. Yet, at the time of writing, *how* death is individualized is in transition. Across the different death topics there is evidence that how to define and understand individualism is being renegotiated.

It is no longer viable to approach death as being contained by the limits of one's individual, biological body. Advances in technology have pushed the boundaries between individual life and death, and in doing so they have raised a set of profound moral and political issues that are set to inform public debate and political contest in the decades to come. These issues pivot on the promise of anti-ageing technology. On the one hand, such anti-ageing technology brings to mind Methuselah, the oldest person mentioned in the Hebrew Bible, who purportedly died at the age of 969. Long lives for the many, rather than the extraordinary few, is for some an exceptionally exciting prospect because it would offer human beings the ability to see their contributions to the world, for good or ill, come to fruition. Shostak (2006) comments, 'How would this kind of life affect living? Would life be endlessly boring for our non-reproductive and endlessly existing descendents or would life be an endless opportunity for creativity and fertilizer for the flowering of civilization?' He raises an intriguing scenario where, 'In an age when individuals can expect to live long enough to see the consequences of their actions, will the notion of passing the buck, such as the national debt, to grandchildren cease shaping the nation's priorities, such as spending for warfare? Are people more likely to be moral when they understand that they will have to face the consequences of their actions in the future?' (Shostak, 2006, p. 157).

But along with the putative boost to morality which might result from increased longevity, there is the prospect of degraded, as well as extended, life. This scenario is well illustrated by Tithonus in Greek mythology. Tithonus was a handsome mortal who fell in love with Eos, the goddess of the dawn. Eos realized that her beloved Tithonus was destined to age and die. She begged Zeus to grant her lover immortal life. But Zeus was a jealous god, prone to acts of deception in order to seduce beautiful gods and mortals alike, and he was not pleased with Eos's infatuation with a rival. In a classic Devil's Bargain, he granted Eos's wish – literally. He made Tithonus immortal, but did not grant him eternal youth. As Tithonus aged, he became increasingly debilitated and demented, eventually driving Eos to distraction with his constant babbling. In despair, she turned Tithonus into a grasshopper. Kellehear (2007) re-phrases this despair as social embarrassment. When the old become decrepit and dependent, their deaths are seen as grossly mis-timed by wider society 'without money, political influence or well-functioning memory, there is no power to "buy" time. Shameful deaths of the present Cosmopolitan Age do not represent a failure of technological achievement but rather – and there is no delicate way to express this – a moral and social failure to provide satisfactory models of social care for dying people at the economic margins of our world' (Kellehear, 2007, p. 248). Anti-ageing technology may present humanity with the fearful scenario of an extended life-span but limited improvement in the quality of life.

The promise of immortality is behind the scientific striving towards an ever-increasing life-span. If bio-medicine were able to break the code of life and thus be able to manipulate the on/off switch embedded in every life form, what would become of us? There are a few possible scenarios – each with attendant worries and dreams. On the one hand, if the code of life could be manipulated directly, it would in theory become possible for human beings to become immortal. Some people, such as the cryogenics/cryonics pioneer, Robert Ettinger, see this as not only possible, but likely. At the time of writing, his body is waiting patiently, frozen in a vat and waiting for technology to catch up with his vision.[1] The capacity to constantly repair and rejuvenate tissue has two interrelated consequences: it produces trans-humans and radically skews the population distribution of young, old and very old. Each has significant consequences for society, and one of them is the end of human society itself. In *Our Posthuman Future* (2003), Francis Fukuyama suggests that our rapidly approaching future world is one filled with two classes of beings – humans who are subject to decay and extinction, and posthuman beings equipped with superior intelligence and blessed with technological immortality. The claim that humans with advanced technological input are posthuman is interesting – it defines humanity through its mortality and vulnerabilities

> which is simply a consequence of being a perishable organism that ages and is subject to inescapable morbidity and mortality, vulnerability defines a shared human world of risk with which we can cope through a shared culture. Collective institutions – law, government, religion and family – are social mechanisms that offer some respite from our ontological vulnerability. Life extending medicine promises to solve the problem of our vulnerability by paradoxically creating a posthuman world. (Fukuyama, 2003)

Speculating on the possible social consequences, Bryan Turner is critical of what he calls the pro-longevity movement, because the debate over ageing rarely confronts the political economy of ageing – that is, who will pay for it; what will the unintended consequences on the environment be; how will it influence family life; and how might it change the balance of power between generations or nations? On the one hand, there is a wish to prolong life, but on the other, there is an indifference to the means of preventing premature death – it assumes a link between wealth and health, and Turner argues it is unjust to value the added years of those who have already lived a long time rather than adding extra years to those whose lives are relatively short because of poverty. For Turner, the consequences of pro-longevity include generational conflict, the exhaustion of basic resources, and massive regional inequalities – very similar to the existing situation – but in this scenario, the only long-term solution to scarcity would be a 'radical reduction in human population' or the colonization of space (Turner, 2010).

Turner offers a Malthusian nightmare, and his concerns are beginning to emerge in cross-national policy conventions where health policy experts are gently but insistently pursuing the question of whether euthanasia should routinely be part of elder-care plans. Turner argues that the prolonging of human life requires and demands social reform if the quality of life is to be maintained, if not improved – if death in old age is perceived as pathological, then it is likely that older adults will compete with others to gain access to scarce medical resources. If, instead, death in old age is considered to be normal, then premature deaths in underdeveloped countries would in turn be interpreted as a priority, since they are incongruent with current norms defining the 'natural' lifespan (Turner, 2010, p. 441). By pushing the biological boundaries between life and death, new dilemmas arise about what it means to be human.

As these questions arise about what it means to be a human being, new patterns of death bring different concerns into view. The kinds of deaths that contemporary individuals face are deeply inscribed by collective relations forged within globalization. Chapter 3 explored how today's intensive, mobile world produces slow, debilitating and degenerative deaths for those in rich and poor populations alike. The epidemiological profile of the world at the time of writing is marked by ever-increasing numbers of people dying slow deaths.

There are two powerful continuities in this social patterning of death and attempts to prevent it. As yet unknown diseases and conditions will emerge, engulf and recede, as will new responses that will attempt to prevent them and protect the populace. Reciprocity and equilibrium will prevail, as will enduring inequalities between the more and the less vulnerable. One consequence of this claim is that the risks that come from new liberal markets, new mobilities and new lifestyles could have profound and potentially devastating consequences for global public health. Current debates are focused on immediate risks. With the spiralling costs of healthcare for those who are slowly dying round the world, especially for those suffering from lifestyle conditions, the argument about promoting *full-cost economics* is made. When products are sold, the companies that make them, and the consumers buying them, have to carry some of the financial burden of the consequences of their production and consumption. Products made to treat non-communicable diseases would cost significantly more, and lift them beyond the purchasing power of the communities within which such diseases do so much damage.

Enduring inequalities look likely to worsen through these new modes of death-dealing diseases and distempers. The battle between humans and pathogens will continue. The movement of people, especially if left unchecked, fuels increasing risks that threaten the precarious epidemiological balance. A vicious cycle of inequality, conflict, forced migration and terrorism becomes an increasingly likely scenario (Knobler *et al.*, 2006, p. 10). One solution that has been proposed is for more extensive and intensive global and regional *surveillance of mobile populations* in the name of global public health, but perhaps potentially in the long run this would in fact serve the interests of incumbent power differentials.

While the fate of millions of individuals is translated into tensions between economics, politics and pathogens, death professions have recalibrated themselves to tailor their expertise in the service of bespoke transnational markets in caring for the wealthy dying and recently dead, stepping up to the globally organized professional economies for these. This marks a radical transformation in the death professions. The shifting global relations between economy and state coincided with a direct challenge to professionalized ways of thinking about and organizing death. Medicalized understandings and practices for managing dying were increasingly regarded as over-medicalized and funeral directors practices as over-commercialized. The over-professionalization of death was seen to disempower the key protagonists – the dying and the bereaved. These professionalized death ways were also seen as being isolating and inappropriate. The social unease with the death professionals led to 'increasing demands for individuals and families to exert greater control over dying and for more meaningful medical engagements and funeral rituals' (Howarth, 1996, p. 16).

Both medical and funeral professionals have undergone a transformation in their practice. Medical as well as funeral professionals have moved away from professional relations premised on autonomy and authority to ones based on collaboration and negotiation. The rise in global palliative care movements and the move to community-based services is a medical case in point. Within the funeral industry, there is a more direct engagement with global economics in the spread of multinational conglomerates *and* responses to and alternatives to this specific mode of providing professional funeral services. Both developments point to a new focus on death care and are evident in the rise of death tourism and bespoke funerals. Where will this new ethics of care for death professionals lead us? A more thorough disengagement from caring for the dying? Pulling against the intensification of bio-medicine suggested by the conclusions reached in Chapter 2? Another possibility may be the formal organization of cross-national death tourism and moves towards mobile death care units that will travel around the world providing specialized death care as and where the consumer and market demands.

Social identity in death is a potential beacon in an uncertain future. Enduring cultural identities are continually achieved – though in new ways with unexpected symbols. This highlights the enduring call of special places and special people within the dizzying mobilities of global living. New icons of place come to the fore and reaffirm people's collective and creative capacities for belonging. For all that is under threat, a sense of who we are and what we are about as individuals and as collectives in a newly forming world endures.

As society changes, so does the way we grieve. The social contexts within which people narrate their grief, and the technologies that are used to do that have changed rapidly in the bridging decades of the twentieth and twenty-first centuries. These broader social changes raise the question of how a world replete with communicative technologies might impinge upon and reconstitute ways of grieving. Online activities have become central to many domains of everyday life, including work, entertainment, health and relationships. Not surprisingly, as people live their lives increasingly online, death and grief have taken their virtual place with the advent of online grief therapy, grief blogs and virtual memorials, to name just three on line grief support strategies. Given that online communication allows for new ways of communicating, it is feasible to suggest that they may also offer new ways of seeking solace.

Debates on mass death tend to approach the relationship between globalization and culture as an ongoing process. Cultures are *always* interacting with each other. Cultural practices are continually changing and being recreated as part of an ongoing process where cultures are informed through various internal and external pressures and influences. Examining the relationship between culture and globalization from this point of view (of cultures as dynamic features), it puts the effects of contemporary global relations on cultures into a longer-range perspective. Much about our current globality is not so different from previous phases of socio-cultural globality. What is of interest is the ways in which engagement across cultures is carried by and through contemporary global relations. A significant aspect of globalization is the varied ways in which cultures and global forces interact. Globalization and cultural diversity is one of the ways in which this issue is thought through. There are arguments on both sides. On the one hand, globalization (of beliefs and traded goods) depletes cultural diversity, while on the other, it can foster diversity and heterogeneity. For example, colonial relations are global in the respect that they span places far removed from each other. Colonial relations are marked by particular types of inter-cultural forms that include either assimilation (you become like us) or separation (you live in a separate way but totally under our control – as in apartheid) of dominating and dominated peoples. It is feared that contemporary global relations replicate the cultural homogenization of assimilation or cultural domination of separation. If we in the present are engaged in archiving the past to enable it to be a resource for our present and our plans for the future; if we are doing this in distinctive and identifiable ways grounded in pragmatic and task-focused connections between infrastructures and imaginaries that manage mass death; if these practices and imaginaries hold the threat of disaster capitalism and the promise of cosmopolitanism, what does the future hold for mass death? Increasing polarization smoothed over with encompassing discourses of a shared humanity and a shared human cause? Suggesting a future of intensified and more numerous mass death scenarios? Increasing equity within and between nations as new forms of political and economic engagement evolve from the ashes of the old, signalling a reduction in the destructive consequences of natural events and a depletion of the struggles that led to self-inflicted mass death? These questions remain unresolved and answers are hard to discern at this juncture.

The place of death in religion and society is the general sociological focus of Chapter 8. It is analysed through a concern with the global as it examines current debates about religion in the sociology of death and dying. The theme of secularization and the shift to a post-secular society and what this means for religion is a significant aspect of current theorization. Even so, death studies literature might not have picked up this theme in relation to the death penalty, suicide or euthanasia, for example, as enthusiastically as one might have expected. Sociologists of death and dying must contend with both religion (as a social institution) and religiosity (as an approach to the world) in any attempt to account for and explain particular formations of religion, death and society. The posited shift to a post-secular world invokes the contemporary contradiction of monotheistic approaches within pluralistic social contexts. How is this issue to be usefully brought to bear as a way of describing and explaining the myriad ways that, for example, suicide, the afterlife and funeral rites are perceived and acted upon in the broader social environs? And how is this way of explaining death through post-secular oriented sociology a way to shed light on globalization's place in all of this? Many studies of death, society and religion suggest there are multiple factors involved in the shaping of the current complex scene. These include the case study of Czechoslovakia discussed in Chapter 8. Globalization is a factor in relations between death, religion and society but cannot claim to be the sole influence.

In light of Tony Walter's prescient prediction that the media is the new church, and Margaret Gibson's reminder that representations of death never replace the real and cannot do justice to a person's own journey towards death, what claims can be made about the rise of reality death? New juxtapositions are apparent from the corpsification of prime-time television to the martyrdom of innocent bystanders. They all point to a shift in death taboos away from the pornography of death towards what one could call reality death. Reality death is the new death taboo. It is the means through which ambiguities affirm social values of what is right or wrong, good or bad. Reality death is now a conduit for mediatized societies to establish and maintain moral order from ambiguity. This is most significantly in the case of problematic deaths – for example, suicide, murder and euthanasia – not only for people's attitudes and formal rules around trying to control them, but also for their more general place in society.

Euthanasia is broadly defined as a professionally assisted death, unlike suicide, when a person takes his/her own life unaided, and murder, when a person dies (unwillingly) by the actions of another person. Euthanasia was valued in Ancient Rome and Greece as a good death, but became deeply problematic during the twentieth century because of the wholesale murder of Jews, gypsies, the mentally ill and physically deformed, and those who opposed the Nazi political system. However, public debates, legislation and the legal practice of euthanasia are emerging once again. This time, global social forces, which include the ageing of the world's population, the global mobility of people and finance, the new struggles for independence and democracy, and the overwhelming mediatization of public debate all force new forms of responsibility and risk on individuals. These in turn force governments around the world to consider more seriously who is entitled to adequate care and protection, especially in the case of the elderly as they approach death.

Many people in wealthy nations are becoming increasingly dissatisfied with the prospect of facing many years of frailty and ill-health as their bodies and minds deteriorate through age. At the same time, there is growing public dissatisfaction with legislation that stops health professionals from helping people to die if and when those individuals decide that is the way they want to do end their lives. Taking the social issue of escalating health care costs for the elderly, are there signs that institutionally organized euthanasia is becoming a more socially acceptable solution for previously wealthy modern societies in the face of financial ruin? What shape would a new degree of public and political acceptance of euthanasia take? Would it be up to the individual to decide, or will bureaucratic imperatives drive the chain of decisions that would lead to someone's medically induced demise? Is it possible to maintain personal autonomy without stepping outside of the law in these new circumstances?

As global relations have an impact on that delicate balance between personal autonomy and the institutions of law and government, both founded on protecting the lives of its people, what principles could fall by the wayside? Or does the turn to global networks spell an end to the relative inequities between peoples and nations? And what effect do these new networks have on death – is poverty increased, thereby escalating death by poverty? Or is it decreased? Or do these new networks simply re-distribute death in unexpected ways?

How the passage from life the death is personally experienced, socially organized, culturally acknowledged and symbolically testified, has always been fluid and contested. Yet there are distinct patterns to that passage and these patterns have been changing. Today, death is no longer shaped by societies organized *en masse*. Instead, it is riven by tensions and social issues informed by global relations. New patterns of disparity are emerging from these, as are unheralded ethical dilemmas about who can and should die.

Amongst all of these newly unfolding challenges for death, one thing is clear. The prospects for death practices in advanced modernity are informed by an optimism for possibilities yet to be imagined, cross-cut by the real danger of re-inscribing enduring social inequalities. How this tension unfolds, and its consequences for death, depend on what we are prepared to try out, examine, question and defend. This is the challenging context for contemporary debates in the sociology of death and dying.

Questions

In review, this chapter claimed that the individualization of death is carried out differently under global social conditions. It also presents some future scenarios to consider.

1. Do you think that human beings will ever become physically immortal? Do you think this is something humans should strive for?

2. Drawing on the different topics covered, outline some of the ways that the individualization of death is being achieved differently under global conditions.
3. Is this difference in death practices enough to persuade us that death in a global age is no longer death-denying? What challenges can be raised against this claim? What are the strengths of its case?

Notes

Chapter 1: Perspectives and Theories on Death and Dying

1. The word *taboo* came into the English language in 1777 by way of Captain James Cook in a journal charting his third voyage around the world as the captain of HMS *Resolution*. According to Holden (2001), 'Cook realised that the term taboo was common throughout Polynesia and meant something or someone that was *set apart* or consecrated for special use or purpose'. Since Cook's time, the understanding of taboo has been greatly refined. The sheer capacity of taboos to set apart and thus make certain things sacred tells us much about what is held dear by a society. As well as being a form of social control (implementing taboos about what is allowed and what is not, and the reprisals that come with breaking the rules is a way to control people's behaviour), taboos also help to classify and order our experience as human beings living in a given society.
2. This is a philosophical position which holds that the methodological rules that apply in natural science could and should be employed in the social sciences. It is useful to note methodological naturalism presupposes that most natural sciences share a common logic and set of procedures, and that there is methodological unity within each discipline in the natural sciences. This presupposition is not borne out in the real world.

Chapter 2: The Social Organization of Death and Dying

1. Cells need to die for there to be life, and all cells have an auto-destruct programme built into them that is called *apoptosis*. In the body, cells are always dying. Blood cells, cells in the skin, those lining the intestine: all are either shed like leaves or degenerate and die. A white blood cell lives for only a few days, and each day we lose millions of cells. To replace all those lost cells and keep the body intact, other cells are constantly dividing. Cell death is therefore the natural state of affairs and so 'in the midst of life we are in death' (*Book of Common Prayer*).
2. The practice of stealing bodies for the dissection table was so rampant that the grave-robbers were known as resurrectionists for their ability to raise the dead.
3. Social death is the social practice of withdrawal and exclusion from existing social relationships *as if* the person is already biologically dead. Social death and physical death are not one and the same thing, and do not always occur at the same

time. Often it is used to refer to situations when people exclude specific individuals or groups from the benefits of society, such as food, water, recognition or acceptance. Social death has been a means of dealing with those who, for whatever reason, are not seen as fitting into the social fabric in an acceptable way.

4. A sad irony of the globalization of bio-medicalization is not lost on contemporary social watchdogs. Communities vulnerable to exploitation through the extraction of their body fluids become exponentially more vulnerable to the risk of infection and disease carried by the equipment used to extract their bio-fluids; to the lack of institutionalized health care available once they are sick; and to the lack of welfare support once they are too ill to work. Isolated rural Chinese communities are, according to the World Health Organization, presenting with HIV/AIDS and hepatitis where the small amount of contact with the outside world has been through mobile blood-bank units. Those people in receipt of the products face similar dilemmas. People needing blood transfusions would have faced death if they had not been given the transfusion – but they were contaminated through this life-preserving procedure.

5. Navarro's mother had authorized the harvesting of his organs, but because he was not brain dead it was determined that the transplant procedure to be used would be 'donation after cardiac death', known as DCD. This requires the withdrawal of life support, leading to death prior to the recovery of organs. As it turned out, Navarro's organs could not be harvested because he did not die within an hour of being removed from life support – he died eight hours later. The prosecution relied on the testimony of a doctor and nurse, who accused Roozrokh of administering drugs to speed up Navarro's death.

Chapter 3:   Patterns in Life and Death

1. An epidemiological tipping point is when small causes have big effects (see Gladwell, 2002).
2. Developed countries have been experiencing negative growth, while developing nations retain high birth rates as their death rates decrease. Regionally, developed nations have been struggling to maintain their increasingly aged populations, while developing nations in such parts of the world as South America, Africa, India and China have seen exponential increases in their populations, and the pressure on resources, food and sanitation that go hand in hand with population growth and urbanization.

Chapter 4:   The Death Industries

1. Assisted death is legal in Switzerland, the Netherlands, Belgium and the State of Oregon in the USA as of July 2009. The Swiss law that allows anyone to help patients die, as long as there are no ulterior motives, dates back to 1942. Article 115 of the Swiss Criminal Code considers assisting suicide a crime if and only if the motive is selfish, and it does not require the involvement of a physician or that the patient is terminally ill.

Chapter 5:   Funerary Rites

1. Alkaline hydrolysis is a disposal process for human remains. The body is placed in a silk bag, which is itself placed within a metal cage frame. This is then loaded into a Resomator. The machine is filled with a mixture of water and lye, and heated under pressure to a high temperature (around 160°C/320°F). The body is broken down into its chemical components and the process takes about three hours. The end result is green-brown tinted liquid (containing amino acids, peptides, sugars and salts) and soft, porous white bone remains (calcium phosphate), which are easily crushed to form a white-coloured 'ash'. The 'ash' is returned to the next of kin of the deceased. The liquid is disposed of either through the sanitary sewer system, or through some other method including use in a garden or green space. This process is championed as using less energy and producing less carbon dioxide and pollutants than cremation (Briggs, 2011).
2. See, for example, various publications from the Cremation in Scotland Project, Durham University Centre for Death and Life Studies http://www.dur.ac.uk/cdals/projects/.

Chapter 7:   Mass Death

1. This idea was explored in chapter 3, which focuses on global demographics.
2. Food security is a term for the availability of food and people's access to it. A person or group has food security when they do not live in hunger or fear of starvation.
3. A significant growth in the popularity of tracing one's past – as a hobby and as a worldwide syndicated source of entertainment (such as the TV programme, *Who Do You Think You Are?*) is a good example of this.

Chapter 8:   Religion

1. The Takbir is the Arabic term for the phrase Allāhu Akbar. Usually translated as God is Great, it is a common Islamic Arabic expression used in various contexts: in formal prayer, as an informal expression of faith, in times of distress, to express victory and to express resolute determination, especially in politically charged contexts.
2. Theodicy – offering meaning to life in the form of a vindication of God's goodness and justice in the face of the existence of evil.
3. Last rites include, for example, Catholic *last rites*, which include the administration of unction (anointment) for the dying person, also the Sacrament of Penance and Holy Communion. People and things are anointed to symbolize the introduction of a sacramental or divine influence, a holy emanation, spirit, power or God: The normal order of administration is: first Penance (if the dying person is physically unable to confess, absolution, conditional on the existence of contrition, is given); next, Anointing; finally, Viaticum (if the person can receive it). Last rites also involve funerary rites and rituals such as throwing in a handful of dust/earth into a grave with the phrase *Ashes to ashes, dust to dust.*

This symbolic rite signifies again the separation of the fate of the material body from (in this case) the spirit or soul. It is also important to realise that last rites do not *need* to be religious. Many funerals, especially in contemporary Western countries, ritualize the release of doves or balloons, or blowing out candles at the committal of a body. These symbols are not strictly religious; they are more spiritual in orientation as they represent the setting free of the spirit from this mortal coil. Similarly, a humanist funeral is neither religious nor spiritual; however, it is symbolic, as it communicates the manner of belief about the after-life (that there is none). That is to say, then, that last rites are always symbolic, though they can take different forms and the form they take indicates the kind of relations that those involved have to otherworldly concerns (http://en.wikipedia.org/wiki/Last_Rites).
4. The death taboo will also be discussed in Chapter 9, while reviewing debates about the representation of death.

Chapter 9:   Representations of Mortality

1. The court case against Heavy Metal Band Judas Priest is another example. Two teenage boys attempted suicide in Reno, Nevada, USA just before Christmas 1985. One succeeded, but the other failed and was left disfigured. Both families attempted to sue Judas Priest for product liability – subliminal messages in their music that the families claimed drove their sons to suicide. Though the case was not upheld, the public debate resulted in calls for warning labels on music deemed to be harmful or obscene, which have now become commonplace.
2. A classic examination of ostensibly neutral and impartial BBC reports revealed how editors manipulated the form and content of images to demonise striking British miners in the early 1970s for political ends (Glasgow University Media Group, 1976).
3. For example, Zigmund Bauman's illustrations of socio-cultural transformations from pre-modern through solid modern to liquid modern times provide unique and powerful hypotheses of how 'death' has been revived for public display and talk in contemporary, liquid modern social life (Higo, 2006). Baudrillard suggests that the changing social context of hyper-reality leads to a loss of refer-ence points that in turn propel people to fear death and render it off-limits; that is, taboo (Baudrillard, 1993).
4. Live Aid is another example of combining the sacred and profane as it combines the marketing of popular music with the imagery of dying children in Africa.

Chapter 10:   Conclusion

1. Cryonics uses ultra cold temperatures to preserve human bodies with the intent of restoring life and good health once the appropriate life-giving technology becomes available.

References

Acts of Parliament

Education (Scotland) Act, 1872, 35 & 36 Vict., c.62, Scotland.
Local Government Act, New Zealand, 2002.
Local Government in Scotland Act, 2003.

General references

Aberdeen City Council (2009) "Local Agenda 21". Available at: http://www.aberdeencity.gov.uk/Regeneration/regen/reg_LocalAgenda21.asp.
Adams, S. (1993) 'A Gendered History of the Social Management of Death in Foleshill, Coventry, during the War Years', in D. Clark (ed.), *The Sociology of Death: Theory, Culture, Practice*. Oxford: Blackwell, pp. 149–65.
AFP-AP Reuters (2004) 'Massive Relief Effort: Toll passes 31,000', *The Press*, Christchurch, New Zealand: B1.
Allen, M. (2007) *Reading CSI: Crime TV under the Microscope*. London: I.B.Tauris.
Altman, D. (1999) 'Globalization, Political Economy and HIV/AIDS', *Theory and Society*, 28(4): 559–84.
American Cancer Society (2008) 'Questions about Smoking, Tobacco, and Health' Atlanta, GA: American Cancer Society.
American Red Cross (2011) 'Text REDCROSS to 90999 to Give $10' Available at: https://american.redcross.org/site/SPageServer?pagename=ntld_nolnav_text2 help; accessed 9 November 2011.
Anden-Papadopoulos, K. (2009) 'Body Horror on the Internet: US Soldiers Recording the War in Iraq and Afghanistan', *Media, Culture and Society*, 31(6): 921–38.
Anderson, B. (1991) *Imagined Communities: Reflections on the Origin and Spread of Nationalism*. London: Verso.
Anderson, H. (2009) 'Common Grief, Complex Grieving', *Pastoral Psychology*, 59.
Arbeit, W. (1994) *From Mortal to Ancestor: The Funeral in Tonga*. Honolulu, HI: Palm Frond Productions.
Ariès, P. (1974) *Western Attitudes toward Death: From the Middle Ages to the Present*. Baltimore, MD/ London: Johns Hopkins University Press.
Armstrong, D. (1987) 'Silence and Truth in Death and Dying', *Social Science and Medicine*, 24(8): 651–7.
Ashby, M. (2009) 'The Dying Human in Palliative Medicine', in A. Kellehear (ed.), *The Study of Dying: From Autonomy to Transformation*. Cambridge: Cambridge University Press, pp. 76–98.
Associated Press (2008) 'The Astonishing Grave Dug for the Mexican Who Died Weighing Half a Ton', *Mail Online*. Available at:www.dailymail.co.uk/

news/article-1072769/Pictured-The-astonishing-grave-dug-Mexican-died-weighing-half-ton.html; accessed 10 November 2011.

Associated Press (2009) 'Reality TV Star Jade Goody Dies after Cancer Fight' (23 March). Available at: http://www.3news.co.nz/News/EntertainmentNews/Reality-TV-star-Jade-Goody-dies-after-cancer-fight-/tabid/418/articleID/96525/cat/56/Default.aspx; accessed 15 July 2009.

Associated Press (2009) *2008 one of worst years for natural disasters this decade*. Retrieved 11 June, from http://www.cbc.ca/news/world/story/2009/01/23/natural-disasters.html.

Associated Press (2010) 'Chinese Investors in Hong Kong Look to Buy New Zealand Dairy Farms for $1.1 billion', *Business News*. Available at http://business.gaeatimes.com/2010/03/24/chinese-investors-in-hong-kong-look-to-buy-new-zealand-dairy-farms-for-11-billion-44903/.

Ater, R. (2010) 'Slavery and Its Memory in Public Monuments.' *American Art*, 2(1): 20–3.

Atkinson, J. M. (1975) *Discovering Suicide: Studies in the Social Organisation of Sudden Death*. London: Macmillan.

Baudrillard, J. (1993) *Symbolic Exchange and Death* (trans. Iain Hamilton Grant). London/Thousand Oaks, CA: Sage.

BBC News (2009) 'Privatisation "Raised Death Rate"'. Available at: http://news.bbc.co.uk/go/pr/fr/-/1/hi/health/7828901.stm.

Beaglehole, R. and Yach, D. (2003) 'Globalisation and the Prevention and Control of Non-Communicable Disease: The Neglected Chronic Diseases of Adults', *Lancet*, 362: 903–8.

Beck, U. (1992) *The Risk Society*. London: Sage.

Beck, U. (2006a) 'Living in the World Risk Society', Hobhouse Memorial Public Lecture. *British Journal of Sociology*, Old Theatre, LSE, Houghton Street, London, 15 February.

Beck, U. (2006b) *Power in the Global Age: A New Global Political Economy*. Oxford: Polity Press.

Beck, U. and Grande, E. (2010) 'Varieties of Second Modernity: The Cosmopolitan Turn in Social and Political Theory and Research', *British Journal of Sociology*, 61(3): 409–43.

Beck, U. and N. Sznaider (2006) 'Unpacking Cosmopolitanism for the Social Sciences: A Research Agenda', *British Journal of Sociology* 57(1): 1–23.

Becker, E. (1973) *The Denial of Death*. New York: The Free Press.

Bell, C. and Matthewman, S. (eds) (2004) *Cultural Studies in Aotearoa New Zealand: Identity, Space and Place*. Melbourne, Australia: Oxford University Press.

Bell, D. (1976) *The Cultural Contradictions of Capitalism*. London: Heinemann.

Bennett, A. (2010) 'Chinese Want to Buy $1.5b NZ Dairy Empire', *New Zealand Herald*. Available at: http://www.nzherald.co.nz/nz/news/article.cfm?c_id=1&objectid=10634177.

Benson, C. and Clay, E. J. (2004) 'Understanding the Economic and Financial Impacts of National Disasters', Disaster Risk Management Series. Washington, DC: World Bank.

Berger, J. (1972) *Ways of Seeing*. Harmondsworth: BBC/Penguin.

Berger, P. (1967) *The Sacred Canopy: Elements of a Sociological Theory of Religion*. Garden City, NY: Doubleday.

Berger, P. L. and Luckmann, T. (1967) *The Social Construction of Reality: A Treatise in the Sociology of Knowledge*. Harmondsworth: Penguin.

Berridge, K. (2001) *Vigor Mortis: The End of the Death Taboo*. London: Profile Books.

Betts, P., Confino, A. and Schumann, D. (2008) 'Death and Twentieth-Century Germany', in A. Confino, P. Betts and D. Schumann (eds), *Between Mass Death and Individual Loss: The Place of the Dead in Twentieth-Century Germany*. New York/Oxford, Berghahn Books, pp. 1–22.

Billings Gazette (2010) 'Obituaries: Nicholas Uzenski'. Available at:http://billingsgazette.com/lifestyles/announcements/obituaries/article_6dc38006-0567-11df-b67f-001cc4c002e0.html; accessed 21 December 2011.

Bilton, T., Bonnett, K., *et al.* (2002) *Introductory Sociology*. Basingstoke: Palgrave Macmillan.

Bloch, M. (1971) *Placing the Dead: Tombs, Ancestral Villages, and Kinship Organization in Madagascar*, Long Grove, IL: Waveland Press.

Boswell, J. ([1769]1952) *The Life of Samuel Johnson LL.D*, Vol. 2. London: Encyclopaedia Britannica.

Bowlby, J. (1980) *Attachment and Loss*. Harmondsworth: Penguin.

Boxing Day Tsunami (2009) 'Facts and Figures'. Available at: http://www.boxingdaytsunami.com/facts-and-figures; accessed 9 November 2011.

Brayne, C., Gao, L., Dewey, M. and Matthews, F. E. (2006) 'Dementia before Death in Ageing Societies – The Promise of Prevention and the Reality' (Public Libraryof Science) PLoS Medicine, 3(10): 1922–30.

Bremborg, A. D. (2006) 'Professionalization without Dead Bodies: The Case of Swedish Funeral Directors', *Mortality*, 11(3): 270–85.

Briggs, A. and Burke, P. (2009) *A Social History of the Media*. Cambridge: Polity Press.

Briggs, B. (2011) 'When You're Dying for a Lower Carbon Footprint'. Available at:http://today.msnbc.msn.com/id/41003238/ns/business-oil_and_energy; accessed 28 December 2011.

Brizio-Skov, F. (2004) *Reconstructing Societies in the Aftermath of War: Memory, Identity and Reconciliation*. New York: Bordighera Press.

Buchanan, D. (2005) 'Death and Bereavement in New Zealand', J. D. Morgan and P. Laungani (eds), *Death and Bereavement Around the World, Vol. 4: Death and Bereavement in Asia, Australia and New Zealand*. Amityville, NY: Baywood.

Bullock, A. *et al.* (1988) *The Fontana Dictionary of Modern Thought*. London: Fontana.

Campbell, K. J. (2001) *Genocide and the Global Village*. Basingstoke, UK: Palgrave.

Canning, J. (2004) 'The Crisis of the Fourteenth Century', in J. Canning, H. Lehmann and J. Winter, *Power, Violence and Mass Death in Pre-Modern and Modern Times*. Aldershot: Ashgate, pp. 9–11.

Castells, M. (2011) *The Rise of the Network Society*. New York: Wiley-Blackwell.

CDC (Centers for Disease Control and Prevention) (2009) 'Smoking & Tobacco Use: Fast Facts', Data and Statisics Fact Sheet. Atlanta, GA: C DC. Available at: http://www.cdc.gov/tobacco/data_statistics/fact_sheets/fast_facts.

Chopra, D. (2006) *Life After Death: The Burden of Proof*. New York: Harmony Books.

CIA (Central Intelligence Agency) (2009) *The World Factbook*. Washington, DC: CIA; available at: https://www.cia.gov/library/publications/the-world-factbook.

Clark, D. (2005) *Cicely Saunders: Founder of the Hospice Movement: Selected Letters 1959–1999*. Oxford: Oxford University Press.

Clayden, A. (2004) 'Natural Burial, British Style', *Landscape Architecture*, 94, 68–77.

CNN (Cable News Network) (1997) 'Mass Suicide Involved Sedatives, Vodka and Careful Planning' (27 March). Available at: http://edition.cnn.com/US/9703/27/suicide/index.html; accessed 15 February 2012.

Cohn, S. K. J. (2004) 'The Black Death: The End of a Paradigm', in J. Canning, H. Lehmann and J. Winter (eds), *Power, Violence and Mass Death in Pre-Modern and Modern Times*. Aldershot: Ashgate, pp. 25–66.

Coles, J. (2008) 'Suicide Doc Sparks Rows', *The Sun* (London). Available at: http://www.thesun.co.uk/sol/homepage/news/article2019734.ece.

Conrad, L. I. *et al.* (1995) *The Western Medical Tradition 800 BC to AD 1800*. Cambridge: Cambridge University Press.

Coser, L. (1992) 'The Revival of the Sociology of Culture: The Case of Collective Memory', *Sociological Forum*, 7(2): 365–73.

Cottle, D. and Keys, A. (2004) 'The Australian Funeral Industry', *Journal of Australian Political Economy*, 54: 32–44.

Crayford, T. (1997) 'Death Rates of Characters in Soap Operas on British Television: Is a Government Health Warning Required?', *BMJ*, 315: 16–49.

Davies, D. (2008) *The Theology of Death*. London: T &T Clark.

Demin, A. (2006) 'Appendix D: Social Aspects of Public Health Challenges in Period of Globalization: The Case of Russia', in S. Knobler, A. Mahmoud, S. Lemon and L. Pray (eds), *The Impact of Globalization on Infectious Disease Emergence and Control: Exploring the Consequences and Opportunities*. Washington, DC, The National Academies Press, pp. 206–27.

DHL (2010) 'Disaster Response Teams' (22 April). Available at: http://www.unglobalcompact.org/docs/issues_doc/un_business_partnerships/UNPSFP_Meeting2010/UNPSFP_2010_DHL_Meier.pdf.

Diamond, J. (1998) *Guns, Germs and Steel: A Short History of Everybody for the Last 13,000 Years*. London: Vintage.

Didion, J. (2006) *The Year of Magical Thinking*. London: Fourth Estate.

Doka, K. (1989) *Disenfranchised Grief: Recognizing Hidden Sorrow*. Lexington, MA: Lexington Books.

Dolan, E. A. (2003) 'British Romantic Melancholia. Charlotte Smith's Elegiac Sonnets, Medical Discourse and the Problem of Sensibility,' *Journal of European Studies*, 33 (3): 237–53.

Dominick, S. A. *et al.* (2009) 'An Internet Tool to Normalize Grief', *Omega*, 60(1): 71–87.

Dougary, G. (2011) 'Interview: Terry Pratchett', *Radio Times*, 11 June.

Douglas, J. D. (1967) *The Social Meanings of Suicide*. Princeton, NJ: Princeton University Press.

Douglas, M. ([1966]2002) *Purity and Danger: An Analysis of Concepts of Pollution and Taboo*. London: Routledge Classics.

Dublin, L. (1963) *Suicide: A Sociological and Statistical Study*. New York: The Ronald Press.

Dueck, R. (2008) 'Renee has been promoted to glory' (17 July). Available at: http://daddydueck.blogspot.co.nz/2008/02/renee-has-been-promoted-to-glory.html.

Durkheim, E. ([1890]1957) *Professional Ethics and Civic Morals*. London: Routledge & Kegan Paul.

Durkheim, E. (1897) *Suicide: A Study in Sociology*. New York: Free Press.

Durkheim, E. ([1912]1995) *The Elementary Forms of Religious Life*. New York: Free Press.

Ehrenreich, B. and English, D. (1973) *Witches, Midwives, and Nurses: A History of Women Healers*. New York: The Feminist Press at CUNY.

Elias, N. (1985) *The Loneliness of the Dying*. Oxford: Basil Blackwell.

Ennis, H. (2007) *Reveries: Photography and Mortality*. Canberra, Australia: National Portrait Gallery.

Erikson, K. T. (1976) 'Loss of Communality at Buffalo Creek', in J. B. Williamson and E. S. Shneidman (eds), *Death: Current Perspectives*. Mountain View, CA: Mayfield, pp. 407–13.

Eyre, A. (1999) 'In Remembrance: Post-Disaster Rituals and Symbols', *Australian Journal of Emergency Management*, 14(4): 23–9.

Fauci, A. (2005) 'The 2005 Robert H. Ebert Memorial Lecture, Emerging and Re-emerging Infectious Diseases: The Perpetual Challenge', Milbank Memorial Fund, 645 Madison Avenue, New York. Available at: http://www.milbank.org/reports/0601fauci/0601Fauci.pdf.

FBI (Federal Bureau of Investigation) (2001) '9/11 Press Release', 28 September.

Fidler, D. P. (2004) *SARS, Governance and the Globalization of Disease*. Basingstoke: Palgrave Macmillan.

Fido, M. (1988) *Bodysnatchers: A History of the Resurrectionists 1742–1832*. London: Weidenfeld & Nicolson.

Finucane, R. C. (1996) *Ghosts: Appearances of the Dead and Cultural Transformation*. Amherst, NY: Prometheus Books.

Fischer, S. (2008) 'Suicide Assisted by Two Swiss Right-to-Die Organisations', *Journal of Medical Ethics*, 34: 810–14.

Fisher, T. (1983) 'There Could Be a McDonald's in Funeral Service', *Mortuary Management Magazine*, January.

Flew, T. (2010) 'Media Convergence', Encyclopædia Britannica Online, 19 October.

Fontana, A. and Keene, J. R. (2009) *Death and Dying in America*. Malden, MA: Polity.

Foucault, M. ([1963]1994) *The Birth of the Clinic: An Archaeology of Medical Perception*. New York: Vintage.

Freeman, R. B. and Cohen, J. T. (2009) 'Transplantation Risks and the Real World: What Does 'High Risk' Really Mean?,' *American Journal of Transplantation*, 9: 23–30.

Freud, S. ([1917]1949) 'Mourning and Melancholia', in J. Riviere (ed.), *Sigmund Freud, Collected Papers, Volume IV*. London: Hogarth Press, pp. 152–70.

Friedman, M. (1962) *Capitalism and Freedom*. Chicago, IL: University of Chicago Press.

Friend, D. (2006) *Watching the World Change: The Stories Behind the Images of 9/11*. New York: Picador.

Fukuyama, F. (2003) *Our Posthuman Future: Consequences of the Biotechnology Revolution*. London: Picador.

Garfinkel, H. (1967) 'Practical Sociological Reasoning: Some Features in the Work of the Los Angeles Suicide Prevention Centre', in E. S. Shneidman (ed.), *Essays in Self-Destruction*. New York: Science House, pp. 171–87.

Geis, G. and Brown, G. C. (2008) 'The Transnational Traffic in Human Body Parts', *Journal of Contemporary Criminal Justice*, 24: 212.

Gellert, G. A. (1995) 'Humanitarian Responses to Mass Violence Perpetrated Against Vulnerable Populations', *British Medical Journal*, 311 (October): 995–1001.

General Register Office for Scotland 2009, *Life Expectancy for Administrative Areas within Scotland 2006-2008*, Edinburgh: General Register Office.

Geneva Declaration Secretariat (2008) *The Global Burden of Armed Violence*. Geneva: Geneva Declaration Secretariat.

Gennep, A. van ([1960]2004) *Rites of Passage*. London: Routledge & Kegan Paul.

George, V. and Wilding, P. (2002) *Globalization and Human Welfare*. Basingstoke: Palgrave Macmillan.

Gibson, M. (2007) 'Death and Mourning in Technologically Mediated Culture', *Health Sociology Review*, 16(5): 415–24.

Giddens, A. (1971) *The Sociology of Suicide*. London: Frank Cass.

Giddens, A. (1991) *Modernity and Self-identity: Self and Society in the Late Modern Age*. Cambridge: Polity Press.

Giddens, A. (1999) 'Runaway World', Reith Lectures, BBC Radio 4, London.

Giddens, A. (2004) 'The Globalizing of Modernity', in D. Held and A. McGrew (eds), *The Global Transformations Reader*. Cambridge: Polity Press, pp. 60–6.

Giddens, A. (2007) *Europe in the Global Age*. Cambridge: Polity Press.

Gilbert, S. M. (2006) *Death's Door: Modern Dying and the Ways We Grieve*. New York: W. W. Norton.

Giroux, H. A. (2006) *Beyond the Spectacle of Terrorism: Global Uncertainty and the Challenge of the New Media*. London: Paradigm.

Gladwell, M. (2002) *The Tipping Point: How Little Things Can Make a Big Difference*. Boston, MA: First Back Bay.

Glaser, B. and Strauss, A. (1968) *Time for Dying*, Chicago, IL: Aldine.

Glasgow University Media Group (1976) *Bad News*. London: Routledge.

Glynn, S. A. (2003) 'Effect of a National Disaster on Blood Supply and Safety: The September 11 Experience', *Journal of the American Medical Association*, 289: 2246–53.

Goethe, J. W. von ([1800]1957) *The Sufferings of Young Werther*. London: John Calder.

Goldberg, P. (2006) 'What Have We Learned?: Memorial 9/11', *The Brian Lehrer Show*, USA, WNYC Radio.

Gorer, G. (1955) 'The Pornography of Death', *Encounter* (reprinted in Gorer 1965).

Gorer, G. (1965) *Death, Grief and Mourning in Contemporary Britain*. London: Cresset.

Goss, R. E. and Klass, D. (1997) 'Tibetan Buddism and the Resolution of Grief: The Bardo-Thodol for the Dying and the Grieving', *Death Studies*, 21(4): 377–95.

Goss, R. E. and Klass, D. (2005) *Dead But Not Lost: Grief Narratives in Religious Traditions*. Oxford: AltaMira Press.

Grossberg, K. A. (2004) 'Outsourcing Enables American Startup to Enter Japanese Funeral Services Industry', *Strategy and Leadership*, 32(6): 37–41.

Guriev, S. and Rachinsky, A. (2009) 'The Evolution of Personal Wealth in the Former Soviet Union and Central and Eastern Europe', in J. B. Davies (ed.), *Personal Wealth from a Global Perspective*. Oxford: Oxford University Press, pp. 134–49.

Hadaegh, B. and Babcock, G. (2005) *A Certain Kind of Death: What Happens to the Unmourned?* Houston, TX: Wellspring.

Hall, J. A. and Jarvie, I. C. (eds) (1992) *Transition to Modernity: Essays on Power, Wealth and Belief.* Cambridge: Cambridge University Press.

Hallam, E. and Hockey, J. (2001) *Death, Memory and Material Culture.* Oxford: Berg.

Harjula, H. (2006) 'Hazardous Waste', *Annals of the New York Academy of Sciences*, 1076: 462–77.

Harrington, D. E. (2007) 'Markets: Preserving Funeral Markets with Ready to Embalm Laws', *Journal of Economic Perspectives*, 21(4): 201–16.

Harrison, T. (1999) 'Globalization and the Trade in Human Body Parts', *Canadian Review of Sociology and Anthropology*, 36(1): 21–35.

HealthGrades (2005) *Second Annual Patient Safety in American Hospitals Report*, May. Denver, CO: HealthGrades Inc.

Heaven's Gate (1997) Home page. Available at: http://www.wave.net/upg/gate/.

Heaphy, B. (2007) *Late Modernity and Social Change: Reconstructing Social and Personal Life.* New York: Routledge.

Hertz, R. ([1960]2004) *Death and the Right Hand.* London: Routledge.

Heyboer, K. (2008) 'Grief blogging: Talking with the blogger behind "A Widow for One Year"'. The Star-Ledger, New Jersey. Accessed 25 July 2012. http://blog.nj.com/jerseyblogs/2008/04/grief_blogging_talking_with_th.html.

Higo, M. J. (2006) 'Four Hypotheses of the Contemporary Revival of Death: Z. Bauman's Contribution to Social Theory on Death and Dying', American Sociological Association 101st Annual Meeting, Palais des congrès de Montréal, Québec, Canada, May/June.

Hilhorst, D. (2005) 'Dead Letter or Living Document? Ten Years of the Code of Conduct for Disaster Relief', *Disasters*, 29(4): 351–69.

Hobbes, T. ([1651]1968) *Leviathan or The Matter, Forme and Power of a Common Wealth Ecclesiasticall and Civil*, Harmondsworth: Penguin.

Hobsbawm, E. and Ranger, T. (eds) ([1983]2008) *The Invention of Tradition.* Cambridge: Cambridge University Press.

Hockey, J. (1994) 'The Acceptable Face of Human Grieving?', in D. Clark (ed.) *The Sociology of Death: Theory, Culture, Practice.* Oxford: Basil Blackwell, pp. 129–48.

Hockey, J., *et al.* (2010) *The Matter of Death.* Basingstoke, UK: Palgrave Macmillan.

Holden, L. (2001) *Taboos: Structure and Rebellion.* London: The Institute for Cultural Research.

Holson, L. M. (2011) For Funerals Too Far, Mourners Gather on the Web, *The New York Times*, 24 January.

Hope, V. (2007) *Death in Ancient Rome.* London: Routledge.

Horizon (2008) 'How Much Is Your Dead Body Worth?', *Horizon*, BBC TV, 31 October.

Horrox, R. (1994) *The Black Death.* Manchester: Manchester University Press.

Hosking, J. (2004) *Mademoiselle and the Doctor*, Enmore, NSW, Australia: Ikandy Films.

Howarth, G. (1996) *Last Rites: The Work of the Modern Funeral Director.* Amityville, NY: Baywood.

Howarth, G. (2007) *Death and Dying: A Sociological Introduction.* Cambridge: Polity Press.

Howarth, G. (2009) 'The Demography of Dying', in A. Kellehear (ed.), *The Study of Dying: From Autonomy to Transformation*. Cambridge: Cambridge University Press. pp. 99–122.

Human Security Report Project (2010) 'The Shrinking Cost of War'. Available at: http://www.humansecurityreport.info/index.php?option=com_content&task=view&id=205&Itemid=91; accessed 9 April 2010.

Humphrey, D. (1973) 'Dissection and Discrimination: The Social Origins of Cadavers in America 1760–1915', *Bulletin of the New York Academy of Medicine*, 49(9): 819–27.

Hurst, S. and Mauron, A. (2003) 'Assisted Suicide and Euthanasia in Switzerland: Allowing a Role for Non-Physicians', *British Medical Journal*, 326: 271–3.

Huyssen, A. (2003) 'Trauma and memory', in J. Bennett and R. J. Kennedy, *World Memory – Personal Trajectories in Global Time*. Basingstoke: Palgrave, pp. 16–29.

Hyman, H. H. (1982) *Health Planning: A Systematic Approach*. Rockville, MD: Aspen.

Ignatieff, M. (2004) 'The Terrorist as Auteur', *New York Times Magazine*, 14 November, p. 50.

IMDb (2010) *The Big C*. Available at: http://www.imdb.com/title/tt1515193.

International Federation of Red Cross and Red Crescent Societies (1992) *Code of Conduct: Principles of Conduct for the International Red Cross and Red Crescent Movement and NGOs in Disaster Response Programmes*. Available at: http://www.ifrc.org/publicat/conduct/code.asp; accessed 22 April 2010.

Jackson, M. (2011) *The Oxford Handbook of the History of Medicine*. Oxford: Oxford University Press.

Jalland, P. (2006) *Changing Ways of Death in Twentieth-century Australia: War, Medicine and the Funeral Business*. Sydney, Australia: University of New South Wales Press.

Johnston, A. (2008) *Ladies, a Plate: Traditional Home Baking*. Rosedale, Auckland, NZ: Penguin.

Jones, E. (2007) *Spaces of Belonging: Home Culture and Identity in 20th Century French Autobiography*. Amsterdam: Rodopi.

Jones, K. E. *et al.* (2008) 'Global Trends in Emerging Infectious Diseases', *Nature*, 451 (February): 990–4.

Jupp, P. (ed.) (2008) *Death Our Future: Christian Theology and Funeral Practice*. London: Epworth.

Jupp, P. C. (2005) *From Dust to Ashes: The Growth of Cremation in England 1820–2000*. Basingstoke: Palgrave Macmillan.

Kearl, M. C. (1989) *Endings: A Sociology of Death and Dying*. New York/Oxford: Oxford University Press.

Kellehear, A. (2007) *A Social History of Dying*. Cambridge: Cambridge University Press.

Kelley, T. (2003) 'Officials Identify Remains of Two Hijackers through DNA'. Available at: http://www.nytimes.com/2003/03/01/nyregion/officials-identify-remains-of-two-hijackers-through-dna.html; accessed 1 March 2012.

Kellner, D. (2004) '9/11, Spectacles of Terror, and Media Manipulation,' *Critical Discourse Studies*, 1(1): 41–64.

Kiernan, B. (2007) *Blood and Soil: A World History of Genocide and Extermination from Sparta to Darfur*. New Haven, CT: Yale University Press.

Kingsepp, E. (2003) 'Apocalypse the Spielberg Way: Representations of Death and Ethics in *Saving Private Ryan*, *Band of Brothers* and the Videogame *Medal of Honor: Frontline*'. Level Up Conference Proceedings: Proceedings of the 2003 Digital Games Research Association Conference, University of Utrecht, The Netherlands.

Kirkwood, T. (2001) 'Brave Old World', Reith Lectures 2001, London, Royal Society.

Klass, D. (1992) 'Religious Aspects in the Resolution of Parental Grief: Solace and Social Support', in K. Pargament, R. E. Hess and K. I. Maton (eds), *Religion and Prevention in Mental Health: Research, Vision, Action*. New York: Routledge, pp. 155–77.

Klass, D. (2007) 'Grief and Mourning in Cross-Cultural Perspective', *Encyclopaedia of Death and Dying*. Available at: http://www. deathreference.com/Gi-Ho/Grief-and-Mourning-in-Cross-Cultural-Perspective.html; accessed 1 February 2010.

Klein, N. (2007) *The Shock Doctrine: The Rise of Disaster Capitalism*. New York: Metropolitan Books.

Knobler, S. *et al.* (2006) *The Impact of Globalization on Infectious Disease Emergence and Control: Exploring the Consequences and Opportunities*. Washington, DC: The National Academic Press.

Koch, T. (2011) *Disease Maps: Epidemics on the Ground*. Chicago, IL: University of Chicago Press.

Koop, C.E., Pearson, C.E. and Schwarz, M.R. (2000) *Critical Issues in Global Health* San Francisco, CA: Jossey-Bass.

Kübler-Ross, E. (1969) *On Death and Dying*. New York: Macmillan.

Kuhlmann, E. (2006) *Shifting Spheres of Opportunity: Professions, Globalisation and the European Project*, European Sociological Association Interim Workshop, Bremen, Germany.

Kumar, H. (2008) 'Kidney Thefts Shock India', *New York Times*, Asia Pacific. 17.March. Available at: http://www.nytimes.com/2008/01/30/world/asia/30kidney.html?scp=1&sq=kidney&st=nyt

Kumar, K. (1996) 'Modernity', in W. Outhwaite and T. Bottomore. (eds), *The Blackwell Dictionary of Twentieth-Century Social Thought*. Oxford: Basil Blackwell, pp. 391–2.

Laderman, G. (2003) *Rest in Peace: A Cultural History of Death and the Funeral Home in Twentieth-Century America*. New York: Oxford University Press.

Lee, R. L. M. (2008) 'Modernity, Mortality and Re-Enchantment: The Death Taboo Revisited', *Sociology*, 42(4): 745–59.

Lefebvre, B. (2006) 'Funeral Co-operatives in Quebec: Lessons from a Success' (Workshop 2), *Communities Under Pressure: The Role of Co-operatives and the Social Economy*, Communities Synthesis Report, Government of Canada.

Lemert, C. (1999) 'The Might Have Been and Could Be of Religion in Social Theory', *Sociological Theory*, 17(3): 240–63.

Lennon, J. and Foley, M. (2006) *Dark Tourism: The Attraction of Death and Disaster*. London: Thomson.

Levy, D. and Sznaider, N. (2006) *Holocaust and Memory in the Global Age*. Philadelphia, PA: Temple University.

Lewis, M. J. (2007) *Medicine and Care of the Dying: A Modern History*. Oxford: Oxford University Press.

Liemt, G. van (2002) *The World Tobacco Industry: Trends and Prospects*. Geneva: International Labour Office.

Lifton, R. J. (1983) *The Broken Connection: On Death and the Continuity of Life.* New York: Basic Books.

Lind, A. (1989) 'Hospitals and Hospices: Feminist Decisions About Care for the Dying', in K. S. Ratcliff (ed.), *Healing Technologies: Feminist Perspectives.* Ann Arbor, MI: University of Michigan.

Lindemann, M. (2010) *Medicine and Society in Early Modern Europe.* Cambridge: Cambridge University Press.

Lisk, F. (2010) *Global Institutions and the HIV/AIDS Epidemic.* New York: Routledge.

Llewellyn, N. (1997) *Visual Culture in the English Death Ritual c. 1500–c. 1800.* Chicago, IL: University of Chicago Press.

Lock, M. (2003) 'On Making Up the Good-As-Dead in a Utilitarian World', in S. Franklin and M. Lock (eds), *Remaking Life and Death: Toward an Anthropology of the Biosciences.* Santa Fe, NM/Oxford: School of American Research Press.

Lock, M. and Nguyen, V.-K. (2010) *An Anthropology of Biomedicine.* Oxford: Wiley-Blackwell.

Loeterman, B. (2002) 'Instructions for the Last Night: Inside the Terror Network, Tracking Their Personal Stories', *Frontline* , 17 January. Transcript available at: http://www.pbs.org/wgbh/pages/frontline/shows/network/etc/script.html.

Lokiit (2009) *Russian Male Death Rates 1950-2008*, Wikipedia. Retrieved: 9 June, from http://en.wikipedia.org/wiki/File:Russian_Male_Death_Rate_since_1950.PNG.

Lupton, D. (2006) 'Sociology and Risk', in G. Mythen and S. Walklate (eds), *Beyond the Risk Society: Critical Reflections on Risk and Human Security.* Maidenhead: Open University Press, pp. 11–24.

Macionis, J. J. (2008) *Society: The Basics.* Upper Saddle River, NJ: Pearson Prentice-Hall.

Mahr, K. (2009) 'Neda Agha-Soltan', *Time Specials.* Available at: http://www.time.com/time/specials/packages/article/0,28804,1945379_1944701_1944705,00.html; accessed 1 September 2011.

Malinowski, B. (1948) *Magic, Science and Religion and Other Essays.* Boston: Beacon Press.

Malthus, T.R. ([1803] 1970) *An Essay on the Principle of Population.* Harmondsworth: Penguin.

Mara, W. (2010) *The Chernobyl Disaster: Legacy and Impact on the Future of Nuclear Energy.* New York: Benchmark Books.

Maris, R. W. (1969) *Social Forces in Urban Suicide*, Homewood, IL: Dorsey Press.

Markusen, E., Christensen, S. and Schreiber, J.L. (1980) *A Viewer's Guide for Joan Robinson: One Woman's Story and Death and Dying, Challenge and Change.* Dubuque, IA: Kendal/Hunt Publishing Company.

McCrone, D. (1992) *Understanding Scotland: The Sociology of a Stateless Nation.* London: Routledge.

McFarland, E. (2010) 'Passing Time: Cultures of Death and Mourning', in L. Abrams and C. Brown (eds), *A History of Everyday Life in Twentieth-Century Scotland.* Edinburgh: Edinburgh University Press, pp. 254–81; 302.

McKay, M. (2011) 'Olympic Luger Dies in Practice'. Available at: http://www.tech-banyan.com/9209/nodar-kumaritashvili-luge-youtube-video; accessed 24 September 2011.

McKeown, T. (1976) *The Role of Medicine: Dream, Mirage or Nemesis?* London: Nuffield Provincial Hospitals Trust.

McKinlay, E. (2001) 'Within the Circle of Care: Patient Experiences of Receiving Palliative Care', *Journal of Palliative Care*, 17: 22–9.

McKinley, J. (2008) 'Surgeon Accused of Speeding a Death to Get Organs'. Available at: http://www.nytimes.com/2008/02/27/us/27transplant.html; accessed 16 March 2009.

McLennan, G. (2007) 'Towards Postsecular Sociology?', *Sociology*, 41(5): 857–70.

McLennan, G. (2011) *Story of Sociology: A First Companion to Social Theory*. London/ New York, Bloomsbury.

McLennan, G. *et al.* (2009) *Exploring Society: Sociology for New Zealand Students*, *3rd edn.* Auckland, NZ: Pearson Education.

McManus, R. (2005) 'Freedom and Suicide: A Genealogy of Suicide Regulation in New Zealand 1840–2000', *Journal of Historical Sociology*, 18(4): 430–56.

McManus, R. (Snr) (2008) 'Scottish funerals'. Interview by R. McManus (Jr), Dunoon, Scotland.

McManus, R. and Schafer, C. T. (2009) *Final Arrangements: Attitudes to Funeral Costs in New Zealand*, Christchurch, NZ: University of Canterbury.

McNeill, W. (1998) *Plagues and Peoples*. New York, Anchor Books.

Meinwald, D. (1990) 'Memento Mori: Death and Photography in Nineteenth Century America', *California Museum of Photography Bulletin*, 9.

Mellor, P. and Shilling, C. (1993) 'Modernity, Self-Identity and the Sequestration of Death', *Sociology* 27(3): 411–31.

Mellor, P. A. (1993) 'Death in High Modernity: The Contemporary Presence and Absence of Death', in D. Clark (ed.), *The Sociology of Death*. Oxford: Basil Blackwell, pp. 11–30.

Mellor, P. A. (2004) 'Religion, Culture and Society in the "Information Age"', *Sociology of Religion*, 65(4): 357–71.

Milicevic, N. (2002) 'The Hospice Movement: History and Current Worldwide Situation', *Archive of Oncology*, 10(1): 29–32.

Mims, C. (1998) *When We Die: The Science, Culture, and Rituals of Death*. New York: St. Martin's Press.

Misztal, B. A. (2003) *Theories of Social Remembering*. Maidenhead, UK/Philadelphia, PA: Open University Press.

Misztal, B. A. (2010) 'Collective Memory in a Global Age: Learning How and What to Remember', *Current Sociology*, 58(24): 24–44.

Mitford, J. (1963) *The American Way of Death*. London: Hutchinson.

Moghadam, A. (2008) *The Globalization of Martyrdom: Al Qaeda, Salafi Jihad, and the Diffusion of Suicide Attacks*. Baltimore, MD: Johns Hopkins University Press.

Mohr, J. (1984) 'Patterns of Abortion and the Response of American Physicians 1790–1930', in J. Leavitt (ed.), *Women and Health in America: Historical Readings*. Madison, WI: University of Wisconsin Press, pp. 117–23.

Moon, G. *et al.* (2007) 'Fat Nation: Deciphering the Distinctive Geographies of Obesity in England', *Social Science and Medicine*, 65(1): 20–31.

Moran, A. (2004) *Australia: Nation, Belonging and Globalization*. London: Routledge.

Morris, R. D. (2007) *The Blue Death: Disease, Disaster and the Water We Drink*. New York: HarperCollins.

Morris, S. M. and Thomas, C. (2005) 'Placing the Dying Body: Emotional,

Situational and Embodied Factors in Preferences for Place of Final Care and Death in Cancer', in J. Davidson, L. Bondi and M. Smith (eds), *Emotional Geographies*. Basingstoke: Ashgate, pp. 19–31.

Mulkay, M. (1993) 'Social Death in Britain', in D. Clark (ed.), *The Sociology of Death*. Oxford: Basil Blackwell.

Naidu, E. (2004) *Symbolic Reparations: A Fractured Opportunity*. Research Report. Johannesburg, South Africa: Centre for the Study of Violence and Reconciliation (CSVR).

Najman, J. M. (2000) 'The Demography of Death: Patterns of Australian Mortality', in A. Kellehear (ed.), *Death and Dying in Australia*. Oxford: Oxford University Press.

National Cancer Institute USA (2005) 'Bereavement, Mourning, Grief'. Available at: http://dying.about.com/gi/dynamic/offsite.htm?zi=1/XJ&sdn=dying&zu= http%3A%2F%2Fwww.nci.nih.gov%2Fcancertopics%2Fpdq%2Fsupportiveca re%2Fbereavement%2FHealthProfessional%2Fpage1.

National Funeral Directors & Morticians Association (2002) 'Death Be Not Proud: Theme Funerals', *Harper's Magazine*, 305: 21–2.

National Research Council (2007) *Tools and Methods for Estimating Populations at Risk from Natural Disasters and Complex Humanitarian Crises*. Washington, DC: The National Academies Press.

Navarro, V. (1976) *Medicine under Capitalism*. New York: Prodist.

Nesporova, O. (2007) 'Believer Perspectives on Death and Funeral Practices in an Non-believing Country', *Czech Sociological Review*, 43(6): 1175–93.

Nichols, B. (1991) *Representing Reality: Issues and Concepts in Documentary*. Bloomington, IN: Indiana University Press.

Nutton, V. (2005) *Ancient Medicine*. London: Routledge.

O'Byrne, D. (2003) *The Dimensions of Global Citizenship: Political Identity Beyond the Nation-State*. London: Frank Cass.

O'Donnell, D. A. (1871) 'Report on Criminal Abortion', *Transactions of the American Medical Association*, 239–58.

Ong, W. J. (1982) *Orality and Literacy: The Technologizing of the Word*. New York: Routledge.

Operation Iraqi Freedom (2009) 'Iraq Coalition Casualty Count'. Available at: http://icasualties.org/iraq/index.aspx; accessed 23 April 2010.

Orent, W. (2004) *Plague: The Mysterious Past and Terrifying Future of the World's Most Dangerous Disease*. New York: Free Press.

Outhwaite, W. *et al.* (1996) *The Blackwell Dictionary of Twentieth-Century Social Thought*. Oxford: Basil Blackwell.

Papadatou, D. (2009) *In the Face of Death: Professionals Who Care for the Dying and the Bereaved*. New York: Springer.

Park, G. R. (2004) 'Death and Its Diagnosis by Doctors', *British Journal of Anaesthesia*, 92(5): 625–8.

Parkes, C. M. (1972) *Bereavement: Studies of Grief in Adult Life*. London: Tavistock.

Parkes, C. M. (2006) *Love and Loss: The Roots of Grief and its Complications*. Abingdon: Routledge.

Parsons, B. (1999) 'Yesterday, Today and Tomorrow. The Lifecycle of the UK Funeral Industry', *Mortality*, 4(2): 127–45.

Parsons, T. *et al.* (1973) 'The "Gift of Life" and Its Reciprocation', in A. Mack (ed.), *Death in American Experience*. New York: Schocken Books, pp. 1–49.

Pearson, E. (2004) *Coercion in the Kidney Trade? A Background Study of Trafficking in Human Organs Worldwide*. Sector Project against Trafficking in Women.

Phipps, E. *et al.* (2003) 'Family Care Giving For Patients At Life's End: Report from the Cultural Variations Study (CVAS)', *Palliative and Supportive Care*, 1: 165–70.

Platt, C. (1996) *King Death: The Black Death and Its Aftermath in Late-Medieval England*. London: UCL Press.

Pope, J. (2008) 'The Globalisation of Medicine: The Emerging Market of Medical Tourists – Estimates , Challenges and Prospects', in J. Bose and B. Sumathi (eds), *Medical Tourism: Perspectives and Specific Country Experiences*. Hyderabad, India: The Icfai University Press, pp. 3–27.

Porter, S. (1999) *The Great Plague*. London: Sutton Publishers.

Powell, D. (2007) '"It Was Hard to Die Frae Hame": Death, Grief and Mourning among Scottish Migrants to New Zealand 1840–1890', *History*. Hamilton, Waikato, NZ: University of Waikato, p. 112.

Powles, J. (1971) 'On the Limitations of Modern Medicine', *Science, Medicine and Man*, 1: 1–30.

Project: Carousel! (2010) 'Is Terrorism the Accident of Global Mass Media?', Centre for Media and Film Studies at the School of Oriental and African Studies (SOAS), University of London. Available at: http://www.projectcarousel.org/?s= Global+Mass+MEdia.

Prothero, S. (2001) *Purified by Fire: A History of Cremation in America*. Berkeley/Los Angeles, CA/London: University of California Press.

Querioz, F. and Rugg, J. (2003) 'The Development of Cemeteries in Portugal c. 1755–1870', *Mortality*, 8(2): 113–28.

Raeburn, G. D. (2010) 'The Changing Face of Scottish Burial Practices, 1560–1645', *Reformation and Renaissance Review*, 11(2): 181–201.

Reid, T. and Goddard, J. (2005) 'Starving Survivors Die As Anarchy Reigns', *The Press*, Christchurch, NZ, p. B1.

Remmler, K. (1997) 'Memorial Spaces and Jewish Identities in Post-Wall Berlin', in J. Peck (ed.), *German Cultures, Foreign Cultures: The Politics of Belonging*, Baltimore AICGS Research Report No. 8 Humanities Program, American Institute for Contemporary German Studies, Johns Hopkins University, Baltimore, MD, pp. 40–53.

Rice, G. (2005) '"Severest Setback" for Maori?', in G. Rice (ed.), *Black November. The 1918 Influenza Pandemic in New Zealand*. Christchurch, NZ: University of Canterbury Press.

Richardson, R. (2001) *Death, Dissection and the Destitute*. Chicago, IL: University of Chicago Press.

Riska, E. (2010) 'Gender and Medicalization and Biomedicalization Theories', in A. Clarke *et al.* (eds), *Biomedicalization: Technoscience, Health and Illness in the U.S.* Durham, NC: Duke University Press, pp. 147–70.

Ritzer, G. (1993) *The McDonaldization of Society*. Thousand Oaks, CA: Pine Forge Press.

Rizvi, F. (2003) 'Globalisation and the Cultural Politics of Race and Educational Reform', *Journal of Educational Change*, 4: 209–11.

Robinson, E. 1990. *One Dark Mile: A Widower's Story*. Massachusetts, MA: University of Massachusetts.

Robinson, W. G. (1997) 'Heaven's Gate: The End?', *Journal of Computer-mediated Communication*, 3(3).

Rosenblatt, P. C. *et al.* (1976) *Grief and Mourning in Cross-Cultural Perspective.* New York: HRAF Press.

Ruby, J. (1995) *Secure the Shadow: Death and Photography in America.* Cambridge, MA: MIT Press.

Rugg, J. (2006) 'Lawn Cemeteries: The Emergence of a New Landscape of Death', *Urban History*, 33(2): 213–33.

Sahu, S. (2009) *Guidebook on Technologies for Disaster Preparedness and Mitigation.* New Delhi, India: Asian and Pacific Centre for Transfer of Technology (APCTT).

Sainsbury, P. (1955) *Suicide in London.* London: Chapman & Hall.

Sappol, M. (2002) *A Traffic of Dead Bodies: Anatomy and Embodied Social Identity in Nineteenth-Century America.* Princeton, NJ: Princeton University Press.

Schafer, C. (2007) 'Dead Serious? Funeral Directing in New Zealand', *Sites*, 4(195–21)

Schiappa, E. *et al.* (2010) 'Can a Television Series Change Attitudes About Death? A Study of College Students and *Six Feet Under*', *Death Studies*, 28: 495–74.

Scottish Government, The (2010) 'Scotland's Population Statistics 2009', News Release, Edinburgh: The Scottish Government.

Searle, C. and Heremaia, C. (2007) Cemetery Plan (2007) Christchurch, New Zealand, Christchurch City Council. Available at: http://www.ssrc.canterbury. ac.nz/research/2006-7/Christchurch_and.shtml] .

Secretary of State for Trade and Industry (1987) *Co-operative Wholesale Society Limited and House of Fraser PLC: A Report on the Acquisition by the Co-operative Wholesale Society Limited of the Scottish Funerals Business of House of Fraser PLC.* London; Competition Commission.

Sharp, L. (2006) *Strange Harvest: Organ Transplants, Denatured Bodies and the Transformed Self*, Los Angeles, CA: University of Calfornia Press.

Shaw, M. (2000) *Theory of the Global State: Globality as an Unfinished Revolution.* Cambridge: Cambridge University Press.

Shimazono, Y. (2007) 'The State of the International Organ Trade: A Provisional Picture Based on Integration of Available Information', *Bulletin of the World Health Organization*, 85(12).

Shiva, V. (1994) *Close to Home: Women Reconnect Ecology, Health And Development Worldwide.* Philadelphia, PA: New Society Press.

Shostak, S. (2006) *The Evolution of Death.* New York: State University of New York Press.

Shrestha, L.B. 2006, *Life expectancy in the United States, CRS report for Congress*, Domestic Social Policy Division, Washington, DC.

Siddell, M. and Komaromy, C. (2003) 'Who Dies in Care Homes for Older People?', in J. S. Katz and S. Peace (eds), *End-of-life Care Homes: A Palliative Approach.* Oxford: Oxford University Press, pp. 43–57.

Sinclair, P. (2007) *Rethinking Palliative Care: A Social Role Valorisation Approach.* Bristol: Policy Press.

Skinner, A. and Zak, J. S. (2004) 'Counseling and the Internet', *American Behavioral Scientist*, 48: 434–46.

Slater, P. (2005) 'Why America is Polarized'. Available at: http://www. philipslater.com/why%20america%20is%20polarized.pdf.

Smith, V. (2010) *Intimate Strangers: Friendship, Exchange and Pacific Encounters.* Cambridge: Cambridge University Press.

Sobchack, V. (1984) 'Inscribing Ethical Space: Ten Propositions on Death, Representation and Documentary', *Quarterly Review of Films*, 9: 283–300.

Spence, A. (1998) *Way to Go*. London: Phoenix House.

Spurr, S. J. (1993) 'The Proposed Market for Human Organs', *Journal of Health Politics*, 18(1): 189–202.

Stack, S. (2003) 'Media Coverage as a Risk Factor in Suicide', *Journal of Epidemiology and Community Health*, 57: 238–40.

Stannard, D. E. (1977) *The Puritan Way of Death: A Study in Religion, Culture, and Social Change*. New York: Oxford University Press.

Starr, D. (1998) *Blood: An Epic History of Medicine and Commerce*. New York: Alfred A. Knopf.

Statistics New Zealand (2009) *New Zealand Life Tables: 2005–2007*, Statistics New Zealand, Wellington.

Steel, G. (2010) *Stardust: Some Thoughts on Death*. Glasgow: St Mungo Museum.

Steering Committee for Humanitarian Response (1992) *Code of Conduct for the International Red Cross and Red Crescent Movement and NGOs in Disaster Relief*. Geneva: International Federation of Red Cross and Red Crescent Societies.

Strange, C. (2000) 'From "Place of Misery" to "Lottery of Life": Interpreting Port Arthur's Past', *Open Museum Journal*, 2.

Stroebe, M. and Schut, H. (1999) 'The Dual Process Model of Coping with Bereavement, Rationale and Description', *Death Studies*, 23: 197–224.

Stuckler, D. *et al.* (2009) 'Mass Privatisation and the Post-Communist Mortality Crisis: A Cross-National Analysis', *The Lancet*, 373: 399–407.

Sudnow, D. (1967) *Passing On: The Social Organisation of Dying*. Upper Saddle River, NJ: Prentice Hall.

Suzuki, H. (2003) 'McFunerals: The Transition of Japanese Funerary Services', *Asian Anthropology*, 2: 49–78.

Swinburn, B. *et al.* (2011) 'The Global Obesity Pandemic: Shaped by Global Drivers and Local Environments', *Lancet*, 9793: 804–14.

Sztompka, P. (1994) *The Sociology of Social Change*. Oxford, UK: Basil Blackwell.

Tait, S. (2006) 'Autoptic Vision and the Necrophilic Imaginary in CSI', *International Journal of Cultural Studies*, 9(1): 45–62.

Takeda, M. B. and Helms, M. M. (2006) '"Bureaucracy, Meet Catastrophe": Analysis of Hurricane Katrina Relief Efforts and Their Implications for Emergency Response Governance', *International Journal of Public Sector Management*, 19(4): 397–411.

Taylor, L. (2005) 'On Pain of Death', *Dispatches* TV programme, Channel 4, UK.

Thornton, K. and Phillips, C. B. (2010) 'Performing the Good Death: The Medieval Ars Moriendi and Contemporary Doctors', *Medical Humanities*, 35: 94–7.

Tierney, K. J. (2007) 'From the Margins to the Mainstream? Disaster Research at the Cross Roads', *Annual Review of Sociology*, 33.

Titmuss, R. (1970) *The Gift Relationship: From Human Blood to Social Policy*. London: George Allen & Unwin.

Tonkin, P. and Laurence, J. (2003) 'Space and Memory', *Architecture Australia*, September/October.

Toqueville, A. de ([1835]1998) *Democracy in America*. Ware: Wordsworth.

Townsend, P. and Gordon, D. (2002) *World Poverty: New Policies to Defeat an Old Enemy*. Bristol: Policy Press.

Turner, B. S. (2007) 'Managing Religions: State Responses to Religious Diversity', *Contemporary Islam*, 1(2): 123–37.

Turner, B. S. (2010) 'Biotechnology and the Prolongation of Life', in C. E. Bird *et al.* (eds), *Handbook of Medical Sociology*. Nashville, TN: Vanderbilt University Press, pp. 435–45.

Turner, V. ([1969]1995) *The Ritual Process: Structure and Anti-Structure*. New York: Aldine.

Tyler, T. R. (2006) 'Viewing CSI and the Threshold of Guilt: Managing Truth and Justice in Reality and Fiction', *The Yale Law Journal*, 115(5): 1050–85.

UNAIDS (2006) *AIDS Epidemic Update: December 2006*. Geneva: UNAIDS/WHO.

United Nations (2005) 'The United Nations Framework Convention on Climate Change'. Available at:http://unfccc.int/essential_background/convention/background/items/1353.php; accessed 15 November 2005.

United Nations (2009) *The Secretary General's High Level Task Force on the Global Food Security Crisis*. Geneva: United Nations Task Force.

United Nations (2011a) *World Mortality Chart*. Geneva: United Nations.

United Nations (2011b) *World Population Prospects*. Geneva: United Nations.

United Nations Environment Programme (2002) *Global Trends in Generation and Transboundary Movements of Hazardous Wastes and Other Wastes*. Geneva: Basel Convention.

Urry, J. (2007) *Mobilities*. Cambridge: Polity Press.

Valentine, C. (2008) *Bereavement Narratives: Continuing Bonds in the Twenty-First Century*. Abingdon/New York: Routledge.

Vickers, J. (2001) *Funerals: A Report of the OFT Inquiry into the Funerals Industry*. London Office of Fair Trading.

Wadmin, W. (2011) 'Christchurch Quake Photos 1: The Red Zone'. Available at: http://www.weatherwatch.co.nz/content/christchurch-quake-photos-1-red-zone-20pics; accessed 8 November 2011.

Waldby, C. and Mitchell, R. (2006) *Tissue Economies: Blood, Organs, and Cell Lines in Late Capitalism*. Durham, NC/London: Duke University Press.

Walker, P. and Williams, R. (2009) 'Prepare for Swine Flu Pandemic, WHO Warns: Health Chiefs Say Plans to Fight Swine Flu Pandemic Needed Now, Especially in Developing World', *Guardian Online*, 28 April. Available at: http://www.guardian.co.uk/world/2009/apr/28/swine-flu-mexico-scotland.

Walter, T. (1991) 'Modern Death: Taboo or Not Taboo', *Sociology*, 25: 293–310.

Walter, T. (1994) *The Revival of Death*. London: Routledge.

Walter, T. (1999) *On Bereavement: The Culture of Grief*. Maidenhead: Open University Press.

Walter, T. (2005) 'Three Ways to Arrange a Funeral: Mortuary Variation in the Modern West', *Mortality*, 10(3): 173–92.

Walter, T. (2006) 'Disaster, Modernity, and the Media', in K. Garces-Foley (ed.), *Death and Religion in a Changing World*. Armonk, NY: M. E. Sharpe.

Weber, M. ([1904]1958) *The Protestant Ethic and the Spirit of Capitalism*. New York: Scribner.

Weber, M. and Turner, B. (1991) *From Max Weber: Essays in Sociology*. Leuven: Routledge.

Whale, J. (1931) Director: *Frankenstein: The Man Who Made a Monster*. United States.

Whittaker, W. G. (2005) 'Funeral Services: The Industry, Its Workforce, and Labor

Standards', Cornell University ILR School Key Workplace Documents, Federal Publications. Available at:http://digitalcommons.ilr.cornell.edu/key work-place/206.

Wikipedia (2012) *Last Rites*. Retrieved: 12 June, from http://en.wikipedia.org/wiki/Last_Rites.

Williams, P. (2007) *Memorial Museums: The Global Rush to Commemorate Atrocities*. Oxford: Berg.

Williamson, J. (1989) 'What Washington Means by Policy Reform', in J. Williamson (ed.), *Latin American Readjustment: How Much Has Happened*. Washington, DC: Institute for International Economics.

Wilson, D. M. *et al.* (2001) 'Location of Death in Canada: A Comparison of 20th-Century Hospital and Nonhospital Locations of Death and Corresponding Population Trends,' *Evaluation and the Health Professions*, 24(4): 385–403.

Worden, J. W. (2009) *Grief Counselling and Grief Therapy: A Handbook for the Mental Health Practitioner*. New York: Springer.

World Bank (2010) 'New Zealand Population', *World Development Indicators*. Washington, DC: World Bank.

World Bank Group (2008) 'Health Transition, Disease Burdens, and Health Expenditure Patterns', *Health Financing Report*, Washington, DC: World Bank.

WHO (World Health Organization) (2008) *The Top Ten Causes of Death*, Fact sheet No. 310. Geneva: World Health Organization.

WHO (World Health Organization) (2010) 'Save Lives by Counting the Dead: Interview with Prabhat Jha', *Bulletin of the World Health Organization*, 88(3): 161–240.

WHO (World Health Organization) (2011) *Health Factsheet: Obesity and Overweight*, Fact sheet No. 311. Geneva: World Health Organization.

World Life Expectancy (2009) 'World Life Expectancy Map'. Available at: http://www.worldlifeexpectancy.com; accessed 30 April 2009.

Wright, M. (2011) 'Quake Victims Suffer Broken Heart Syndrome', *The Press*, Wellington, NZ.

Yach, D. and Bettcher, D. (2000) 'Globalisation of Tobacco Industry Influence and New Global Responses', *Tobacco Control*, 9: 206–16.

Yahoo Voices (2010) 'Luger Nodar Kumaritashvili Dies in Horrific Crash'. Available at: http://www.associatedcontent.com/article/2693655/luger_nodar_kumaritashvili_dies_in.html?cat=14).

Younge, G. and Jones, S. (2005) 'Family's Dismay after "Alistair Cooke's Bones" Stolen by New York Gang', *The Guardian*, 23 December. Available at: http://www.guardian.co.uk/media/2005/dec/23/bbc.usnews; accessed 18 February 2008.

Youngner, S. J. *et al.* (1999) *The Definition of Death: Contemporary Controversies*. Baltimore, MD: Johns Hopkins University Press.

Zelikow, P. (2004), National Commission on Terrorist Attacks upon the United States (The 9/11 Commission).

Zurubavel, E. (2003) *Time Maps: Collective Memory as the Social Shape of the Past*. Chicago, ILL: University of Chicago Press.

Index